MORAL RELATIVITY

MORAL RELATIVITY

David B. Wong

UNIVERSITY OF CALIFORNIA PRESS
Berkeley   Los Angeles   London

University of California Press
Berkeley and Los Angeles, California

University of California Press, Ltd.
London, England

Copyright © 1984 by The Regents of the University of California

Library of Congress Cataloging in Publication Data

Wong, David B.
  Moral relativity.

  Bibliography: p. 237
  Includes index.
  1. Ethical relativism.   I. Title.
BJ1031.W65   1984   170'.42   83-18073
ISBN 0-520-04976-4

Printed in the United States of America

1 2 3 4 5 6 7 8 9

To my mother and the memory of my father

Contents

Preface

I conceived this book on the basis of three convictions. The first is that metaethics could benefit from new developments in theories of truth, reference, and translation. Philosophers who gave us the established metaethical theories of the twentieth century, such as G. E. Moore, C. L. Stevenson, and R. M. Hare, formulated their analyses of moral language given a certain philosophy of language. The new philosophy of language forms part of the foundation of my argument for a new analysis of moral language and for the thesis that there is no single true morality. The second conviction is that mainstream moral philosophy suffers from an ignorance of the moralities of Eastern cultures. It is particularly important to remedy this ignorance in discussions on the issue of whether there is a single true morality. I begin the remedy by discussion of Confucianism and Taoism, two ancient Chinese philosophies. The third conviction is that the growing field of normative ethics needs some connection with a revived metaethics. I attempt to forge a connection between the metaethical thesis that there is no single true morality and normative issues such as abortion and the inequality of respect for human beings that exists in American society.

Analytic philosophers who have a basic knowledge of recent philosophy of language (who have a general idea of what Alfred Tarski, Donald Davidson, Willard Quine, Hilary Putnam, and Saul Kripke have done) should have no trouble with this book. Philosophers who have no such knowledge, and the general reading public, can get a general sense of what is happening in the sections on philosophy of language. The greatest portion of the argument for moral relativity and its implications should be completely accessible to them, and this book is intended for them as much as it is intended for specialists in ethics and those with knowledge of philosophy of language.

Gilbert Harman, Tyler Burge, Hector-Neri Castañeda, Richard Wasserstrom, and David Shatz have been extremely helpful to me in providing detailed criticism and encouragement. I appreciated the fairness and helpfulness of the comments from Professors Harman and Castañeda, since my disagreements with them are quite apparent in this book. Alan Berger and Fred Sommers helped me with some of the sections on philosophy of language. Laura Weisberg and Craig Ihara helped with the chaper on Taoism and equal worth. My editors, John Miles and Shirley Warren, have skillfully steered me through the process of preparing the manuscript for publication. Izchak Miller and the people of the Feldberg Computer Center at Brandeis were merciful and patient in dealing with my anxieties and puzzlement over the mysteries of word processing. Finally, I would like to thank my wife, Laura Weisberg, and Sam and Lillian Weisberg, for their emotional and material support. I also hope that some of the wisdom my wife gave me is reflected in this book.

1 Introduction to the Strategy of Argument for Moral Relativity and its Normative Implications

1.1 *Explaining moral experience*

In this book, I defend a theory built around the claim that there is no single true morality. My strategy is to argue that the theory gives us the best explanation of moral experience. Let me begin an outline of this strategy by identifying the main difficulty in explaining moral experience: reconciling the features of experience suggesting that morality is objective with other features suggesting that it is subjective.

When applied to morality, the terms 'objective' and 'subjective' each connote a family of characteristics. That is, the characteristics are not necessarily related but are frequently found together in descriptions of the nature of morality. When a philosopher calls morality objective, for instance, he or she is making several and perhaps all of the following claims:

1. Moral statements have truth values;
2. There are good and bad arguments for the moral positions people take;
3. Nonmoral facts (states of affairs that obtain in the world and that can be described without use of moral terms such as 'ought, 'good,' and 'right') are relevant to the assessment of the truth value of moral statements;
4. There are moral facts (that may or may not be claimed to be reducible in some way to nonmoral facts);
5. When two moral statements conflict as recommendations to action, only one statement can be true;
6. There is a single true morality.

When morality is called subjective, several and perhaps all of the above claims are denied.

For examples of features of experience suggesting moral objectivity, note that we commonly call moral beliefs true or false, that we give arguments for or against these beliefs, and that we judge these arguments to be good or bad. One may, for instance, regard arguments for segregation of the races as objectively unsound as any argument for the conclusion that the earth is flat. We also find that some people seem to mature in making moral judgments. Iris Murdoch gives us the example of a mother who feels hostility toward her daughter-in-law, judging her to have a juvenile and vulgar character. The mother, however, reflects on her own attitude, concluding that she has been snobbish, narrow-minded, and certainly jealous. Looking again at the daughter-in-law, she now finds her to be refreshingly simple and spontaneous.[1] The mother now has moral reason to act differently toward her daughter-in-law. This example suggests that there are facts (whether they be moral or nonmoral) relevant to the assessment of the truth value of moral judgments, and that people can learn how their interests and emotions color their perceptions of these facts and become more "objective."

The features of moral experience suggesting claims 1 through 3 are often taken as evidence for 4. There is no strict entailment here, but it may be argued that 4 is a plausible explanation of why 1 through 3 are true. Even those who believe there are irreducible moral facts usually say that the moral is "supervenient" on nonmoral facts, in such a way that change in the former must be accompanied by change in the latter. A feature of moral experience suggesting 5 is that we normally take a person who has admitted to the truth of a moral statement to be admitting to a reason to act in accordance with that statement when it has implications for how he or she is to act. For instance, if the mother in Murdoch's example now admits to the truth of the statement that she ought not to act coldly to her daughter, she is normally taken as admitting to a reason to act differently. If a person were to admit to the truth of each of two moral statements that were incompatible as recommendations to action, such as "You ought not to act coldly" and "You ought to act coldly," then the person would seem to be admitting that morality can tell us to do an act X and at the same time to not do X. Finally, people who hold 6 — I will call them "absolutists" — may argue that it is a plausible inference from claims 1 through 5.[2] If moral statements are true or false in virtue of their correspondence to moral facts, it may be inferred that there is a single true morality that accurately depicts these moral facts. Or if we think of a morality as a set of compatible recommendations to action, we may conclude that there can be only a single true morality in the light of 5.

For examples of features of experience suggesting moral subjectivity, note the deep disagreement over issues such as the permissibility of abortion. Conservatives point to the potential of the fetus to have a rich life. They point to its continuous development from conception and challenge the liberal to point out the stage of development that makes the difference between having and not having a right to life. Liberals respond by pointing out qualities in human beings that are morally relevant to the way they ought to be treated — possession of a conception of self, of desires, of rationality — and argue that fetuses possess these qualities *only* potentially. Their conclusion is that the latter do not have a serious right to life, or at least a right that is serious enough to override a woman's desire for an abortion (see chapter twelve for a more extensive discussion of abortion). Nonmoral facts about the development of fetuses do not seem to provide a rational resolution, and it is difficult for many to conceive of a moral fact of the matter as to whether or not the fetus is a person with a right to life.

Also, note that comparative ethics, sociology, and anthropology give a wealth of evidence for the existence of significant diversity in moral belief, across societies and within many of them. In this book, I will focus on differences between virtue-centered and rights-centered moralities, and differences between interpretations of each type of morality. A virtue-centered morality gives a central place to the concept of a good common to all members of a community. The common good is made possible and is at least partially defined by a way of life in which all members cooperate to achieve it. The

shared life is defined by a system of roles that specifies the contribution of each member to the sustenance of that life. The
virtues are identified as the qualities necessary for the performance of one's role and thus for successful contribution to
the common good. A rights-centered morality does not give a
central place to the common good and a shared life. Rather, it
emphasizes the notion of what each member of the community
is entitled to claim from other members. The moral bonds of
the community are founded on mutual respect, demonstrated
by recognizing the rights of each—rights such as those to freedom, property, and well-being. The list of rights may vary,
just as the list of virtues in the other type of morality may vary.

Ancient Greek morality is virtue-centered and constitutes an
interpretation of that type. So does ancient Chinese Confucianism and the morality of the Zuni Indians. The moralities
of modern Western Europe and North America have become
various interpretations of rights-centered morality. Now the
question is whether we can claim that one of these fundamentally different types is closer to the moral truth and
whether one interpretation of each type is the true interpretation. If we attribute to the members of a society a mistaken
belief in an interpretation of one of these ideals, can we
explain *how* they made the mistake? The inability of absolutists to provide persuasive answers to such questions, together
with the apparent irresolvability of disagreements such as the
one over abortion, has led some moral philosophers—I will call
them "relativists"—to deny 6 and usually one or more of the
other claims for moral objectivity (5, quite often 4, and sometimes all the claims).

To talk about the ways in which different theories of morality deal with the features of experience suggesting moral objectivity and the features suggesting subjectivity, it will be useful
to divide theories into broad types. To call a theory "objec-
tivist" or "subjectivist" will not be useful, because many analyses, including my own, will deny some and accept some of
claims 1 through 6. The best strategy is to classify theories as
relativist or absolutist, as denying or accepting 6, and then to
make finer discriminations within each category according to
denial or acceptance of the other claims for moral objectivity
and according to different ways of arguing for, qualifying, or

fleshing out the claims accepted. It is the thesis of this book that a certain kind of relativist theory provides maximal reconciliation of the features of experience suggesting objectivity with the features suggesting subjectivity.

This maximal reconciliation is made possible by replacing the philosophy of language presupposed by previous theories with a more satisfactory one. The next two sections show why and how a new philosophy of language is used.

1.2 Why we need new analyses of moral language

Twentieth-century theories of the nature of morality have focused on moral language in the attempt to solve the problem of reconciling the opposing features of moral experience. Because the theories have failed, many philosophers have turned away altogether from the analysis of moral language. I believe this is a mistake and that a much more successful analysis can be given.

Philosophy of language has changed since the established metaethical analyses were developed. Many of these analyses rest on theories of meaning that now have been revised or rejected. Emotivist theories such as Stevenson's were premised on a verificationism that has lost all credibility. The analytic-synthetic distinction underlies Moore's open-question argument against naturalism in favor of the existence of a non-natural property of goodness ("Is pleasure really good after all?" is an open question; therefore, 'good' cannot be defined as pleasure, and the same holds for any other natural property). It underlies Hare's argument against naturalism in favor of the existence of an "evaluative" element of moral meaning (if the answer to the above question were analytic, we could not use 'good' to commend pleasurable things; therefore, 'good' must have an element of meaning that allows the use of commendation). Both arguments presuppose that we ought to be able to consult our linguistic intuitions and discover what statements are analytic or true by virtue of their meaning and what statements are not true in this way or synthetic. This is just the kind of assumption Quine so forcefully attacks (see chapter two for more discussion of this attack).

New developments in the philosophy of language include

not only the rejection of verificationism and the attack on the analytic-synthetic distinction, but new ways of approaching the study of meaning. The work of Tarski and Davidson on truth has motivated the study of a term's meaning through identification of the way it contributes to the truth conditions of statements containing it. Also, Kripke and Putnam have contributed new theories about the manner in which the reference of terms is determined. All this work provides a new context for the study of moral terms. Finally, Quine and others have developed theories of how the languages of alien cultures may be translated. Their theories may be applied to the problem of how to interpret apparent differences in moral belief across different societies and groups within a single society. The problem of resolving the disagreement between absolutists and relativists then becomes one of determining whether people of different societies and groups are talking about the same things when they use moral terms.

The new developments in philosophy of language require a reevaluation of previous analyses of moral language and the proposal of new ones. I will examine previous relativist analyses and show how their deficiencies can be remedied by adopting a framework for the analyses of moral language that is based on the new developments. Chapter two will treat the work on truth; chapter five, reference theory; and chapter eight, translation theory. Each new development will support part of the argument that new relativist analyses provide a maximal reconciliation of the features of experience suggesting moral objectivity with the features suggesting subjectivity.

1.3   *Reconciling moral objectivity with subjectivity*

Not surprisingly, previous relativist analyses are liable to be weak in their explanations of features suggesting objectivity. In chapter two, I will show how the relativist analyses of Stevenson and Hare exemplify such weakness, and will argue that the recent work on truth will provide a framework for developing analyses that can account for a greater measure of moral objectivity. In chapter three, I discuss the more recent analyses of Harman and Castañeda within the framework. They account for a greater measure of moral objectivity but still need improvement. Chapters four, five, and six present the recommended relativist analyses of moral "A ought to do X" statements (where 'A' is a place holder for the name or description of an agent and 'X' for the description of an action) and "X is a good Y" statements (where 'X' is a place holder for the name or description of an object, person or action, and 'Y' for the description of a class). Consideration of the new theories of reference will play a role in the development of these analyses. Under them, claims 1 through 4 are accepted, while 5 and 6 are denied. It will be possible to offer a plausible explanation as to why 5 and 6 are mistakenly believed by some to be true. My analysis, therefore, allows for a considerable measure of moral objectivity and explains why some have thought there is more when there isn't.

I will then turn to absolutist analyses of moral language in chapter seven, dividing them into three broad categories: Kantian (such as those given by Nagel and Gewirth), Aristotelian (McDowell and Foot), and Platonic (Moore and Platts). Not surprisingly, these analyses are weakest at explaining features of experience suggesting moral subjectivity—the existence of apparently irresolvable moral disagreements and apparent diversity of belief such as that concerning virtue-centered and rights-centered moralities. Chapters nine, ten, and eleven involve comparisons between virtue-centered and rights-centered moralities, between ancient Greek and Chinese virtue-centered moralities, and between the rights-centered moralities of Rawls and Nozick. The theory of translation in chapter eight will provide the framework for these comparisons. I will construct an explanation of the disagreement and diversity that will be consistent with the recommended relativist analyses and will argue that the explanation is better than any that absolutists could offer.

When taken together, then, chapters two through eleven constitute the argument that a recognition of moral relativity is part of the best explanation of moral experience—an explanation that provides maximal reconciliation of those features of experience suggesting objectivity and those features suggesting subjectivity. In the last two chapters of this book, however,

I turn from problems of explanation to the problem of what we should do, having recognized the existence of moral relativity.

1.4   *The normative implications of moral relativity*

The recent turn away from metaethics has been motivated only partly by the perceived failure of previous analyses of moral language. Analytic and nonanalytic philosophers have come to perceive a certain emptiness in the analytic approach to morality. They have tired of books that mention moral issues of the day almost incidentally, as mere examples of the use of moral language. Hence the increased emphasis on the resolution of issues such as abortion and affirmative action, and on theories of justice such as those developed by Rawls and Nozick. And hence Rawls' proposal that "for the time being we put aside the idea of constructing . . . a systematic account of what we regard as objective moral truths . . . Since the history of moral philosophy shows that the notion of moral truth is problematical."[3] But surely Rawls' argument against dealing with the problem of moral truth would be more convincing if the problem had not had such a long history, going back at least to Socrates and Plato. *When* will we have a sufficiently deep understanding of moral conceptions? The continuing investigation of substantive moral conceptions may produce insights that make the notion of moral truth less puzzling, but the mere possibility does not warrant a blanket prohibition of all attempts at doing metaethics.

It must be granted that most metaethical theories have been irrelevant to normative issues. This irrelevance, however, is not an inherent feature of metaethics. One of the gravest normative problems with which we must deal is the existence of deep and apparently irresolvable moral disagreements such as abortion. We must know how to act when no single side in a disagreement can show that it has the best arguments. Should each side continue acting on its own convictions, or should each modify its actions in the light of its inability to justify its convictions to the other? In other words, should each show tolerance in the light of a metaethical fact? It is the thesis of chapter twelve that the inability to justify one's actions to the people one affects is relevant to the rightness of one's actions, given a certain kind of morality that many of us accept. My claim runs counter to the popular view that metaethics has no implications whatsoever for normative issues. I suspect that what motivates the acceptance of such a view is the fear that recognition of moral relativity can only result in a weak-minded, wishy-washy ethic of tolerance that accepts the worst forms of evil, an ethic that is often invoked by the question, "Who's to say what's moral or immoral?" I will show that this fear is unjustified.

The final chapter begins the project of showing that the recognition of moral relativity can make a positive contribution to the resolution of an important moral problem — that of bringing about a society in which the equal worth of every person is truly affirmed and recognized. I argue that previous attempts to justify the principle that every person has equal worth are inadequate. I also point to sociological evidence for the conclusion that it is extremely difficult for many people to truly believe that they have equal worth even if they give lip service to the principle. The evidence shows that we constantly compare ourselves with others, and that when we come out worse in a comparison, our sense of self-worth is often lowered. My suggestion is that we need to be able to look at ourselves and others without judging in terms of "better than" or "worse than." To describe what this ability would be like, I make use of the Chinese philosophy of Taoism and argue that its seemingly outrageous advice to "forget morality" is actually of great moral value. I attempt to describe what a society would be like if it truly promoted the unconditional acceptance of equal human worth. Both chapters twelve and thirteen, then, show that the recognition of moral relativity can be part of a larger normative ethic and social philosophy, that once we recognize moral relativity we can integrate it with the rest of our moral concerns.

2 The Importance of Moral Truth

2.1 *The purpose of surveying the analyses of Stevenson and Hare*

Let me begin by considering well-known analyses that are consistent with moral relativity — those of Stevenson and Hare. Since they are well-known, and well-criticized, there is no need for detailed exposition and criticism. The purpose of this chapter is to relate their shortcomings to the need for a new framework for analysis. The framework I will construct from the work of Tarski and Davidson on truth allows us to take the notion of moral truth much more seriously than Stevenson and Hare do.

2.2 *Stevenson's moral individualism*

Stevenson's analyses are motivated by the desire to account for irresolvable moral disagreements such as abortion. The idea is to claim that such disagreements consist of two possible components — conflict in belief and conflict in attitude. The latter involves oppositions in purposes, preferences, desires and aspirations, when at least one side seeks to change the attitudes of the other. Securing agreement in belief does not always secure agreement in attitude. For instance, everyone may have the same beliefs about the medical facts on fetuses but some will desire to permit abortion while others desire to prohibit it. When a moral disagreement rests on such a conflict and not on conflict in belief, each side may seek to persuade the other

10

through nonrational methods: appealing to emotions by dis-
playing the pictures of aborted fetuses or describing the misery
of unwanted children, and so on.

Let us see how Stevenson's analyses conform to this view of
moral disagreement:

A ought to do X ≡ I disapprove of A's not doing X; do so as well

This is good ≡ I approve of this; do so as well.

The imperative parts of the right-hand sides represent the
"emotive meaning" of 'ought' and 'good'. Such meaning is an
emotional "charge" carried by the words—a dispositional
property enabling the speaker to express his or her attitudes
and to change or intensify the attitudes of the audience.[1]

Stevenson does justice to the apparent irresolvability of some
moral disagreements at a severe cost. By making moral statements expressions of attitude, and by contrasting disagreements in belief with disagreements in attitude, Stevenson
assimilates approval to personal taste. If Stevenson is right,
many moral language users are mistaken in believing (claim 2
of chapter one) that moral argument may be correct or incorrect. They also would be mistaken in believing in the possibility of one becoming more mature in moral judgment. The
problem is that Stevenson provides little explanation of why
moral language users could be so mistaken.

His analyses gain whatever plausibility they possess by illegit-
imately borrowing from an impersonal element we normally
associate with approval. George Pitcher correctly points out
that expressing approval of something is maintaining that
there are reasons for being favorably disposed toward that
thing and that it is implying that anyone in the same position
ought to approve.[2] Approval is an attitude purporting to have
an impersonal authority behind it. Stevenson's method of
explaining the irresolvability of certain moral disagreements
can, however, work only by ignoring that impersonal element.
And of course, he must, if 'ought' is used to express the impersonal element, as Pitcher believes. That is why Stevenson *ille-*
gitimately borrows from the impersonal element of approval.

His analyses lose plausibility when we substitute the clause "I approve" with some phrase that is purely personal in connotation, such as "I like." When one makes a moral statement, one implies that there are reasons for the pro-attitude expressed, reasons one believes ought to be accepted by anyone else in the same position.[3]

2.3 *Hare's principled moral individualism*

The above considerations have led many relativists to prefer R. M. Hare's analyses of moral statements, since these analyses are compatible with relativism but avoid many of the liabilities to which Stevenson's are subject.

He interprets "A ought to do X" statements in the following manner:

If A does not do X, A will be breaking a universal 'ought' principle to which I hereby subscribe.

Universal 'ought' principles of the form "All P's ought to be Q's" are interpreted as universal quasi-imperatives of the form "All P's being Q's, please." I call them "quasi-imperatives" because they may apply to all moral agents, past, present, and future, unlike ordinary imperatives.[4] Under Hare's analysis, "A ought to do X" statements comprise a kind of second-order normative language, used to talk about the logical implications of imperative language.

Hare interprets "X is a good Y" statements in terms of 'ought', via an analysis of 'better than':

X is a better Y than Z ≡ If one is choosing a Y, then if one chooses Z, one ought to choose X.[5]

Then Hare is able to say

X is a good Y ≡ X is better than Y's usually are.

Making a value statement is subscribing to an 'ought' principle telling people to choose Y's that have certain properties, if they're going to choose Y's at all, and it is saying that X has these properties to a greater degree than the average Y.[6]

Hare's analyses are compatible with the moral phenomena that have motivated relativism. Take the apparent irresolvability of some moral disagreements. If the two sides to such disagreements have subscribed to different universal 'ought' principles that require incompatible actions, and if the choice of principles is not founded on some mistake in reasoning or ignorance of some fact statable without the use of moral terms, then an irresolvable disagreement is the result. Similarly, variation in moral belief across societies and different groups within a single society can be the result of the choice of different universal 'ought' principles. The result is moral relativism.[7]

At the same time, Hare avoids some of the liabilities of Stevenson's analyses. In his analysis of how 'ought' and 'good' are used to prescribe and commend, Hare explains how speakers are expressing and attempting to evoke *principled* pro or con attitudes toward an object, person or action. For instance, speakers of "A ought to do X" statements express a negative attitude toward A not doing X by subscribing to quasi-imperatives requiring X. In making disapproval of A not doing X a matter of having reasons based on universal principles, Hare is able to avoid the fusion between this attitude and personal taste that made Stevenson so vulnerable. The reasons for disapproval apply to any other action with the same relevant properties. And Hare is able to say that in making an "A ought to do X" statement, a speaker implies that anyone ought to have a negative attitude toward A not doing X, given the universal 'ought' principle to which the speaker subscribes.

If a group of speakers agree on a set of universal 'ought' principles, then they can agree that there are good and bad arguments for moral positions, and that nonmoral facts are relevant to the assessment of such positions (claims 2 and 3 of chapter one). Good arguments establish that an action X recommended by the speaker for A is indeed required by some universal 'ought' principles held by A. Facts concerning X and the circumstances under which it would be performed could be relevant to the question of whether X is indeed

required by one of A's universal 'ought' principles. Since Hare
is prepared to assert that there is often wide agreement on such
principles within a society, he can claim that he does justice to
at least some aspects of our moral experience that have supported the view of morality as objective.

The measure of objectivity allotted is not enough, however.
We can see this by focusing on the radical change in content
that occurs when we move from "A ought to do X" statements
about particular agents to universal 'ought' principles. The
former are analyzed as statements about what is required of an
agent by a universal quasi-imperative, and the latter are identified with the quasi-imperatives themselves. The former could
have truth values if we interpret them not only as the speech
acts of subscribing but as reports by the speaker that an act is
entailed by some principle to which he or she subscribes. The
latter cannot be interpreted in any way that clearly indicates
they have truth values. But in everyday discourse, people do
not hesitate to apply "That's true" to universal 'ought' principles, so unless Hare can find a way of explaining why people
would mistakenly apply a predicate to an item that could not
bear it, he must give an interpretation of 'true' when applies to
universal 'ought' principles that is compatible with his analysis.
Presumably, this interpretation would have to be based on a
nonrealistic theory of truth — one which does not hold that
truth consists in some relation between the truth bearer and
items in the world.

One possibility is to assert something like the "redundancy
theory of truth" — to say p is true is simply to say p. When p is
an ordinary imperative, however, the equivalence does not
hold, because we don't say imperatives are true or false. Why
are quasi-imperatives different in this respect? Another possibility is to say that 'true' when applied to universal quasi-
imperatives has a meaning different from the one it has when
applied to indicatives such as "The cat is on the mat." Perhaps
it means something analogous to "warranted assertability";
Hare's quasi-imperatives may be justifiable in the sense of
tending to satisfy needs, desires, or purposes. The problem
with this proposal is that different imperatives will satisfy different needs, desires, and purposes, whether they belong to the

same agent or to different ones. It is a moral question as to which of these needs, desires, and purposes are to be satisfied. In fact, we could frame possible answers to the question in terms of 'ought' principles. Explicating moral truth as warranted "commandability" seems to have led us into a circle.

A third interpretation of the use of 'true' as applied to universal 'ought' principles is that it is merely used as a sign of assent to a quasi-imperative, of willingness to abide by it. But again in this case, Hare would have to explain why we use 'true' to signal assent to imperatives only when they are dressed in 'ought' clothing. The fact that we apply the truth predicate to universal 'ought' principles seems to indicate that we are signaling our admission of the *correctness* of abiding by them or the existence of a reason for abiding by them. It is probable, therefore, that the identification of universal 'ought' principles with quasi-imperatives will not lead to an adequate explanation of why the truth predicate is applied to such principles.

It is also doubtful that Hare can give an adequate explanation of why we make certain inferences when someone applies the truth predicate to "A ought to do X" statements about particular agents. Consider the fact that when George applies "That's true" to a statement such as "George ought to pay back the money he borrowed from John," we normally take George to be acknowledging a reason for his paying back the money (this may not hold if George is completely amoral and recognizes the existence of his obligation to John but is completely unmoved by it). That is, we assume that George is expressing the belief that he has such a reason, and that he knows we are entitled to assume this upon hearing his admission of the truth of the statement. Under Hare's analysis, we have problems accounting for this linkage between admission of truth and admission of reasons for acting (recall that this linkage was the motivation for claim 5 of chapter one).

Recall that we may interpret the statement about George as having a truth value, under Hare's analysis. We may interpret the speaker as reporting that the act is entailed by a quasi-imperative to which he or she subscribes. But under this analysis, George need not be admitting anything about having reasons for paying back the money when he admits the statement to be true, for all he is admitting is that paying back the money is required by the *speaker's* principle and not necessarily any principle of his own.

In reply to this objection, Hare could try the redundancy theory of truth again. This time, the theory is not obviously inapplicable, since an "A ought to do X" statement about a particular agent is not a universal quasi-imperative but is a genuine statement about the action required of the agent by such an imperative. In saying "That's true" about the above statement, George could be repeating the uttered sentence type and thus announcing his own subscription to a principle requiring him to pay back the money. But this reply assumes that when George says, "That's true" of a statement containing an indexical such as 'I', he is in effect repeating the sentence type and using 'I' to refer to himself. This is not what usually happens. Suppose that George says, "I ought to pay back the money," and Thomas says, "That's true." We would interpret Thomas as confirming George's obligation, not admitting to one that applies to himself.

The lesson to be drawn from Hare's problems is that there is a cognitive content of such statements that his analyses do not reveal. This lesson must be drawn unless Hare gives us a plausible explanation of why we have fallen into massive confusion in the ways we apply the truth predicate to 'ought' statements. Furthermore, some of the objections that have been made against his analysis of 'ought' also may be made against his analysis of 'good'. For instance, under his analysis, when student A says, "Professor Wordsworth is a good teacher," he is commending the professor as a teacher according to his 'ought' principle for choosing teachers. But if student B says, "What A said is true," she is not merely agreeing that the professor meets A's standards, but is saying that the professor meets *her* standards, or that A's standards are reasonable ones.

2.4   *Using the work of Tarski and Davidson on truth*

The lesson of the preceding discussion is that we need to be able to attribute truth values to moral statements, universal principles included, and in such a way that the recognition of their truth can be linked with an admission of reason for action. Moreover, we should make possible the distinction between good and bad arguments for moral statements and the recognition of the relevance of facts (moral or nonmoral) to the assessment of moral positions.

The way to begin to do this is to present a truth conditions analysis of moral statements that gives the desired results. We should attempt to analyze the necessary and sufficient conditions under which moral statements are true, as these statements are made in different societies and groups. And if we analyze moral statements in this way, we have a convenient way of posing the issue between absolutists and relativists. If the absolutists are right, the truth conditions of important types of moral statements will be the same across different societies and groups. If the relativists are right, then these truth conditions will vary, or we will fail altogether in attempting to present truth conditions.

To simply set before ourselves the goal of giving truth conditions for moral statements, however, is not setting up a definite target. A truth conditions analysis could be totally trivial and uninformative. For instance, one could say that the statement "One ought never to have an abortion" is true if and only if one ought never to have an abortion, and leave it at that. Let us clarify, therefore, what a useful truth conditions analysis should be like.

In the philosophy of language our conception of a truth conditions analysis has been shaped by Tarski's definition of 'true' as a predicate of sentences in a formalized language — the object language L. Tarski's aim was to explicate the notion that the truth of a sentence consists of its correspondence with reality. He started by asking what we would mean by saying that the sentence "Snow is white" is true. He answered that we would mean that snow is white, or

s is true if and only if snow is white

where 's' is the name of the sentence. Tarski stipulates as a condition of adequacy for any acceptable definition of truth for L that it should have as a consequence all instances of the (T) schema:

s is true if and only if p

where 's' is replaced by a description of a sentence of L and 'p' replaced by that sentence if L is part of the meta-language (the language in which the truth definition is given), or by its translation if not. Tarski points out that we could view each instance of (T) as a *partial* definition of truth, in that each instance specifies the truth conditions of a specific sentence. The conjunction of all instances of (T), therefore, for each sentence of L, would constitute a complete definition. It is not possible to give a conjunctive definition, however, because the number of sentences of a language may be infinite.

Tarski's solution was to take those formal languages in which all sentences could be constructed from a limited stock of constituent elements—names and "sentential functions" (or open sentences) for instance. Sentential functions comprehend what we normally call predicates, and they may have "free variables," as in "x is white" and "x is greater than y." A sentence such as "Snow is white" may be defined as a sentential function with no free variables. The idea is that a truth definition will specify how the truth values of sentences of L depend on the semantic properties of their constituent elements. Axioms of the truth definition assign these semantic properties to the constituents and reveal the semantic outcome of possible combinations of these constituents.

The relevant property of sentential functions is "satisfaction." For instance, "x is white" is satisfied by snow and by other white things; "x is greater than y" is satisfied by the ordered pair $<2,1>$. Intuitively speaking, satisfaction is a relation between the functions and the objects (or ordered sequences of objects) "referred to" by those functions. Tarski's formal definition of satisfaction is recursive. Definitions are given first for the simplest sentential functions and then the conditions are stated under which compound sentential functions are satisfied. The truth conditions of sentences may then be given in terms of satisfaction conditions of their constituents. For instance, suppose we have existential quantification of a sentential function with one variable — "($\exists$x) (x is white)." Then the truth conditions of the sentence depend on the satisfaction conditions for sentential functions with one free variable and the satisfaction conditions for all existentially quantified sentences. There should be clauses of the truth definition stating these conditions.[8]

Tarski restricted his truth definition to formalized languages. It was Donald Davidson who made the next move of proposing that the semantic theory of a natural language be modeled on a truth definition. Beginning with the recognition that the definition works by giving necessary and sufficient conditions for the truth of every sentence, he argued that giving truth conditions is a way of giving the meaning of a sentence.[9] He suggests that we construct a systematic model of the way truth conditions of complex sentences of natural language are determined by the semantic properties of their constituents. The model requires us to state not only what the truth conditions are but *how* they are determined.

There is much that is useful in Davidson's proposal. If we show how the constituents of moral statements contribute to their truth conditions, then we have a good chance of getting clearer on the nature of moral truth. In this book, we shall focus on "A ought to do X" and "X is a good Y" statements. The idea will be to show how 'ought' and 'good' contribute to the truth conditions of those statements, and we can only benefit by striving to come as close to the Tarskian ideal as possible.

Of course, we must recognize that there will be differences between a truth conditions analysis of natural language and Tarski's truth definition for a formal language. For instance, Tarski's definition applies to sentence types of a formal language. But in natural language, different sentence tokens of the same type may be used to make inequivalent statements. One reason for this is the fact that natural language contains indexicals like 'I', 'now', and 'here'. A strategy for meeting this difficulty is to apply the truth predicate to utterances of sentences by particular persons at particular times and places. In addition, we may want to speak of potential utterances, since we don't want to restrict ourselves to sentences that have been uttered.[10] In effect, statements become truth bearers, and we may think of statements as equivalence classes of sentence tokens. But since all tokens of the same type will not be in the same class (for the reasons stated above), and since tokens of the same class need not be of the same type, we would need (in a fully developed truth definition for natural language) identity criteria for being a member of an equivalence class.

There is a much more serious complication in giving a truth definition for a natural language. Tarski stipulated that p be a *translation* of s in the schema "s is true if and only if p" when L is not part of the meta-language. We are faced with the task, therefore, of saying what an adequate translation is. We could turn to the platitude that an adequate translation preserves meaning and then try to say when meaning is preserved. But this would be to turn Davidson's proposal inside out, since he wanted to use truth definitions to elucidate meaning and not the other way around. At this point we could part company with Davidson and remind ourselves that we are primarily interested in obtaining truth conditions for moral statements and not in capturing all aspects of their meaning. So why can't we derive constraints on translations of truth conditions from the platitude that meaning is to be preserved?

The reason is that we don't have clear ideas about what it is to preserve meaning. In his classic attack on the analytic-synthetic distinction, Quine showed how difficult it was to articulate a useful notion of synonymy. Against the idea that sameness of meaning is fixed (i.e., immune to revision) by linguistic convention, Quine proposed the powerful idea that our system of beliefs faces "the tribunal of sense experience not individually but only as a corporate body."[11] When trouble strikes, no statement is immune to revision. And conversely, any statement may be held true no matter what, if we are willing to make radical enough revisions elsewhere in the system. It follows that it is impossible to separate that part of the use of a word that reflects its meaning from that part that reflects firmly held collateral information.

I am not at all sure that this holds for all words. "Unmarried man" is definitely the primary meaning of 'bachelor', and not just a piece of firmly held collateral information about bachelors.[12] But Quine is right about enough words, and in particular scientific words, so that we are not entitled to any confidence in the project of deriving constraints on translation from the platitude about preserving meaning. Scientists say things about mass and energy that were never dreamt of in Newton's world. So what is to be done?

We should ask how we actually go about translating a group's language and how we distinguish good translations from bad ones. I do not believe that an adequate translation will necessarily capture all aspects of meaning, but we would probably have captured an important aspect and will have a notion of adequate translation. The latter is what is needed for a truth conditions analysis of natural language. In chapter eight, I will argue for a certain principle that can serve as the guiding maxim for translating the truth conditions of a group's language. I save the argument and detailed clarification of the principle for that later chapter because the principle will do most of its work at that point in the book. For now, I will be content to state the principle of the best explanation: our translation of a language should fit with the most plausible overall theory of the people who use the language. A translation of a group's language has implications for our theory of the members' propositional attitudes — the content of their beliefs, desires, hopes, fears, and so on. The content of imputed propositional attitudes, and the relations among them and the world, should be included in the best explanation of the group's linguistic and nonlinguistic behavior.

Before ending this chapter, let me counter a possible objection to the project of giving truth conditions of moral language as I have described it. Under Tarski's truth definition, reference and satisfaction constitute the conventional correspondence relations between parts of the truth bearer on the one hand and objects and sequences of objects on the other, and so he gives a correspondence conception of truth or at least a realist conception (under which truth concerns a relation between language and the world, whether or not this may be a "correspondence" relation) in this respect.[13] It could be asked why such a conception of truth should be presupposed here.

One answer that could be given is not very satisfying, though true: I believe in a realist conception, and, in the absence of a plausible noncorrespondence realist conception, I believe in a correspondence conception. A second answer, however, is that many of the main issues this book is concerned with cannot be stated when any other conception of truth is presupposed. Take the coherence conception of truth, which is the main competitor to realism. Under that conception, the truth of a statement consists of support on the whole by the rest of the theory that contains it. Truth ceases to be an arbiter between different theories. It is applied only within theories. But those who have asserted that there is a single true morality claim that a morality can be false even if it is perfectly coherent and is part of a perfectly coherent theory of the world. When a coherence conception is presupposed, then, we cannot make sense of what they want to say. Still, it may be replied that they shouldn't be able to make sense of that.

There is no easy answer to such a radical reply. A book such as this must have some substantive presuppositions. There are issues concerning absolutism and relativism, however, that can be intelligibly stated under a coherence conception of truth and that are addressed in this book. For instance, we will discuss the issue of whether there is more than one coherent morality or more than one coherent set of fundamental moral principles (even though these principles may differ in their application to the different circumstances of different groups or societies). Such an issue seems to be the closest coherentist analogue to the issue of absolutism versus relativism that is stated under a correspondence conception. But if this is the issue a coherence theorist would rather discuss, I believe that much I will have to say in chapters nine, ten, and eleven will be a strong argument for the coherentist analogue of the relativist position.

There is now enough framework for beginning the project of giving truth conditions for moral statements. The next chapter will consider previous relativist analyses that unequivocally attribute truth values to moral statements and principles, that allow for a greater measure of moral objectivity than Stevenson's and Hare's analyses allow, and that therefore can be considered within the framework of the truth conditions project.

3 Relativist Analyses of Morality as Social Creation

3.1 Harman's analysis of morality as social creation

Stevenson and Hare analyze moral statements as if they are founded on pro-attitudes adopted by the individual speaker. An alternative move is to analyze moral statements as if they are founded on resolutions of the *group* to act in certain ways. This may be a more promising move, because it may enable us to explain why the truth of a moral statement is important to a speaker's audience as well as to the speaker. Moral truth becomes relative to the group, instead of individuals. Gilbert Harman's analysis is premised on the theory that morality is constituted by an implicit agreement among members of a group, each intending to comply as long as the others comply.[1] When speakers make "A ought to do X" statements, they presume that they are parties to an implicit agreement along with A and their audiences. They are saying that X is the course of action for A supported by the best reasons, given the motivational attitudes appropriate to being a party to the agreement and given a set of initial conditions that pick out relevant features of the context of action. Once we allow that different groups can have different agreements, relativism follows.

Harman's analysis implies that 'ought' contributes to the truth conditions of "A ought to do X" statements by serving as a sentential function with free variables. His analysis makes possible the distinction between good and bad arguments for moral positions (claim 2 for moral objectivity in chapter one), since there can be good and bad arguments for X being the course of action for A that is supported by the best reasons, given an implicit agreement and a set of initial conditions. Such arguments can cite nonmoral facts (claim 3 for moral objectivity). Harman also allows for moral facts (claim 4) that are reducible to facts about which actions are supported by an implicit agreement.

And this analysis does address Hare's problems in accounting for other aspects of moral objectivity. Remember that Hare couldn't account for the motivation of claim 5 for moral objectivity: that an admission of the truth of a moral statement is normally taken as an admission of a reason to act in accordance with it. Now consider an "A ought to do X" statement when it is addressed to an agent A who shares an implicit agreement with the speaker. A's admission to the truth of the statement is A's admission that X is supported by terms to which he or she has agreed and intends to carry out. Note, however, that this connection between admission of truth and admissions of reasons for acting holds only *within* a group with a common agreement. Harman argues that this is all the connection there is, pointing out that his theory of morality as implicit agreement can explain why it is odd to say Hitler morally ought not to have ordered the killing of the Jews. The explanation, says Harman, is that we cannot conceive of Hitler as a party to any implicit agreement to which we could be parties. Harman, therefore, can maintain that he accepts claim 5, for under his analysis two "A ought to do X" statements conflict only when they constitute conflicting recommendations based on the same implicit agreement.

Undoubtedly, Harman allows for a greater measure of moral objectivity than does Hare, while allowing for relativity at the same time. Yet there are certain aspects of moral experience suggesting that morality possesses an objectivity independent of any implicit agreements made within groups. For one thing, many of us recognize some basic moral duties that would survive a situation in which there were no implicit agreements. Suppose that in the next Great Depression, the fabric of society unravels into a Hobbesian war of all against all. Many of us think we would still have the elementary duty not to kill each other for amusement, even if we know that others had no intention of reciprocating. Under Harman's theory, this belief is false, and involves a misapprehension of the nature of morality. But in the absence of a good explanation of how so many of us came to be so mistaken, we had better look for another conception of morality.

True, it does sound odd to say Hitler morally ought not to have ordered the Holocaust, but the oddness is explainable in a manner that does not suppose Harman's theory. When a person such as Hitler is so completely beyond the reach of moral motivation, there is little practical point in making an obvious understatement, either to him or to those within the pale, who don't need the lesson. The statement sounds odd partly because it is a toothless one about a matter that is of the most practical import. It is odd partly because it misleads in failing to suggest the enormity of Hitler's crimes. This explanation does not require Harman's theory of morality as implicit agreement.[2]

There is another aspect of moral experience suggesting that the objectivity of morality is independent of whatever implicit agreements are made: we criticize people for the agreements they make. Suppose we see another society with rules working to the extreme disadvantage of a majority of the population because a powerful elite was able to impose that agreement on them. We can say that the elite ought not to have taken advantage of the weaker position of others. Harman can reply that an agreement is subject to criticism on the grounds of coherence, a requirement that includes the avoidance of arbitrary distinctions. Perhaps the elite have rules of fair dealing among themselves, and it is possible to criticize as arbitrary the limited application of these rules. There is no guarantee, however, that we will always find rules of fair dealing, even among an elite, and it isn't necessary for the intelligibility or correctness of our criticism of an agreement that we find within it such rules. It is enough that no such rules are applied to dealings between the elite and the others.

An analysis of "A ought to do X" statements that relativizes them to implicit agreements, therefore, has advantages over the moral individualism of Stevenson and Hare. But such an analysis does not explain the full measure of objectivity we attribute to morality.

3.2 *Castañeda's analysis of morality as social creation*

An alternative view of morality as social creation is suggested by the work of Hector-Neri Castañeda. He, like Hare,
believes that "A ought to do X" statements constitute a kind of
second-order normative language, to be (partially) analyzed in
terms of what it says about imperatives; but under Castañeda's
theory, the relevant imperatives are those to which a *group*
subscribes, not individuals. And he is not committed to saying
that a group comes to subscribe to a set of imperatives through
implicit agreement.

The theory contains useful machinery to talk about imperatives and related parts of practical discourse.[3] Different imperatives may have a common element in that they may
demand of one and the same agent conceived in the same way,
the same action. Consider the order, "Jones, you'd better bring
Mary home," and the request, "Jones, please bring Mary
home." Castañeda calls the common elements "prescriptions"
and uses infinitive clauses of the form "A to X"[4] as canonical
expressions for them. Another part of practical discourse is an
"intention," a possible appropriate answer to the question
"What shall I do?" when asked of oneself as in a monologue.
Prescriptions and intentions combine to form the class of
"practitions."

Imperatives and intentions normally have a "pushing
aspect" in that their use is normally accompanied by the intention that the imperative contribute causally to the agent doing
the action in question. Castañeda notes that "A ought to do X"
statements frequently do not have a pushing aspect. This is
most evident when 'ought' is used in a context of deliberation.
Suppose Smith promised Jones to wait for his friend. Inasmuch
as Smith did this, he ought to wait. But inasmuch as he promised his wife not to wait for Peter, who turns out to be Jones'
friend, he ought not to wait for Jones' friend. When Smith
deliberates upon these two "A ought to do X" statements, trying to decide what to do, neither has a pushing aspect. Rather
these statements formulate alternative courses of action. They
point to reasons for acting in one way or another.

Castañeda takes this difference with respect to pushing

aspects to be indicative of a sharp distinction between the practical roles of imperatives and intentions on the one hand and of "A ought to do X" statements on the other. The latter can be instruments of deliberation in a way that the former cannot be. And yet, there is a close relation between "A ought to do X" statements and imperatives. Children are first taught what they ought or ought not to do through imperatives addressed to them. Castañeda's strategy for the analysis of "A ought to do X" statements recognizes this close relation while preserving the differences:

A ought to do X ≡ there is a consistent set B_i of both true propositions and at least partially endorsed practitions that implies the practition A to do X.[5]

The 'ought' is subscripted to allow for the difference between moral 'ought's, prudential 'ought's, and so on.[6] For instance, it can be said that Smith ought to keep his promise to Jones, referring to a moral obligation Smith has incurred. But it can also be said that he ought to keep his promise to Jones if he wants to avoid Jones' retaliation. These different uses of 'ought' correspond to different sets of propositions and practitions. The true propositions in each set B_i identify the factual considerations — reasons for action — that purportedly weigh in favor of endorsing the practition A to do X. For instance, the fact that Smith promised Jones to wait for his friend is a consideration or reason weighing in favor of endorsing the practition Smith to wait for Jones' friend. A practition that may be included in B_i is the practition that all agents are to keep their promises under a specified set of conditions. The idea of true propositions as reasons explains why "A ought to do X" statements frequently lack a pushing aspect. To point out a reason for A to do X is not necessarily to have the intention of having one's statement contribute causally to A doing X. Notice also that Castañeda's analysis allows for indicating reasons without actually specifying them, and it does seem that we do not need to make such specifications in making an "A ought to do X" statement.

In referring to the "implication" of practitions, the analysis presupposes that there is a logic of practitions. As Castañeda shows, this logic parallels the logic of propositions. For instance, the propositional argument

All students took the course
John is one of the students
Therefore, John took the course.

is parallel to the practical argument

All of you students, take the course
You, John, are a student
Therefore, John take the course.[7]

At this point, it may be asked what rational basis a group of moral language users has for accepting a particular set B_i of practitions. A practition is rationally accepted to the extent that it promotes the realization of a "total hierarchic complex" of ends and "procedural conventions" to which the group subscribes. There is a "hierarchy" because ends allow comparison and ranking. "Procedural conventions" limit means to the achievement of ends, an example of such a convention being a constitution. For Castañeda, subscription is not specially associated with a speech act (as it is for Hare), nor need it originate with an implicit agreement (as with Harman). A person subscribes to a certain end or convention if he or she can be truly said to want in some degree that the end be achieved or the convention obeyed.

The basic idea of Castañeda's analysis of "A ought to do X" statements is that these statements are used to identify practitions that follow from sets of practitions and true propositions that are rationally acceptable in terms of a given context of ends and procedural conventions. We have a moral "A ought to do X" statement when a certain context is invoked. The relevant context has three dimensions.

The "ethical" dimension concerns the human desire to resolve internal conflicts within the self. The agent's needs, wants, and goals all impose requirements that frequently pull him or her in many different directions. There is also what the agent has agreed to do, which may conflict with other requirements. The "euergetical" dimension concerns conflicts involving possible conduct that affects other people. The end is to resolve the conflict. Morality is the ideal that demands from each agent a rearrangement of the powers and inclinations that make up his or her motivational nature, so that his or her actions are reconciled with the ends and inclinations of others, and may often further the ends of others. The specific resolutions a morality offers compose a moral code. Now Castañeda has a general conception of the content of the ideal: it demands that each agent rearrange his or her motivational nature so that his or her actions collide *as little as possible* with the ends and inclinations of others. It is the ideal of "maximal compatible self-fulfillment of all agents."

There may be a discrepancy between a moral code and the ideal, caused by a misconception of the ideal or by misjudging the circumstances in which the ideal applies. The "metathetical" dimension of the moral context, therefore, concerns the resolution of conflicts between a moral code and the ideal. Resolution may result in revision of the code or a revolution in which most of it is overturned. In this third dimension morality also furnishes guidelines for the solution of conflicts between agents on those occasions when they are not bound by common institutional agreements, and when each experiences no internal conflicts of requirements.[8]

At this point, we have an overall sketch of Castañeda's analysis of "A ought to do X" statements. It must be noted that he does not present the analysis as a *definition* of these statements, mainly because there is a difference in the subject matter of the two statements on either side of the biconditional. An "A ought to do X" statement is about the agent A and the doing of X. It concerns people and the issuing of imperatives or intentions to them. The right-hand side is about a practition and its inferential relations to propositions and other practitions. The two statements, therefore, cannot be synonymous. Castañeda conceives of his analysis as a third-order statement schema that provides the truth conditions of "A ought to do X" statements, just as the truth table for the connective of conjunction provides the truth conditions of conjunctions but not the definition of 'and'.[9]

His analysis is compatible with relativism because it allows for the existence of differences in moral codes. These differences need not be the result of error or ignorance. The existence of such differences is inevitable because every agent has a large number of possible types of self-fulfillment. Morality may narrow the range of such types to provide a "consistent maximal harmonization of all agents' self-fulfillment," but there are different ways of restricting the range.[10]

As I noted above, a crucial difference between the relativistic analyses of Harman and Castañeda is that the latter does not require the vulnerable conception of morality as constituted by implicit agreement. Instead, a group's morality is founded on practitions and procedural conventions to which its members subscribe. While the conventions may be the result of implicit agreement, the practitions may not even be the object of conscious choice. This accords with the plausible observation that most people learn morality through explicit teaching or through watching models, without ever having agreed to it. Another advantage of Castañeda's analysis is that it allows for criticism of existing moral codes through the distinction between the ideal of morality and its application.

Castañeda's analysis shares with Harman's the virtue of accounting for a great measure of moral objectivity (claims 1 through 4 of chapter one). He is able to attribute truth values to universal 'ought' principles. He accounts for the difference between good and bad arguments for moral positions, for the relevance of nonmoral facts in such arguments, and for moral facts, which are reducible to facts about practitions. It is not clear that he accepts claim 5 for moral objectivity (that whenever two moral statements conflict as recommendations to action, only one can be true), since he allows that the ideal of morality is consistent with more than one moral code. He can explain, however, why we have motivation for believing 5, which is the perceived connection between A admitting the truth of an "A ought to do X" statement and A admitting a reason to do X.

Under his theory, a moral language user is liable to belong to a group the members of which subscribe to a common set B_i. Within that group, a user who says that another member A ought$_i$ to do X, is saying that A has reason to do X based on the set B_i to which A subscribes. If the user learns moral language within a group that subscribes to a common B_i, he or she will come to learn the connection between admission of truth and admission of reason to act as a regular connection (even though it may not hold across groups). The inference to 5 is understandable, though mistaken.

The first doubt I would like to raise about Castañeda's analysis concerns the relation between the ideal of morality and the truth conditions of "A ought to do X" statements. Suppose a practition A to do X is implied by a set B_i of true propositions and practitions endorsed by a group to which the speaker and A both belong, but suppose also that the group's endorsement of the practitions in B_i is founded on some misconception of the ideal of morality. Is the statement true because the practition in question is in fact implied by B_i or is it false because the practitions in B_i do not measure up to the ideal?

According to Castañeda, the answer depends on what dimension of morality is being considered: the ethical, euergetical, or meta-thetical. A ought to do X given the established moral code, but perhaps every acceptable revision of the code would call for A not to do X. Castañeda believes that morality has its own built-in rankings for the solution of such a conflict.[11] Oppositely, the ranking is not a simple one. Castañeda remarks that the duty to adhere to a new moral code "must not bring in new errors and must not jeopardize the stability and security that members of the community" who live by the established code "need in order to engage in their life projects."[12] Accordingly, he gives stringent conditions to be met before a new code overrides the established one. For instance, A must know that "it is highly probable that his action, if performed, would bring about the substitution of the new ethical system S for the old ethical system S."[13]

This condition seems too stringent, too conservative in its thrust. Castañeda may be overestimating the amount of stability and security that people need to engage in their life proj-

ects, and in any case, the instability caused by A acting contrary to the old code must be weighed against the possibility
that defects of that code will become entrenched if people such
as A conform to it. Furthermore, to require that A *know* that
his or her action will bring about the needed change is to
strangle the possibility for moral reform or revolution in all but
the most exceptional situations. Almost always, reformers and
revolutionaries act individually or in small groups, and the
most they can have is the reasonable hope that others will
follow suit.

These disagreements I have with Castañeda bring out a
more fundamental point, however. The issue of resolving conflicts between the moral ideal and the established code is a
moral issue. To resolve these conflicts, we must move beyond
the established code and refer to some ideal — an ideal of moral
change. This ideal provides some principled means of taking
into account the sorts of considerations Castañeda and I have
raised. In other words, an ideal of morality may not only contain some general ideas on how people are to act and feel
toward one another but also some ideas on how they are to act
and feel in a world where established codes are defective and
need change. My claim is that if A really ought to act according to an established code, or if A ought to act according to a
revised code, considering all relevant dimensions of morality
and priority rankings, then there must be a practition directing A to do so that is a member of a set adequate from the
standpoint of an ideal of morality and moral change. It is better to make it explicit in an analysis that a true "A ought to do
X" statement must be founded on an adequate set.

A second doubt to be raised concerns Castañeda's characterization of the ideal of morality. Remember that his ideal is
the consistent maximal harmonization of all agents' self-
fulfillment. This characterization is broad enough to embrace
a variety of moral codes, but it is skewed toward a particular
kind of morality. For instance, it is antiutilitarian in the sense
that it rules out any code intended to maximize total happiness
summed over a population of agents. It is Kantian in stressing
the value of the individual and his or her autonomy.[14] In contrasting his ideal of morality with utilitarianism, Castañeda
argues that the criterion of the greatest happiness for the great-

est number leads to injustices and cruelties. But this argument comes too close to saying that utilitarianism is wrong because it fails to meet the Kantian ideal, for many a classical utilitarian would be willing to defend the practices and institutions that meet the criterion of the greatest happiness, whether or not a Kantian would call them unjust or cruel.

Of course, the utilitarian's willingness to disagree with the Kantian doesn't by itself show that his or her disagreement should be taken seriously — as equally right or equally moral. The superiority of the Kantian ideal, however, should not be presupposed at this stage in the analysis of "A ought to do X" statements. Right now, we want an analysis that will give us an understanding of what kinds of claims Kantians and utilitarians are making when they make "A ought to do X" statements; but we also want an analysis that will not automatically commit us to the judgment that utilitarians are wrong. That matter can be determined only after we have an idea of how the truth conditions for Kantians and utilitarians are fixed. Presumably, the fixing of these conditions will determine whether the Kantian ideal is superior to the utilitarian ideal. Let me borrow a distinction from Rawls to summarize the reasoning here. If we want an analysis that allows for moral relativity, we need a "thin" conception of the truth conditions of "A ought to do X" statements that will not presuppose the adequacy or inadequacy of any single ideal of morality. Later, we will need a "full" or comprehensive conception of the truth conditions that includes a description of how these conditions are fixed for any group of language users.[15] Once we have the full conception, it is possible to go about determining whether the Kantian ideal of morality is really superior to other ideals, utilitarian and nonutilitarian. And it is important to note that there are nonutilitarian, non-Kantian ideals. Much modern moral philosophy seems premised on the assumption that the only possibilities are Kant and utilitarianism. In this book, I shall not in fact concentrate on the opposition between these two, but on the opposition between rights-centered ideals (Kant falls into this broad category) and virtue-centered ideals (those that emphasize the common good of a shared life instead of individual autonomy).

This leads me to the point that Castañeda's ideal leaves out those moralities that emphasize the self-fulfillment to be found in social relationships, instead of emphasizing the need to prevent collisions between agents who are separately pursuing individual plans of fulfillment. For Aristotle and for Confucius, to be human meant to have friendships, or to be part of a family, and to be part of a community. Their conceptions of how agents ought to behave were governed by the ideal of sustaining this essential good. From the perspective of relativism, Castañeda's ideal of morality is arbitrarily restrictive. He does not give sufficient argument to show that other possible ideals are invalid.

The same conclusion is suggested by the possible objection that his ideal is too permissive from the perspective of some moralities. Castañeda allows that different moral codes may be equally valid from the standpoint of the ideal since there are different ways of restricting each agent to a range of types of self-fulfillment. Aristotle was not so tolerant. He thought that the highest form of self-fulfillment had to include the contemplation of truth. Medieval Christian moralists had a different list of virtues but no inclination to allow for different roads to self-fulfillment. Are we to say that they misconceived the ideal of morality? That is a possibility, but another possibility is that Castañeda has simply transferred the liberal and tolerant spirit of his morality into an absolute ideal. He does not account for the fact that other ideals narrow the range of adequate moral codes to a much greater degree than his does. Now I do not mean to imply that these other ideals should be taken to be equally right, but Castañeda has not ruled out the possibility that they are. And as I say above, we want to allow for such a possibility at this stage of the analysis.

A final doubt concerns Castañeda's analysis of "A ought to do X" statements as statements about practitions and propositions but not about agents and actions. This certainly does not fit our intuitive apprehension of the logical behavior of the names and descriptions for which 'A' and 'X' are place holders. They are *used,* not mentioned. Castañeda recognizes this, and that is why he presents his analysis as giving the truth conditions only and not the full meaning of "A ought to do X" statements. The problem is that a truth conditions analysis should tell us something about the contribution of various parts of the statement to the truth conditions of the whole and two parts of "A ought to do X" statements are names and descriptions of nonlinguistic items. An analysis that refers to practitions and propositions, and not agents and actions, does not reveal the manner in which the relevant terms contribute. At the least, Castañeda should explain why these names and descriptions do not contribute to truth conditions in the way we expect them to.[16]

He has said that normative statements appear to be about objects and actions because they are patterned on the language of natural facts, providing "the users of the language of action with the model of empirical facts so that they can imagine the nonnatural properties rightness, wrongness, obligatoriness as inhering in objects or actions." Since we can get along without the language of 'ought' as far as truth conditions are concerned, substituting the talk of imperatives and intentions, the deontic properties are not really of this world. But this bit of gloss confuses us more than ever, because there is no clear explanation of why our normative language should be modeled after empirical facts so that we can talk about deontic properties that are not of this world. Castañeda suggests that it is "a product of that metaphysical nature of man in which Kant was greatly interested," but this is not an explanation.[17]

Castañeda could reply that his analysis *does* explain why "A ought to do X" statements lack a pushing aspect on many occasions, why they may be used as instruments of deliberation about reasons for action, and why at the same time we can make such statements without actually specifying the reasons for A doing X (since such statements merely assert the existence of reasons). But we should be able to provide an alternative explanation of these facts that does not make a mystery of the way that crucial terms in an "A ought to do X" statement contribute to its truth conditions. I will show how this can be done under my own analysis.

To summarize, given that our aim is to develop the most plausible truth conditions analysis compatible with relativism, it is necessary to develop one that allows for greater relativity in what counts as a correct set of practitions within the moral context. At the same time, we want an analysis that makes more explicit the connection between the truth of a moral "A ought to do X" statement and the adequacy of the set of practitions to which the statement makes reference. It is also desirable to have an analysis that explains how the names and descriptions for which 'A' and 'X' are place holders contribute to the truth conditions of the statements, or if that is not possible, we want an explanation of why there appear to be names and descriptions of agents and actions in the statements. Concurrently, we have found useful Castañeda's idea of morality as founded on a set of practitions and an ideal for those practitions. His idea allows us to view morality as a social creation (practitions are accepted out of the need to resolve internal conflicts in requirements when these affect others and the need to resolve interpersonal conflict of interest) without committing us to view it as implicit agreement. Furthermore, his idea of analyzing "A ought to do X" statements as statements about the justifiability of practitions allows us to explain the fact that 'ought' finds its home in deliberative and reason-giving contexts.

4 The Recommended Relativist Analysis of Moral "A ought to do X" Statements

4.1 *Rules and moral statements*

In developing an analysis that avoids the weaknesses of previous relativist analyses and incorporates their strengths, let me begin by instituting a change in terminology. 'Rule' will be used in roughly the same way as Castañeda's 'practition'. The canonical expression of a rule is "A is to do X" or "If C then A is to do X," where 'C' is a place holder for a sentence type used to identify conditions under which A is to do X. A rule can be the content of various imperatives or intentions. We may think of it as an equivalence class of sentence tokens, characteristically used as a directive to some agent or agents to perform some action or type of action.

In common usage, 'rule' is used to refer to things with such a use and sometimes to those statements containing terms such as 'ought', 'must', and 'obligatory' that have the effect of requiring agents to adhere to some policy of action. It is no great distortion of common usage to restrict the reference of the term to the directives containing no explicitly normative terms. I prefer to use a term like 'rule' instead of Castañeda's 'practition' because the former is a term of common usage, and using it in the analysis of "A ought to do X" statements will help to illustrate my thesis that the use of 'ought' evolved in a natural way from common normative language of the first order.

My thesis is that rules were the first means by which people began to formulate and to recommend to each other actions or policies of action. At first, they may have used rules of the simplest form "A is to do X." As they became more sophisticated

and reflective about the use of their rules, they noted conditions under which this or that policy of action was to be carried
out, and they used rules of the form "If C, A is to do X." They
went on to develop general rules of the form "If C, everyone is
to do X," from which more specific rules about particular
agents could be derived. It was useful to develop a language
for talking about which rule applied to agents given certain
conditions, or which rule applied to agents given certain rules
applying to all agents. An "A ought to do X" statement may be
interpreted as telling us (in part) that by not doing X, A would
be breaking a rule under certain conditions that obtain. But
how are we to distinguish a moral "A ought to do X" statement
from the other kinds?

As the culture of a group or society develops, it becomes possible to distinguish different sets of rules the uses of which have
different points: the set of rules intended to identify the necessary or efficient means of achieving a given end; the set for
defining social manners or etiquette; and the set for resolving
internal conflicts of requirements (stemming from an individual's different needs, desires, and goals) that affect others and
for resolving interpersonal conflicts of interest in general. The
latter set gives rise to morality. An "A ought to do X" statement may be interpreted as telling us (in part) that under certain conditions that obtain, A would be breaking a rule belonging to that set of rules for resolving internal and interpersonal conflicts.

It may be asked why morality doesn't have the same function
as law with respect to the resolution of interpersonal conflict
and as that of psychotherapy with respect to the resolution of
internal conflict. The functions of morality do overlap with
those of law and therapy, but morality has both functions.
This is partly how it is distinguished from others. To the
extent, furthermore, that therapy refrains from proposing a
comprehensive ideal of the way people ought to be and behave, it is much more limited in its attempts to reconcile internal conflict. Many contemporary therapies address themselves
solely to the elimination or management of disfunctions that
prevent a person from fulfilling his or her major goals, whatever they may be. To the extent that therapy does propose a

comprehensive ideal of the person (Freud approached this), it becomes more like a morality (that is why some call Freud a moralist). Similarly, legal systems are characteristically more limited than morality in performing the function of reconciling interpersonal conflict. For instance, our legal system generally does not punish or require compensation for broken promises between friends. Appendix A gives a fuller discussion of the point of moral rules and more details on which sets of rules would be allowed as moral and which would be excluded.

It is more informative, however, to talk of a "system" of rules than a set, for there may be priority orderings of the rules to take care of cases of conflict. For example, promise-keeping and truth-telling give way to saving lives (for most of us, though not for Kant). In Rawls' theory of justice, maximizing equal liberty is not to be sacrificed for the just distribution of other primary social goods, such as income and wealth.

There are many possible systems of rules that would fit the description of a moral system. Which one would be relevant to a moral "A ought to do X" statement? Applying the lesson learned in the discussion of Castañeda's analysis, we will make it explicit that true moral "A ought to do X" statements are founded on moral systems that are adequate with respect to some ideal of morality (that includes an ideal of moral change). The simplest way to do this is to analyze such statements as referring to an "adequate" moral system (Roger Wertheimer utilizes the notion of adequacy in his analysis of "A ought to do X" statements, though his analysis is nonrelativistic and does not use the notions of rule or practition).[1] Now it may be objected that a potential circularity threatens if we insert a term such as 'adequate' into the analysis. Is an adequate moral system one that we *ought* to follow?

Of course, but we need not explicate adequacy in terms of 'ought'. Instead, we may think of standards for moral systems of the form "M is to be F," where 'M' is a place holder for the description of a moral system and 'F' for a description of some characteristic of moral systems. Standards are part of the most basic normative language, along with rules, and their function is the specification of ideals to be fulfilled. An adequate moral system meets the standards for moral systems. A complete list of such standards specify the ideal of morality. Castañeda's ideal — that a morality harmonize the maximal self-fulfillment of all agents — could be spelled out in terms of standards. One would expect that his ideal would be satisfied by a Kantian morality that is centered around the principle of humanity as an end in itself — that one is never to treat humanity, whether in one's own person or those of others, as a means only but always as an end in itself. Speakers accept a moral system with the implicit presupposition that it is adequate.

'Adequate moral system' is not used frequently in ordinary moral discourse. The term is a modest idealization in the sense that I have chosen it as a more explicit rendering of what people have in mind when they use terms such as 'the right moral rules'. In the next chapter, I will discuss the way moral language users fix the semantic contribution of 'adequate moral system' to the truth conditions of "A ought to do X" statements. This is a convenient way for me to discuss the way users fix the semantic contribution of terms such as 'the right moral rules'.

4.2   *An analysis of the moral "A ought to do X"*

With the above introduction to rules and adequate moral systems, let me state an analysis of moral "A ought to do X" statements as referring to these things:

By not doing X under actual conditions C, A will be breaking a rule of an adequate moral system applying to him or her.

Notice that the subject matter of the analysis includes the agent A and the possible action X.[2] Under my analysis, the names or descriptions of the agent and action are used and not mentioned, in contrast to Castañeda's analysis. This move preserves what seems to be an a logical feature of "A ought to do X" statements.

The insertion of the clause "under actual conditions C" is founded on the view that an "A ought to do X" statement is always implicitly or explicitly relativized to such a clause.[3] What we ought to do is relative to the circumstances in which we take action. The moral reasons for this or that action are often based on what we have done or been in the past (such as having made a promise or assumed an office with responsibilities) and what others have done. Or they depend on the predictable effects of actions.[4] This feature allows an explanation of *prima facie* obligations, pairs of which can hold even when they are obligations to do conflicting actions. To adapt an example of Castañeda's, let us suppose Smith may have an obligation to wait for Jones' friend, under the condition that Smith promised Jones to wait for that friend. Smith may also have an obligation not to wait for Jones' friend, under the condition that he promised his wife not to wait for Peter, who turns out to be Jones' friend. Notice that the obligations are not "detachable" from their conditions. We cannot treat the clause "under the actual conditions that" as an 'if' as in "If . . . then . . ." and perform a *modus ponens*. If it is true that Smith promised Jones to wait for Jones' friend, then we are *not* entitled to conclude that Smith has an obligation to wait for Jones' friend *simpliciter*.

Relativizing "A ought to do X" statements to a conditions clause also helps to explain the function of *ceteris paribus* clauses when these are attached to the statements. "Other things being equal, A ought to do X" can be construed as implicitly relativized to a set of conditions of which the speaker is aware and of which he or she assumes the audience is aware. The clause is usually used when the speaker is not familiar with many of the other conditions obtaining in the situation in question and wants to warn the audience that there may be other considerations which weigh against A doing X. Or the speaker may know of such conditions, but may want to establish the moral implications of one aspect of a complex situation in the course of deliberating over what ought to be done, all things considered.

This brings me to another kind of moral "A ought to do X" statement, which purports to be a final or conclusive prescription to action. In Castañeda's example, it is concluded that Smith's obligation to his wife is the stronger, and that he ought not to wait for Peter. It is this kind of 'ought' that possesses a "pushing aspect," as Castañeda calls it, in contrast to 'ought's that express *prima facie* obligations. This final 'ought' may be subsumed under the above analysis.[5] It is an 'ought' relativized to all relevant conditions, including Smith's promise to Jones and his promise to his wife. This explains why the final 'ought' is action-guiding in a way that others are not. After having taken into account everything that is relevant, the speaker is ready to make a final recommendation for action.

We may now analyze several kinds of conditions that "A ought to do X" statements may be relativized to, given what I have laid down so far. Statements like "If John made a promise to Joe, then he ought to keep it" give sufficient conditions for the existence of a *prima facie* obligation ("By not keeping the promise to Joe, under the condition that John made a promise to Joe, John will be breaking a rule of an adequate moral system applying to him"), but they do not commit the speaker to the actuality of these conditions. Or they give sufficient conditions for a final, overriding obligation ("By not keeping the promise to Joe, under the condition that John made a promise to Joe, and all other relevant actual conditions, John will be breaking a rule..."), but again, they do not commit the speaker to the actuality of the explicitly mentioned conditions. The context of utterance determines which kind of statement is being expressed, while the conditioning clause has the effect of canceling out the claim that the conditions to which the statement is being explicitly relativized are actual. We may interpret statements such as "John ought to give money to Joe only if he promised to give it" as giving necessary conditions for the existence of a *prima facie* or final, overriding obligation, while not committing the speaker to the actuality of these conditions. Finally, there are conditions of defeasibility, which specify when an obligation is canceled (if Susan marries Fred on Wednesday, it's not the case that Joe ought to keep the promise he made on Monday to marry Susan on Friday). We may treat such conditions as corresponding to necessary conditions for the existence of a *prima facie* or final, overriding obligation (so Joe has a *prima facie* obligation to marry Susan on Friday only if she has not married anyone else since he made the promise).

Let me point out certain explanatory virtues that my analysis shares with Castañeda's. My analysis allows for true "A ought to do X" statements identifying *prima facie* obligations to lack a pushing aspect. When a speaker relativizes such a statement to some relevant condition but does not commit himself or herself to saying they are all the relevant conditions, there may be no intention for the statement to contribute causally to A doing X. Also, my analysis shows how "A ought to do X" statements may be used as instruments of deliberation, to point to reasons for action without actually specifying them. Reasons may be relevant conditions C, which may be left implicit, or they may be rules of an adequate moral system.

Note that the analysis contains a reference not only to an adequate moral system but an adequate moral system applying to the agent. Why the qualification? It is desirable to allow for a kind of variation in moral systems that does not stem from a variation in what we would ordinarily classify under the "conditions C" clause. Castañeda provides an example of what I have in mind: he believes that monogamy is morally right in a community approximately evenly distributed between members of the sexes, who are heterosexual, and who satisfy other appropriate conditions, but that in an entirely different situation, in which the female population is, say, only ten percent of the total population, the polyandric family is right.[6] Rawls provides another example: the lexical ordering of his two principles of justice means that the liberty of individuals may be restricted only for the sake of obtaining a better balance within the total system of liberties, not for the sake of achieving a more just distribution of other primary social goods such as income and wealth; however, Rawls believes that it may be reasonable to forgo certain political liberties (some may have more votes than others, or the votes of some may be weighted more heavily, or a segment of society may be without the franchise altogether) and rights of fair equality of opportunity, "when the long-run benefits are great enough to transform a less fortunate society into one where the equal liberties can be fully enjoyed."[7]

The kinds of conditions to which Castañeda and Rawls refer are not of the same order as conditions such as having made a promise or the predictable effects of a single action. Differences in the former result in systematic and widespread differences in the moral rules that apply to societies. These conditions concern the human and material resources available to whole groups and societies. They also include the ways in which the environment is affected by other groups and societies. A group that is under constant threat of attack by marauding enemies may tolerate aggression and violence in its members simply because these qualities are needed in its defense.

What this implies is that a number of moral systems may be equally adequate from the standpoint of an ideal of morality. How may we allow for this in terms of the analysis? Let us call the set of systems that satisfy the sentential function "Y is an adequate moral system" the "extension" of the term 'adequate moral system'. Then we may say that the extension may contain a number of moral systems that conflict with each other with regard to the content of rules or to priority orderings among the same rules. Which moral system applies to a given group or society depends on conditions of the sort just described. There may be, furthermore, more than one system that is appropriate to the conditions of a group or a society. In this case, choice among the equally adequate and equally appropriate systems would be "optional." That is, the relevant system would be determined by the subscriptions of the members of the group or society (I use 'subscription' in Castañeda's sense, referring to desires to act in accordance with a system of rules).

There is one other potential source of relativity in what one morally ought to do. The extension of 'adequate moral system' could vary, as the term is used in different groups and societies. This would correspond to variation in the ideal of morality, and to indicate such a possibility, we could add a subscript to the term: 'adequate$_i$ moral system'. I have not formally included the subscript in the above analysis of moral "A ought to do X" statements, because it would be misleading to do so in one important respect. The term is not learned as varying in extension, as are indexicals, for instance. A competent language user could have 'adequate moral system' or 'the right moral rules' in his or her idiolect, and be completely unaware that it could vary in extension. It is as analysts of moral language, not necessarily as users, that we attach the subscript to 'adequate'.

Now it may be asked why I treat 'adequate moral system' as a single term with varying extensions if I admit that the term is not *learned* as a single term with varying extensions. Why not say that where the extension varies, there are different terms? One reason is that tokens of the term make the same *kind* of semantic contribution to the truth conditions of moral "A ought to do X" statements, even though they may have different extensions. That is, they pick out a subset of moral systems, one of which is then applied to pick out the action required of the agent in the circumstances.

Another reason is that treating tokens with different extensions as tokens of the same term is a way of conveying the sameness of their potential *use*. Moral systems are all action-guiding systems. Tokens referring to a subset of these systems all have the potential of being used to tell agents what to do. This sameness of use explains how there can be a pragmatic conflict between different moral "A ought to do X" statements, even though these statements refer to different sets of adequate moral systems. A speaker B may say of A that he ought to do X under conditions C. A speaker D may say of A that he ought not to do X under the same conditions C. If 'adequate moral system' has different extensions in the idiolects of B and D, both statements may be true, and there is no conflict between the statements generated by their truth conditions. There is, however, at least a potential pragmatic conflict, because both statements may have the illocutionary force of prescription and they would be *conflicting* prescriptions. This stems from the fact that moral systems are all action-guiding systems and there is no *a priori* reason to think that an agent would fall within the scope of just one adequate moral system or just one set of them that constitutes one extension of the term. Allowing for such pragmatic conflict where there is no conflict on the level of truth conditions is a way of explaining how there can be the kind of moral disagreement that allows no resolution, by reference to facts of any kind.

Obviously, relativity in the extension of 'adequate moral system' is an important kind of relativity in what one ought to do, and its existence or nonexistence must be at the heart of the debate between relativists and absolutists. It is, therefore, important to clarify the ways in which the extension comes to be fixed for the term. In developing a theory on this matter, we must take into account the term's complex structure. It is a noun phrase containing two adjectives. The adjectives have a special logical character.

To define this character, let us distinguish between the attributive position for an adjective and the predicative position. The former is revealed by the schema "Y is an AM," where 'M' is a place holder for a noun and 'A' for the adjective in question, while the latter is revealed by the schema "Y is A and Y is an M." The adjective 'moral' and 'adequate' are both found in the attributive position. Now some adjectives occurring in this position are analyzable in terms of their corresponding occurrences in predicative positions, but some are not. The adjective 'red' as it occurs in "Sam is a red flea" is analyzable as "Sam is red and Sam is a flea." On the other hand, the adjective 'large' as it occurs in "Sam is a large flea" is *not* analyzable as "Sam is large and Sam is a flea." Adjectives like 'large' are called "attributive adjectives." 'Moral' and 'adequate' fall into this class. "Y is a moral system" does not imply "Y is moral and Y is a system." It is as inappropriate to uncouple 'moral' from 'system' as it was to uncouple 'large' from 'flea'. Similarly, "Y is an adequate system" does not imply "Y is adequate and Y is a system" (consider also "George is an adequate plumber").

The fact that attributive adjectives should not be uncoupled from the nouns they modify is a clue to the way they might contribute to the extensions of the noun phrases in which they occur. We may think of them as operators on sentential functions with n variables (such as "Y is a system"), forming more complex functions (such as "Y is a moral system" or "Y is an adequate moral system"). These operators correspond to functions which take sets of n-tuples of the domain (under a certain description, such as "system of rules" or "moral system of rules") to sets of n-tuples of the domain. As was noted when 'adequate moral system' was first introduced, we could spell out the notion of the adequacy of a moral system with the use of standards of the form "M is to be F," where 'F' expresses a characteristic possessed by all adequate moral systems. The same could be done for the notion of a moral system, and in fact this was implicitly done when 'moral system' was defined above.

Given this sketch of the logical structure of the term, we are now ready to ask the crucial question of the next chapter: "How is the extension determined for a given group of moral language users?" The way we answer this question will affect the way we decide the question of absolutism versus relativism.

5 The Analysis of "A ought to do X" Statements Completed

5.1 *Applying theories of reference*

To answer the question of how the reference of 'adequate moral system' is determined, we must have an idea of the theories of reference we could apply. There are two broad categories: "descriptive" and "causal" theories. I do not claim that these are the only kinds of theories of reference. Indeed, I shall be discussing below the possibility of combining elements of both kinds and applying the new theory to 'adequate moral system'. Other than a combination of the two kinds, however, at present I do not know of other theories of reference that are even remotely plausible when applied to 'adequate moral system'.

The descriptive theory has its roots in Frege and has been given more recent formulations by Strawson and Searle. According to this theory, the reference of a term is just the set of things that uniquely satisfies a set of descriptions associated with the term. These descriptions are embedded in the beliefs of those who use the term. Now descriptive theorists want to allow that some descriptions associated with a term are false of the reference, so they must propose ways to distinguish those descriptions that fix reference from those that do not. Some descriptive theorists have said that the reference is that which renders a majority of associated descriptions true.[1]

Such a proposal seems excessively democratic. There are degrees of firmness with which a description is held to be true of a term's reference. Take a man who believes in witches, and let us say that he associates with the term 'witch' the descriptions "is able to ride on broomsticks through the air" and "is a human being with supernatural powers." If he were forced to choose between the two descriptions (told that one had to be false), there would be no doubt which one he would choose. Some descriptions associated with a term, furthermore, are secondary to others in the sense that they are clearly derived from other descriptions with the help of collateral information (here I disagree with an implication of Quine's attack on the analytic-synthetic distinction: in some cases, we can identify some information as clearly collateral), and they would be withdrawn by users of the term if they came to believe that the information was false or that the derivation was invalid. For instance, if the man who believed in witches lived in Salem, Massachusetts, in the late 1600s, he might have come to associate with 'witch' some descriptions derived from observation of people to whom the term was applied. If he were to be convinced, however, that those people did not in fact have supernatural powers, he would no longer be willing to apply the derived descriptions to witches. So an alternative to simple majoritarianism is taking into account the degree of firmness to which a description is associated with a term and the possibility of its being primary or secondary to other descriptions with which it is incompatible. Of course, I do not pretend to have stated a complete descriptive theory of reference, nor to have solved all the problems of such a theory, but I believe that I have sketched the main outlines of what a descriptive theory would have to look like once a complete statement is given.

Such a theory does seem well-suited to some terms. 'Witch' is one of them. We use the term with the intention of referring to whatever satisfies certain descriptions, and if a speaker does not believe anything satisfies the descriptions, he or she will believe there are no witches. On the contrary, the descriptive theory does not seem well-suited to other terms in a language. In particular, the references of some terms are such that it is possible for speakers to have largely false beliefs about their nature.

Kripke's causal theory of the reference of proper names is based on this insight. According to that theory, we assign to tokens of a name uttered by a speaker whatever referent we assign to the tokens of the same name uttered by the person from whom the speaker acquired the name; and the causal chain begins at a dubbing ceremony in which there is a pointing to the object to be named or an identification of it through descriptions.[2] The chain of reference transmission is distinguished from any chain through which beliefs about the nature of the referent are passed from speaker to speaker. Not only does this theory allow speakers to have largely false beliefs about an object to which they are referring, it allows them to be largely ignorant of the nature of the object, to the extent that they could not pick it out if asked.

Kripke and Hilary Putnam both have argued that the descriptions we associate with the extensions of natural kind terms do not necessarily pick out those extensions. The extensions are determined in part by the actual nature of the particular things serving as paradigms of the references. That actual nature may not be fully known to the typical user, nor perhaps to anyone at a given time. Putnam points to 'gold' and its cognate term in Greek to illustrate his assertion. The Greeks may have identified as gold metals that were not gold because their identification methods were relatively crude. This does not mean difference in extension; they simply had some false beliefs as to which metals were gold.[3]

If we were to apply a causal theory to natural kind terms analogous to Kripke's theory of proper names, we would talk about a time when the extensions of the terms were fixed that is analogous to the time of a dubbing. It is more realistic to say that over a period of time a number of people used pointing and descriptions to propose partial or tentative extensions for terms such as 'gold'. At the end of the period, there is general agreement that an extension has been picked out for the term. Let us call this process of fixing the extension an "E determination." Once it is performed, each speaker resolves to use the term with the same extension as the speaker from whom he or she acquired the term. Any speaker could have false beliefs about the extension, but the extension could still be preserved.[4]

Now Kripke's and Putnam's theories seem better suited to proper names and natural kind terms than the descriptive theory, but it is doubtful that they provide us with a *general* account of how the reference of these terms is fixed and transmitted. Gareth Evans has shown that Kripke's causal theory does not adequately account for proper names that have undergone certain changes in reference. His example is 'Madagascar', corrupt form of the name that originally stood for a part of the African mainland and that was taken by Marco Polo to stand for the African Island. Surely, the name now stands for the island no matter what it originally stood for. Evan's solution is to propose a theory of reference that is causal in a broad sense, since he agrees with Kripke that beliefs do not pick out the references of proper names. Very roughly, his theory is that the referent of a term may be that object or set of objects causally responsible for the speaker's possession of information about the object (much of this information may be false), whether or not it is at the dubbing end of a Kripkean chain of intentions to corefer (this is not the case with Madagascar). If there is more than one object causally responsible for a speaker's beliefs, the referent is the one that is *dominantly* responsible, where dominance is a function not only of amount of information but spread of information contributed by an object.[5]

The lesson to be drawn from this discussion of descriptive and causal theories of reference is that no one theory is likely to be the most applicable to all terms with reference. To the question of which theory is most applicable to a given term, we have to answer that it all depends. A descriptive theory is most applicable when speakers use a term with the intention of referring to whatever satisfies certain descriptions. In such a case, the possibility that speakers may be largely mistaken about the nature of a referent (if it exists) is ruled out, though the possibility of some (perhaps many, if we move away from simple majoritarianism in counting descriptions) false beliefs about a referent is not ruled out. Causal theories seem most applicable when speakers use a term with the intention of referring to whatever the persons from whom they acquired the terms refer to (under Kripke's theory), or with the intention of referring to something that is causally responsible for a community's beliefs about it (under Evans' theory). In such cases, the possibility that speakers may be largely mistaken about the nature of a referent is admitted. The choice of which theory to apply will depend on the particular evidence we have for the nature of the intentions of speakers who use the term in question, and it will depend on what is the most plausible fit (or lack of fit) between beliefs about the referent and its actual nature. It is also possible, as I shall argue below, that a combination of the two theories is the most suitable for a given term.

5.2   A causal theory of moral reference?

It may be thought that we can dismiss the causal theory in the case of 'adequate moral system' because it is a description with a complex internal structure and so is quite different from the proper names and natural kind terms for which that theory seems suited. After all, don't different components of the term each make a contribution to the determination of its extension? How is this captured under the causal theory?

These considerations are not conclusive. A description with a complex structure may be used like a name. Its reference may be fixed and transmitted from speaker to speaker in a way that is more accurately described by a causal theory. In fact, many names were originally composed of descriptions. Take "The One with Whom One Usually Rubs Noses," a translation of an Eskimo name, or "The Holy Roman Empire." The question of what theory of reference applies to 'adequate moral system', therefore, is still an open one. Descriptions that moral language users associate with 'adequate' and 'moral' may be indicative of their beliefs about the nature of the referent, but the referent may be fixed and transmitted in a way that is described more accurately by the causal theory. Let me begin discussion of that question by describing how causal theories could be applied to the term. Then we can evaluate the suitability of the theories along the dimensions mentioned above.

If we were to apply a Kripkean causal theory to 'adequate moral system', we would begin by positing a period of E determination for the term, corresponding to such a period in the case of natural kind terms. During this period, a group will pick out a set of moral systems as the adequate ones. They will do this through a set of descriptions. Remember that Kripke and Putnam allow dubbings through description. In fact, almost everything I will say about the course of events during an E determination will apply to the way in which the extension would be fixed under the descriptive theory. The primary difference between the two theories lies in the stories told about transmission of reference once it is fixed.

The reference-fixing descriptions will set the nature of an adequate moral system and are equivalent to standards for adequacy. For instance, the standards may stipulate that a moral system is to have rules that accord equal consideration to the interests of every person. There would have to be other standards that spell out what it is to accord equal considera- tion — to refrain from interfering with a person's freedom of action except under a specified set of conditions, for instance.

During the period of E determination, a group of speakers may formulate standards of adequacy at the same time that it develops the practices and institutions that constitute its way of life. The group, however, may formulate standards in a period of reflection on a way of life that has already taken shape. In his study of ancient Egyptian morality, James Breasted observed that the earliest thinkers did not use distinctively moral terms. Instead, they talked of "what is loved" and "what is hated." It was quite a while before such terms were partially displaced by terms that are the correlates of our 'right' and 'wrong'.[6] A group may develop standards of adequacy by using the relationships between people in one of its institutions as a model for relationships between people in general. For instance, the dominant moralities of ancient Egypt and China emphasize filial piety as the most fundamental virtue from which all others grow.[7] Patterns of behavior required in the family are taken as models for behavior in the larger com- munity. More generally, it is possible, as Alasdair MacIntyre suggests, that moral rules are first formulated in order to define the duties of people who assume roles in the social order, such as that of king or warrior or shepherd.[8] There are different kinds of processes through which a group may settle on the standards for adequate moral systems. They *could* settle on them via an implicit agreement of the sort Harman has in mind. Certain standards, however, may gain acceptance throughout the group because some of its members present them as sanctioned by a powerful and wise deity. Or one segment of the group may favor certain standards and gain acceptance for them because of its power and influence. It is probable that a mixture of such factors go into a group's selection of standards.

What happens after an E determination? Under a Kripkean theory we would say that a causal chain of reference transmission forms, the links of which are the intentions of each speaker to refer to the same set of adequate moral systems as those to which the person from whom the term is acquired refers. Over generations, a moral tradition is born. This theory would allow for gaps between custom and moral ideal and for the development of misinformation about the nature of the adequate moral system. For instance, it is always in the self-interest of some people forming links in the chain of reference transmission to spread misinformation about the nature of the rules. An example would be a slaveholding class that promotes the doctrine that the possession of people is morally permissible, even though the rules of an adequate moral system for that class prohibit the practice (more on this below). When many rules are systematically distorted, and when a group still has the intention of referring to the same rules originally determined as adequate, we have radical moral error.

We have seen what kinds of intentions would be attributed to users of 'adequate moral system' under a Kripkean theory. Is this implication of the theory plausible? In some cultures, people say that their morality is the morality of their ancestors—a stable system of rules and an ideal to which the rules are thought to conform are handed down from generation to generation.[9] The Kripkean intentions seem to be present here. The theory, however, does not accord well with the intentions of users during times of moral reform and revolution. A person may adhere to a moral tradition in the sense of subscribing to many of its rules but may come to believe that the founders of that tradition were too limited in their conception of an adequate moral system. That person would have little interest in referring to exactly the set of moral systems the founders had in mind when performing the original E determination.

One example of this is an important kind of change that may occur within a moral tradition: an expansion of the circle within which the moral rules are held applicable. This circle embraces the domain of agents who have duties and the domain of patients who are owed certain duties. Moralities typically start as systems limited in application to the group in which they originate. Hobhouse tells us that in Rome a defeated enemy was in principle rightless. The conquered were put to death in large numbers.[10] Later, the Stoics advocated better treatment for slaves. Seneca argued that the slave was a human being with rights and dignity.[11] Christianity was a force for widening the moral circle, condemning murder of any kind without regard to nationality or race.

How does such change occur? Many moral rules arise from the need to regulate interpersonal conflicts of interest, and when a group is relatively self-contained, with little or no interaction with outsiders except for war and occasional trade, the moral rules are naturally limited in application to those whose conduct they are intended to regulate. This may be particularly true, as May and Abraham Edel suggest, for groups or societies in which the moral rules were originally intended to regulate and define family and kin relationships.[12] The performance of duties is owed to specific people occupying particular social roles or statuses. As a group expands, however, and takes in those who were previously regarded as distant outsiders, there may be pressure to recognize their moral status.

When different families or clans cooperate to fulfill their needs, they must have rules to structure their cooperation and to resolve their conflicts. The solution is to extend some moral rules that previously applied only *within* the family or clan to relations between the different families and clans. Similarly, when larger groups interact, moral rules that previously applied only within each group are extended to relations between groups. To the extent that two groups cooperate voluntarily, they will need to regulate their interactions by rules that both acknowledge as binding. An example of a needed rule is one that requires the keeping of agreements, which would be crucial for structuring economic interaction. Another example would be a rule requiring reciprocation of aid. Even when one group conquers another, there usually will come a time when the dominating group needs some degree of voluntary cooperation from the dominated. Domination through sheer force takes up too many resources for policing, and there are tasks one cannot force someone to do, but which require enduring, voluntary commitment. For such reasons, an "in" group will extend some of its moral rules to a former "out" group it dominates. Note that the Stoic ideal followed Alexander's conquest of the Persian empire and the breakdown of the Greek city states.

The result is a reexamination of a moral tradition. While the founders may have been content to limit application of the moral rules to their own group, the heirs of the tradition will recognize that at least some of the moral rules apply to former "out" groups. Of course, the heirs will usually want to maintain some superiority of status over the former "outs." While some consideration is owed to the former "outs," their interests are not equal in importance to those of one of "us." But once *some* of the moral rules apply to the former "outs," the question arises as to what justifies the difference in moral status. Since kinship or membership in a community does not make a difference with respect to the application of some rules, why does it make a difference with respect to the application of others? Hence the argument for superiority will refer to other traits which differentiate the "ins" from the "outs." Is it trait F? But many of the "outs" have trait F. Perhaps it is trait G. But some "ins" don't have trait G. The heirs may not be able to find a relevant trait to justify their superior status and, from the moral point of view, they will have to give it up.

It may be asked whether this process of gradual inclusion is a necessary consequence of the nature of morality. I see no logical necessity in the fact that kinship groups usually unite into larger groups. And if a larger group remains isolated from the rest of the world, it may have no occasion to question whether its rules should be extended beyond its boundaries. Its morality will remain a purely tribal morality, and I see no compelling reason based on the concept of morality for it to be otherwise. But *once* social, political, and economic factors move a group into some degree of voluntary cooperation with others, to the extent that it applies *some* moral rules to its treatment of former "outs," then I do think that there is a logic that compels an expansion of the domain in which moral rules are applied. Membership in a group per se will no longer be an adequate justification for difference in moral status. The compelling logic is simply a requirement of consistency in practical reasoning. If *some* directives from a moral system but not others, apply to the treatment of a group, then there must be a morally relevant reason for that difference in application. Once some moral rules have been applied to the treatment of a former "out" group, there is a logic compelling the application of the other rules to them (or the discovery of morally relevant reasons for not doing so), but there is no logic compelling the application of moral rules to "out" groups in the first place.

Assuming that such a process of gradual inclusion takes place within a moral tradition, it is not plausible to say that members of a moral tradition simply resolve to use a term such as 'adequate moral system' or 'the right moral rules' with the intention of preserving the reference of the past. What may take place is the formation of a new ideal of morality and along with it a new extension for the terms. In fact, this sort of moral change can occur continuously through a moral tradition. In light of such a possibility, it seems better not to posit a two-stage sequence in which the extension of 'adequate moral system' is determined by description and then passed along from speaker to speaker through the intention to corefer. It is truer to the continuousness of moral change to say that the formulation and reformulation of standards of adequacy, which under a Kripkean theory would be limited to the period of E determination, can occur any time over the history of a moral tradition. There is no *one* discrete period in which the set of adequate moral systems is picked out by description.

Given this conclusion, a causal theory like Evans' may be more appropriate. Under such a theory, the referent of the term is the set of moral systems that plays an appropriate role in a causal explanation of speakers' beliefs about the nature of adequate moral systems. It does not commit us to the Kripkean view that there is a discrete period during which the set of adequate moral systems is fixed. It, furthermore, shares with

Kripke's theory the implication that speakers may have false beliefs about the nature of adequate moral systems.

The case of an important, false moral belief shows how Evans' theory could account for it. Early Christians laid down as the core of their conceptions of the moral ideal a rule that all human beings are to be treated as beings with worth and dignity. But they held slavery to be compatible with such a rule —rendering to Caesar the things that were Caesar's and to God the things that were God's.[13] While this may have justified the toleration of slaveholding by non-Christians, it hardly justified the possession of slaves by martyrs, abbots, bishops, popes, churches, and monasteries.[14] There is inconsistency here, and those who desired to maintain slavery tried to justify its existence in various ways. There were the claims about the natural inferiority of enslaved races that are still made to this day. In the southern United States, there was an attempt to justify slavery as a form of paternalism. Involuntary labor was transformed into legitimate return for the protection and direction of masters. It was claimed that slaves acquiesced to their fate, that they willingly became part of the "family" of which the white master was the father.[15]

In these attempted justifications, we have an illustration of how people can distort, through self-interest, self-deception, or simple misinformation the true implications of what is for them the set of adequate moral systems. But these justifications illustrate how an adequate moral system may play a causal role in the acquisition of false moral beliefs. In justifying the permissibility of slavery by claiming that slaves could not take care of themselves and that they willingly placed themselves in the hands of their masters, white slaveholders paid inadvertent homage to the rule that skin color alone is not to count as a reason for treating someone differently. They recognized that they had to give consideration to the interests of slaves, even if false doctrines allowed slavery to masquerade as consideration of their interests.

Another way in which speakers may come to have a distorted view of the adequate moral systems to which they refer is through false beliefs about the consequences of certain actions or failures to act. A group may regularly sacrifice some of its members to a deity it believes would cause catastrophic famine if not placated. In such cases, we would not be understanding that group correctly if we simply said that human life is cheap under its morality. Supernatural beliefs may justify a vast array of practices that we may initially think are unjustifiable under any conception of an adequate moral system that is remotely like ours. It may be, however, that the set of adequate moral systems that plays an appropriate role (along with supernatural beliefs) in a causal explanation of the belief in the justifiability of these practices is similar to the set to which we refer.

5.3   *The case for applying the descriptive theory*

Given these kinds of cases in which a set of moral systems plays an appropriate role in a causal explanation of speakers' false beliefs about them, we may think that a causal theory such as Evans' is the one to adopt. We must note, however, that in all such cases, speakers do have some knowledge of the rules of adequate moral systems. In their attempt to justify the possession of slaves, masters implicitly acknowledged the need to justify restricting the freedom of human beings, regardless of their skin color. In the case of speakers who acquire a distorted view of which rules are contained in adequate moral systems through false beliefs about the consequences of certain actions or failures to act, we must note that the speakers are only able to acquire this distorted view by combining their false beliefs with a knowledge of some rules of adequate moral systems. These observations suggest that some of the descriptions associated with 'adequate moral system' can be construed as fixing the reference of the term.

This would be consistent with a fact that absolutists like to point out: there are substantive moral beliefs that we cannot conceive to be false. Do we doubt that a person's skin color (in and of itself) is irrelevant to how we ought to treat him or her?[16] This indubitability is explained by saying that we have a reference-fixing description that connects the adequacy of a moral system with a consideration of the interests of human beings regardless of their skin color. Why would this become a reference-fixing belief? We are the heirs of a tradition (or traditions) that has undergone the process of transformation from a kinship or tribal morality, which no longer accepts membership in a group per se as a morally relevant reason for refusing to apply moral rules in our treatment of others. Skin color is like membership in a group. Once we have recognized that some moral rules apply to our treatment of people of a certain color, we must explain why other rules do not apply. Another example of a substantive moral belief we cannot conceive to be false is that we ought not to torture people for our amusement. This belief also would correspond to a reference-fixing description. Why? One of the primary functions of a morality is the resolution of interpersonal conflict. A system of rules that allowed torture for amusement could not possibly achieve this function.

In the discussion of the descriptive theory of reference, I concluded that we could not simply identify the referent of a term as the item or items that satisfied a majority of all associated descriptions. Rather, these descriptions have to be weighted, with some counting more in the determination of reference because of the relative firmness with which they are associated with the term and because they are basic relative to other descriptions (that is, other descriptions of the referent are derived on the assumption that they apply to the referent). According to such criteria, the description that connects the adequacy of a moral system with the consideration of the interests of human beings regardless of their skin color would probably count as a reference-fixing description, and the belief in the permissibility of slavery would turn out to be false. Similarly, such criteria would imply that the belief in the permissibility of human sacrifice would not embody reference-fixing descriptions, because the descriptions they embody are derived from other descriptions of adequate moral systems and (we assume) false beliefs in the supernatural. The way in which a causal theory like Evans' accords with certain features of our moral experience, therefore, leads us to the conclusion that a *descriptive theory* is also applicable to 'adequate moral system'.

Is there some difference between the descriptive and causal

theories when applied to the term? Only if there is a case in which a system of rules plays an appropriate role in a causal explanation of speakers' beliefs about it and if they have no knowledge that would embody descriptions picking out that system. But the relativistic analysis that we are developing here is premised on the theory of morality as social creation, on the theory that there is such a thing as morality only because people have needs to resolve internal and interpersonal conflicts and because they develop rules to meet these needs. But how do we develop them? By conceiving them under certain descriptions. That is, moral rules are creations of the human mind, and as such, we could not fail to have some knowledge of them. Otherwise, we would have no rules.

At this point, we see a convergence between the descriptive theory and a causal theory such as Evans', when they are applied to a reference such as the set of adequate moral systems. By the very nature of the referent, it is created and fixed as the referent through the formulation of descriptions of it. Yet once fixed, it functions in a causal explanation of the acquisition of beliefs about it in such a way that Evans' theory is applicable. Both are true: certain descriptions associated with 'adequate moral system' fix the referent of the term, *and* the referent, once fixed, plays an appropriate role in a causal explanation of speakers' beliefs about it. In the end, we have a theory with causal and descriptive elements in it. The kind of name we give it is a matter of convention. I prefer to think of it as a primarily descriptive theory since fundamental features of adequate moral systems are fixed through descriptions, but it is a descriptive theory with causal elements incorporated into it since knowledge of the fundamental features can lead moral language users to have true or false beliefs about what else is in the systems and what follows from them.

There is another way in which this primarily descriptive theory could have causal elements incorporated into it. Within a moral tradition, some speakers could defer to others in the sense that they accept what these others say about the content of adequate moral systems and intend to refer to whatever systems these others refer to. This possibility is most likely to be realized in a hierarchical social system in which some classes of a society see other classes as superior to them in authority and wisdom. In medieval Europe, the moral teachings of the Church may have been accepted with such deference, and here it is possible for a system of rules to play an appropriate causal role in the explanation of some speakers' beliefs about it and for these speakers to have very little knowledge of the content of the system. They may be taught what is thought necessary to perform their station in life but nothing else. Here we would have to acknowledge a Kripkean causal element in the reference determination of 'adequate moral system' for some speakers, but ultimately the reference is fixed by some descriptions embodied in the beliefs of other speakers. This possibility is realized only in some societies and cultures. In contemporary American society there does not seem to be such deference with respect to reference transmission, since there are no generally acknowledged moral authorities.

Let me discuss the ways in which the descriptive-causal theory could allow for false beliefs about the nature of adequate moral systems. As we have already seen, it allows for many false beliefs about the content of the referent, through simple misinformation about relevant facts, self-deception, and false beliefs about the consequences of actions or failures to act. There is another way in which the theory could allow for false beliefs: if the set of adequate moral systems contains more than one member for a group of speakers, different members of the set may be applicable to different groups and societies, depending on variable conditions such as the availability of human and material resources. It could very well be a complex matter to determine which system is applicable to a given group or society, requiring much knowledge of human psychology, political science, sociology, and economics. The possibility for error is endless. False doctrines about human nature, about the way economic systems work, and so on, could all result in false beliefs about which adequate moral systems apply, given the conditions of a group or society.

A final note on the descriptive-causal theory: it can incorporate everything that was said about the ways in which an E determination of 'adequate moral system' comes about—that the formulation of standards for adequate moral systems may arise from reflection upon a way of life that has already taken shape, or that it may be simultaneous with the growth of that way of life, and that it may begin with the formulation of rules for the family and kin groups and spread outward to larger social units. We do not limit, however, the E determination to one initial period of a moral tradition. We allow for the reference to change at any time in that tradition, when the moral beliefs that embody reference-fixing descriptions (standards for the adequacy of moral systems) change.

5.4 Advantages over the previous relativist analyses

Let me complete the initial presentation of the analysis of moral "A ought to do X" statements by listing the ways in which it avoids the weaknesses of previous relativist analyses and incorporates their strengths.

The theory of reference applied to 'adequate moral system' does not commit us to Harman's view that morality is constituted by implicit agreement. It allows a speaker to apply moral rules to people who do not belong to the group for which the extension of the term was originally determined and who have no implicit agreement with the group. Members of a group can judge the moralities of other groups by application of their own term 'adequate moral system'. The recommended relativist analysis makes explicit the way in which the truth of moral "A ought to do X" statements depends on what follows from a moral system that is adequate in terms of an ideal of morality, as Castañeda's analysis does not. Also, remember that Castañeda's conception of the ideal morality ruled out the possibility of different, equally valid ideals of morality. The recommended relativist analysis allows for different extensions of 'adequate moral system'. Finally, Castañeda's analysis did not explain why moral "A ought to do X" statements are about agents and actions instead of just practitions and intentions (or rules). The recommended analysis explains how the names and descriptions that 'A' and 'X' are place holders for contribute straightforwardly to the truth conditions of these statements.

My analysis renders 1 through 4 true. With respect to 4, we can say that moral facts are reducible to nonmoral facts about agents, rules, and empirical conditions. My analysis also makes possible an explanation of the motivation for 5. That is, we can explain why admitting the truth of a moral "A ought to do X" statement is normally taken as admitting a reason to act in accordance with it. The explanation begins with a definition: a group or society in which the extension of 'adequate moral system' is the same for all of its members is a "moral community." When a member of such a community makes a moral statement to other members, he or she is in part purporting to identify the action required by the set of systems according to which every member wants (at least to some degree, if he or she subscribes to any moral system at all) to be guided. Normally, determining the truth or falsity of that statement is determining whether there is a reason for the subject of that statement to act in a certain way. A regular connection between admission of truth and admission of a reason for acting holds within a moral community.

Morality fully serves its purpose only within a moral community, for moral truth is interesting to us only when it provides us with reasons for action. A society in which each person is a moral community unto him- or herself does not have a viable morality. Morality would vanish (as it might have among the Ik, if Turnbull's description of their life is correct[17]), or a new morality would have to develop that would gain the allegiance of substantial numbers of people. If one learns, therefore, to use moral language in a society where morality is indeed a viable action-guide, it will be in a society that either contains some genuine moral communities, perhaps constituting a single moral community, *or* one in which its members mistakenly *believe* they belong to moral communities. A group may believe that it constitutes a single moral community when in fact the extension of 'adequate moral system' varies over segments of the group. It is usually striking differences in moral belief that raise in people's minds the possibility of moral relativity, and there may not be many such differences within a group.

It is crucial to note that in a society containing genuine moral communities or one in which such communities are mistakenly believed to exist, people will associate an admission of truth with an admission of a reason for acting. In these socie-ties, a person is likely to grow up and learn moral language in a genuine or perceived moral community. He or she will learn moral language in a context in which everyone expects a con-nection between admission of truth and admission of reasons for acting. The connection is learned as a regular one, and it would be natural to carry the expectation that it will hold into moral discourse and debate with members of other groups or societies, especially when a speaker does not believe there is more than one moral community. In such discourse and debate, both sides expect the connection to hold. Each side, therefore, would be reluctant to admit the truth of the other side's moral position unless it were willing to concede that it had reason to act according to the other position. I, therefore, can account for the motivation behind the belief that when-ever two "A ought to do X" statements prescribe incompatible actions, only one statement can be true, even though I render this claim (5 of chapter one) false.

At the same time, the recommended analysis provides a number of ways to explain the diversity of moral belief and the existence of apparently irresolvable moral disagreements. By allowing for the extension of 'adequate moral system' to vary over different groups and societies, it allows for two sets of moral beliefs that conflict pragmatically to be equally true (a more detailed explanation will be given in chapters nine, ten, and eleven where specific cases of apparent variations in moral belief are considered). It allows for different members of one extension to be applicable to different groups or societies, and this also accounts for some diversity in moral belief. Finally, it allows for some diversity through the existence of *false* moral beliefs. The recommended analysis, therefore, can account for many of the features of moral discourse that motivate claims for moral objectivity and at the same time account for the diversity of moral belief as well as the existence of apparently irresolvable disagreement that motivate claims for moral subjectivity.

There is another explanatory virtue of the analysis—it allows us to make an interesting and important distinction between different *kinds* of moral relativity in what ought to be done. First, there is the kind of relativity stemming from variations in what is identified by the "conditions C" clause. Second, there is the kind stemming from the possibility that the extension of 'adequate moral system' contains more than one member and that different members may apply to different groups or societies according to their varying conditions. Third, there is the kind stemming from possible variations in the extension of 'adequate moral system'. Now the first kind is admitted by both relativists and absolutists and is not the issue between them. The second, however, is important to the issue. Sometimes anthropologists who argue for moral relativity point to differences in moral belief among societies and then connect these differences to differences in the conditions of these societies. It is possible that these cases can be subsumed under the second kind, which I shall now dub "environmental relativity." If so, the absolutists have won a victory, at least those who are willing to admit that there is a *range* of acceptable moral systems. In any case, the third kind is at the heart of the debate between relativists and absolutists. Both the second and third kinds are important, and we must be careful to note that what may be evidence for one may not be evidence for the other.

5.5   *The general use of "A ought to do X" statements*

The remaining task in the analysis of moral "A ought to do X" statements is to show how they are related to other statements of this kind. Already mentioned are the prudential "A ought to do X" statements, such as "You ought to return the money you stole if you don't want to get caught." There is also the 'ought' of etiquette, and the so-called "expectation" 'ought', as in "I've checked the ignition system, the gas, the battery, and the car ought to start with no trouble."

It is plausible to hypothesize that there is a general use of "A ought to do X" statements, out of which the different uses evolved. I give the general use the following analysis:

By not doing X under conditions C, A will be breaking an appropriate rule that applies to him or her.

'Appropriate' is an attributive, like 'adequate'. It corresponds to a function that singles out a rule from the set of all rules that is to be applied to the situation at hand. What is appropriate depends not only on the situation but on the purpose of the speaker in making the statement. For instance, when someone says, "One ought always to thank the host before leaving a party," the point is to instruct the audience in etiquette. Or the speaker's purpose may be to identify an action that is necessary and/or sufficient for an end, as in "If you want to start the car, you ought to put it in gear." The clause "that applies to him or her" covers the possibility that a rule may apply to one group or society under a given set of conditions but not apply to another group or society under a different set of conditions. The rules of table manners that apply to contemporary American society would be ludicrous when applied to a society in which there is massive starvation and poverty.

We can see how the different uses of 'ought' could spin off from the general use. When we begin to distinguish large classes of "A ought to do X" statements that are made with the same purpose in mind, we begin to list the different uses. The moral 'ought' was born of the need to settle on a relatively fixed system of rules with the point of resolving internal conflicts between requirements and resolving interpersonal conflicts of interest. The "appropriate rule" becomes the rule contained in an adequate moral system applying to the agent. The expectation 'ought' is interesting because it seems to lack the normative force possessed at least potentially by all other 'ought's. It is plausible that this 'ought' resulted from the human tendency to anthropomorphize nature, to impute an intelligence and will to things. This tendency goes along with viewing the regularities of nature as the conformance of things to norms governing their behavior. When we cannot explain the occurrence of an exception to a regularity, we may view it as a violation. If the car doesn't start when all its systems appear to be in good order, it is breaking a norm, not doing what it ought to do. We want to punish it (kick it), until we discover that we have not put it in gear.

6 The Recommended Relativist Analysis of "X is a good Y" Statements and Consideration of Objections

6.1 *Evaluating according to standards*

It is possible to present a relativist analysis of moral "X" is a good Y" statements using the same ideas as those underlying the 'ought' analysis. Value language developed out of a more basic normative language: standards, which have been mentioned already in the explication of 'adequate moral system'. Standards of the form "M is to be F" do not just spell out conceptions of adequacy for moral systems. They are included *within* moral systems and apply to persons, actions, and states of affairs, all subjects of moral evaluation. Standards, as well as rules, help to resolve internal conflicts in requirements and interpersonal conflicts of interest. Note that the question of how to resolve conflicts in one's requirements is as much a question of what kind of person to be (or what kind of husband, wife, father, or mother to be) as it is a question of how to act. A person with virtues—traits of character such as patience, courage, and kindness—will have distinctive ways of dealing with interpersonal conflicts. Encouraging the cultivation of these qualities may be a way of providing people means to deal with those conflicts, besides the prescription of rules of action for them. In fact, some moralities give standards of character a more prominent place than rules of action. This is true of ancient Greek and Chinese morality, as we shall see in chapter ten.

A straightforward analysis of moral "X is a good Y" statements that utilizes the concepts of standards and adequate moral systems is the following:

Under actual conditions C, X satisfies those standards for Y's contained in adequate moral systems applying to X.

A standard for Y's has the form "a Y is to be F." An X satisfies a standard for Y's when it is a Y and when it possesses the property, in whatever specified degree, predicated of Y's in the standard. The clause "Under actual conditions C" is explicitly or implicitly given in the context of utterance and serves to identify certain parameters for the evaluation of X.

For instance, an act may be called good under the condition that its point is to fulfill a certain end. Fasting is a good action under the condition that its point is to symbolize a commitment to end starvation and hunger. It is questionable as a means to losing weight. Or people who occupy certain roles may be called good under certain conditions. Parents who give financial assistance to their adult children are good parents under the condition that they do not render their children dependent on them. The clause "applying to X" allows for the possibility that among the set of adequate moral systems, there are some that do not apply given the human and material resources of the society containing X, or that more than one system could apply to X under a given set of social conditions, and that the relevant system is the one to which the relevant group of speakers subscribe. Finally, we must note that the above analysis is compatible with relativism because it allows for different extensions of 'adequate moral system', with different standards. The explanation of how the extension is fixed is the same explanation given in connection with the moral 'ought'.

6.2 *A general analysis of "X is a good Y" statements*

As in the case of 'ought', we need to explain how moral value statements are related to other value statements. G. H. Von Wright has done a thorough job of compiling a list of familiar uses of 'good' and of grouping these uses under some main headings. He groups talk of a good knife, good car, good house, and a good way of doing something, such as unlocking a door, under the heading of "instrumental goodness." Such talk concerns the value of implements, tools, instruments, or the activities involving these things. Talk of a good chess player, runner, scientist, or artist comes under "technical goodness," which concerns people who are good *at* some activity and who require special training to be good at it. Another kind of goodness is utilitarian — that which favors some end or purpose in general, such as a good plan, good luck, good advice, and a good opportunity. A subcategory of the useful is the beneficial — that which promotes the special end of the welfare of a being. Talk of physical exercise as good for health falls into this category. There are more categories, and Von Wright observes that there are uses that fall completely outside his list or somewhere between the categories he developed. Examples are good manners, good times, and good books.[1]

This multiplicity of uses of 'good' makes it unwise to give separate truth conditions analyses of each use. It is particularly unwise to try to identify a system of standards corresponding to each use. We just don't have systems of standards especially devoted to defining technical or instrumental goodness. And there is a good reason for such a lack. Even if we limit ourselves to one kind of goodness — instrumental or technical, let us say — that goodness is relative to a multiplicity of ends, purposes, and interests. A good car may be a plain but reliable vehicle, given the interest in getting where we want to go as frequently as possible. On the other hand, a good car may be one with graceful lines and a wealth of luxury features if our interest is in showing off our means. A good runner may be a world-class sprinter who cannot run twenty miles, or he or she may be a relentless plodder who sets records in fifty-mile races. Each distinctive set of ends, purposes, and interests would seem to have its appropriate standards of goodness.

A truth conditions analysis of "X is a good Y" statements that does not require a set system of standards for each use is the following:

Under actual conditions C, X satisfies the appropriate standards for Y's.

Appropriateness is a function of the ends, purposes, and interests specified in the "conditions C" clause and of the nature of the Y's in question. Moral goodness is a special case and derivative from the general use: "X satisfies the appropriate moral standards for Y's" when these standards are derived from the adequate moral system applying to X.

Since there is a strong need to codify the standards for persons and actions when these have to do with resolving internal and interpersonal conflicts, it becomes possible at some stage in the development of a value language to distinguish a set system of standards belonging to an adequate moral system. This is how moral goodness is singled out.

Note that both the general analysis and that of moral value statements explain the manner in which 'good' functions as an attributive adjective like 'adequate' and 'appropriate'. One cannot infer from "Willie Sutton was a good bank robber" that "Willie Sutton was good and he was a bank robber." 'Good' operates on the noun phrase to produce a complex predicate with an extension that is a subset of the extension of the noun phrase. It selects a subset under a description such as "bank robber" from the extension of the noun phrase according to the appropriate standards. It is a straightforward matter to extend the analysis to explain evaluative comparisons. When X is a better Y than Z, under conditions C, X satisfies to a greater degree the appropriate standard that applies to X and Z. This strategy reverses Hare's, which defined 'good' in terms of 'better than' (a good Y is better than most Y's usually are). Like Bernard Williams, I find no contradiction in the idea that the game of cricket can flourish so much that most cricketeers are pretty good.[2]

6.3 *Possible objections to the analyses*

It might be objected that I have strayed from the correspondence conception of truth that was supposed to be the foundation of my analysis. I have analyzed "A ought to do X" and "X is a good Y" statements in terms of rules and standards of moral systems that people have developed to resolve internal and interpersonal conflicts. I have pointed out that moral language users may have misconceptions about the nature and implications of these rules and standards, but in the end, the true nature of the rules and standards depends on the criteria for adequacy of moral systems that people lay down in fixing the reference of 'adequate moral system'. Doesn't this amount to a coherence conception of truth? Am I not saying that the moral truth is whatever is consistent with people's fundamental moral beliefs—those beliefs that correspond to the reference-fixing descriptions of 'adequate moral system'?

There is an important sense in which this criticism is just. By analyzing moral statements as statements about normative structures created by the human mind, I am taking the position that there is no irreducible moral reality independent of human invention and choice. My analyses allow for no correspondence between such an independently existing moral reality and true moral statements. If this is what one expected from a correspondence theory of moral truth, then it is just to say with disappointment that my theory makes moral truth a matter of coherence.

There is an important sense, however, in which my analyses are genuinely founded on a correspondence theory.[3] I analyze moral statements as making reference to rules and standards, items in the world that are distinct from moral statements. The fact that the existence of these rules and standards is not independent of human will and invention does not make my analyses any less consistent with a correspondence theory of truth. Nor is it made any less consistent by the fact that the reference-fixing descriptions associated with 'adequate moral system' correspond with fundamental moral beliefs of moral language users. My analyses are in a strict sense founded on a correspondence theory.

That is why they are not vulnerable to the general criticism that a correspondence theory of truth is a more plausible theory than the coherence theory (a claim I tend to believe). If someone is disappointed because my analyses behave in some respects *as if* they were founded on a coherence theory of truth, then the real objection is that I don't analyze moral statements as statements about a moral reality existing independently of human will and invention. I will consider such analyses in the next chapter on absolutism, where I explain why I think they are unsatisfactory. My analyses of moral statements as concerning adequate moral systems are, furthermore, made possible by assuming a correspondence theory of truth, and these analyses have real explanatory power over any that could be given by assuming a coherence theory. My analyses explain the fact that we criticize as false the morality of another group of language users, even when that morality is a coherent system of moral beliefs very different from ours. When we criticize that morality, we take the group's recommendations for action, state them in our moral language, and evaluate them as false according to our standards for the adequacy of moral systems. Under a coherence theory, evaluations of moral truth are made only within a moral tradition and not across different ones. This is because the theory defines truth simply as a matter of coherence within a morality. But as a matter of fact we do not limit ourselves in the way the coherence theory predicts, and my theory can explain why.

Other possible criticisms concern my claim that moral objectivity can be explained in a manner compatible with a relativist analysis of moral statements. Absolutists will claim, of course, that I have missed some aspects of moral objectivity, so let me anticipate what aspects they would mention.

They would claim that even though the recommended relativist analyses allow for the criticism of existing moralities, based on a conception of the adequacy of a moral system, they allow for different sets of adequate moral systems corresponding to different ideals. But aren't ideals of morality also subject to rational criticism? In reply to this objection, let me first point out that in developing an ideal of morality a group may make many factual assumptions. Those concerning human nature and religion are particularly relevant. For instance, when a group determines a set of moral systems as adequate, it may deem certain rules part of an adequate moral system for them because it believes the rules to be commanded by a deity with superior moral wisdom. Or a group may assume that all adequate moral systems must be of a certain nature because there are innate human traits that make other moral systems wholly impractical or the effects of attempting to conform to them harmful. Some believe that women are unsuited for anything but the duties of housewife and mother or of careers that suit "womanly" qualities, such as nursing. They express moral disapproval of women who do not take their appropriate places in life and attempt to perform "masculine" tasks. If the factual assumptions about women are false, and if they play a crucial role in the fixing of the extension of 'adequate moral system', the term may have no extension at all, at least with respect to rules concerning the duties of women as women. The recommended relativist analyses, therefore, imply that ideals of morality are susceptible to rational criticism.

Still, it may be replied that as long as a group does not make false factual assumptions, it can determine any set of systems, no matter how evil or perverse, to be the set of adequate moral systems within the constraints of what counts as a moral system. But let me point out that it is only in the logical sense of possibility that a group can conduct so arbitrary a determination of adequate moral systems. In practice, a group will be limited in its attempt to develop an adequate system of rules and standards that will provide a relatively effective resolution of the conflicts a morality is intended to resolve. That is why rules permitting torture on whim are not found in adequate moral systems. There are constraints imposed by the availability of human and material resources. There are those imposed by the willingness of all affected parties to subscribe to a given system of rules. If some segment of society is frustrated by a moral system, the segments who are more advantaged under the rules must find ways of keeping that frustration from causing excessive instability. These ways may involve force, deception, concessions to the disadvantaged, or a mixture of these strategies. As was noted in the last chapter, slaveholders in the American South felt the need to justify the legitimacy of holding property in people by taking a paternalistic stance toward their slaves. Genovese cites a study that concludes that slaves in the American South of the nineteenth century lived as well in material terms as a substantial portion of the workers and peasants of Western Europe and better than the mass of Russian, Hungarian, Polish, and Italian peasants.[4]

The way in which self-interest can work to reenforce moral rules is illustrated by another observation of Genovese's:

A slaveholding community did not intervene against a brutal master because of moral outrage alone; it intervened to protect its interests. Or rather, its strong sense of interest informed its moral sensibilities.[5]

It is much too easy an argument — and too frequently repeated — to lament that everything is permitted once relativism is admitted. This is to arbitrarily associate with relativism the ludicrous view that a group could choose a morality as one chooses what to have for breakfast, with as much neglect of the past history of the group and of its present conditions, such as the availability of its human and material resources and the balance of power among its classes. It was noted in the last chapter that once a group begins to cooperate with other groups, it has a strong motivation to apply some rules of its moral system to its relations with the others. And having done that, the requirements of consistency in practical reasoning may compel it to extend other rules to the other groups, or to give a morally relevant reason for not doing so. This is how kinship, membership in a group, and skin color get eliminated as reasons for excluding a group from the domain in which moral rules apply.

So far, I have been discussing constraints on the group's choice of a morality. What about constraints on the individual's choice? Let me first note as context for this discussion that relatively few people choose the morality they accept. Most simply learn it as they learn the moral language, and they accept it as they learn it. Now, let us focus on the few who reflect on the possibility that there is more than one morality and who have come to the point where they can conceive of adopting a morality other than the one they originally learned. These individuals operate under the same constraints on the group I mentioned above, if they still want to remain members of the group.

In addition, there are internal constraints arising from individual psychology. To accept a morality is to adopt a set of desires and intentions with respect to oneself and others, and the adoption of a new morality may require a set of desires and intentions that an individual may find impossible to have.

Take an extremely ambitious and successful businessman whose life has been focused on the goals of achieving a high level of material comfort and leisure for himself and for his family. Because of his business, he has traveled widely, learned about other ways of life, and in the abstract he may come to the view that the libertarian, Nozickian morality he has lived his life by is not the only true morality. He might even concede that the egalitarian, socialist morality he found realized in an Israeli kibbutz might be true. Perhaps he is vaguely attracted to it because his life is not as satisfying as he thought it would be. Yet he may dismiss the possibility of coming to accept this morality as pure fantasy. He may be right. He may not be able to overturn lifelong habits of wanting to acquire wealth, instead of wanting to share it. He may find it impossible to forsake the kinds of comfort to which he has become accustomed. He could *try* to accept this morality; he could *choose to try* to change himself, but it would be silly to say he could simply choose to change himself. Or take someone who by nature is a deeply sympathetic, caring person who gains a great deal of satisfaction from helping others. If this is an enduring trait, it would act as a constraint on the kind of morality he or she could adopt. An unlikely candidate, for instance, would be an elitist morality that confers worth on people only if they possess certain desirable traits. Here again, it would be silly to say that he or she could simply choose such a morality, notwithstanding Sartre's romantic existentialism.

A more restrained absolutist may say that even if relativism does not permit any moral system to be adequate, it does deny that there is a single true morality, and it is a common belief that there is such a thing. Now in fact, these beliefs are not as widespread as absolutists seem to think. Any teacher of ethics should be familiar with the problem of overcoming in students an unthinking bias in favor of relativism. They come to that view all too easily on the basis of perceived disagreement in fundamental moral beliefs. And they may very well say that both sides in such disagreement have positions that are "true for them." Absolutists, however, can make the more modest claim that *many* intelligent and informed people have the belief that there is a single true morality, and if relativists want to say the belief is mistaken, they do have the obligation to explain how these people could acquire such a belief.

This is a serious objection, and there is more than one possible way to reply to it. Let us consider the way in which John Mackie replies to it. There is much that is useful in what he says, but I disagree with him on some important points. His way of explaining the belief in a single true morality is to build that belief into the meaning of 'ought' and 'good' as used in moral contexts. To understand how he does this, consider first his analysis of the general use of 'good':

X is good $\equiv$ X is such as to satisfy requirements or wants or interests of the kind in question.

"Requirements (etc.) of the kind in question" is deliberately vague to allow for the different ways in which requirements are fed into the context of utterance. If one says that something is a good knife, the relevant requirements are determined by the function of knives. If one calls a sunset good, the relevant interests are probably those of typical people who like to look at sunsets. Use of 'good' in moral contexts involves the supposition that "there are requirements which are simply there in the nature of things, without being the requirements of any person or body of persons, even God." To be morally good will then be such as to satisfy these intrinsic requirements.

Mackie's analysis of the general use of 'ought' is as follows:

A ought to do X $\equiv$ There is reason for A's X-ing.

Different uses of 'ought' introduce different kinds of reasons for acting. The "prudential" 'ought' refers to reasons based on some want, purpose, or ideal that the agent has. The moral 'ought' is thought to refer to intrinsic requirements arising from the nature of the situation or from the nature of things.[6] These analyses are not relativistic at all. That is why I did not consider them in the previous chapter. What makes Mackie's *theory* of morality relativistic is his view that there are no intrinsic requirements, even though people believe there are. In other words, Mackie thinks absolutists are right about how the moral 'ought' and 'good' are to be analyzed, but he thinks that the meaning of these terms embodies a radical error. How is it that people came to make this error?

Mackie says that one partial cause is the human tendency to project moral attitudes onto the world. This tendency is analogous to that of reading feelings into objects. A fungus that fills one with disgust comes to possess the quality of foulness. Another partial cause is that morality is a social creation — something invented to regulate interpersonal relations — and so we sense that it has a source external to the individual. The social nature of the source is obscured to most of us, partially because such obscurity is useful for encouraging conformance to morality. If we think that moral requirements are somehow in the nature of things, we will be more inclined to conform to them without question.[7]

Mackie's explanation of why people err in believing in a single true morality has a severe cost. He has built into the meaning of 'good' and 'ought' a false presupposition that makes all moral statements containing these terms false or without truth values. Such a consequence is neither necessary nor makes for the best explanation of our moral experience.

It is not necessary because a major part of Mackie's explanation of why people come to believe in a single true morality could be combined with the recommended analyses of moral "A ought to do X" and "X is a good Y" statements. That is, these statements could have genuine truth conditions concerning the rules and standards of adequate moral systems, but some speakers could come to believe that the rules and standards of an adequate moral system arise from the nature of things in the ways Mackie describes. We need not incorporate this belief into the truth conditions of moral statements. It may be that this belief goes into the fixing of the extension of 'adequate moral system', but the recommended relativist analyses do not commit us to the view that it always goes into the fixing.

Mackie's moral skepticism does not make for the best explanation of moral experience because not everyone arrives at a belief in a single true morality via a belief that moral requirements arise from the nature of things. A common path to absolutism is via the belief that the reason for having a morality is the fulfillment of human nature. Some believe that a successful and wealthy criminal who preys on others cannot be truly happy. They believe that one's life would be barren if one does not realize the human potential to care for others and to take satisfaction in their satisfaction. They believe, furthermore, that only a certain set of moral systems could provide for the greatest fulfillment. A philosophical representative of such a view is, of course, Aristotle. Not only is this view distinct from a misguided objectification of moral attitudes and from a failure to recognize the social source of morality, it is not obviously false.

It is a serious challenge for relativists. I will argue in the ninth, tenth, and eleventh chapters that what constitutes human fulfillment varies with different groups and societies, and that such variation results in different extensions for 'adequate moral system' as the term is used among different groups and societies. If this kind of variation exists, it is not difficult to explain why absolutists should fail to recognize it. Our conceptions of what constitutes human fulfillment are to a large extent shaped by our personal experience, observations of those around us, and what we are taught on the subject. Relatively few of us have been in the position of being pressed to confront an alien conception of human fulfillment and to understand it. Even fewer of us will be pressed to justify our judgments of alien conceptions as misguided or perverse. In any case, the general point I am making here is that there are many paths to a belief in absolutism. Mackie has described some of them and there are others. The recommended relativist analyses are compatible with all of them.

Returning to the original absolutist objection, we should explain what seems to be a belief many intelligent, reasonably informed people have. We are not required to make it true. I sketched some plausible paths along which these people could have arrived at such a false belief. I, therefore, have not allotted morality all the objectivity some people believe it has, but I have explained why they could have come to acquire false beliefs in that much objectivity.

7 Absolutist Analyses of Moral Statements

7.1 Three kinds of absolutist analysis

This chapter will set out some absolutist analyses to compete with the relativist analyses recommended in the last three. The question is whether relativist or absolutist analyses will fit with the best explanation of our moral experience. There will be no attempt to present a single set of best analyses for absolutism, as there was for relativism. I do not think there is one such set. Instead, I will set out three kinds of analyses representing three absolutist traditions in moral philosophy.

The first tradition stems from Kant. Its central claim is that the single true morality satisfies standards of rationality for practical reasoning. The second tradition stems from Aristotle, and its claim is that the single true morality provides the fullest realization of human potential or the greatest satisfaction of human needs and desires. The third tradition stems from Plato, and its claim is that there are irreducible moral properties upon which the single true morality is founded. I will sketch analyses of moral statements that fit with each of these traditions, and will point out the main problems that beset the analyses.

7.2 Gewirth's Kantianism

Alan Gewirth has presented the most detailed and comprehensive argument that substantive moral principles are derivable from a standard of rationality for practical reasoning.

The standard he has in mind is that an agent is not to logically contradict him- or herself in making practical judgments. Gewirth argues that an agent would violate this standard in not recognizing the "generic rights" of those with whom he or she interacts.

Gewirth begins his argument from the viewpoint of an agent who must value the "generic features" of his or her actions — freedom and purposiveness — because these make it possible to pursue the ends he or she implicitly regards as good. Goods such as physical integrity, food, clothing, and mental equilibrium constitute his or her well-being, enabling the agent to act with some hope of fulfilling his or her purposes. The next and most crucial step in Gewirth's argument is the claim that the agent must implicitly hold that he or she has rights to the necessary conditions of freedom and well-being: "the agent holds that other persons owe him at least noninterference with his freedom and well-being...on the basis of his own prudential criteria, because such noninterference is necessary to his being a purposive agent."[1] Why must the agent make such a claim? The answer is that "It would be contradictory for the agent to accept both that he or she must have freedom and well-being and that other persons may interfere with his or her having these, where the criteria of the 'must' and 'may' are the same, consisting in the agent's own requirements for agency."[2] From the fact that the agent must attribute to him- or herself the rights to freedom and well-being, it follows that he or she must attribute the same rights to others. This step is licensed by the logical principle of universalizability: "if some predicate P belongs to some subject S because S has the property Q, then P must also belong to all other subjects that have Q." Since the agent must hold that the property of being a prospective, purposive agent is a necessary and sufficient condition for his or her claim to the rights of freedom and well-being, the agent must recognize similar rights for all other prospective, purposive agents. The principle requiring such recognition is the "principle of generic consistency" (PGC).

The argument fails at the most crucial step. Gewirth claims that each agent must claim a right to freedom and well-being on prudential ground that these goods are necessary for his or her purposive agency. Why *must* the agent make such a claim? The most natural interpretation is that the agent must see as a matter of logic that the claim is entailed by his or her needs for freedom and well-being. But the alleged entailment does not hold, if the claim is interpreted as rights-claims usually are. To see this, suppose an agent A makes a claim against another agent B, asserting her right to freedom and well-being. This claim is taken to entail certain duties on B's part (such as that of noninterference with A) *if* it is valid. The claim is valid if and only if A's needs for freedom and well-being constitute legitimate grounds for B to act in the appropriate ways. I can think of only two ways in which we could see such a claim as valid. We either see A's needs as self-evident grounds for B to act in the appropriate ways, or we see that the status of her needs as legitimate grounds is justified by some further principle Gewirth has not given.

Consider the first possibility. To say A's needs constitute self-evident grounds for her rights-claim is to beg the question. A's needs provide *A* with a reason for *wanting* B to act in the appropriate ways toward her. But it is not self-evident that A's needs provide *B* a reason for acting in the appropriate ways. In fact, we sometimes recognize that our needs do *not* give us a valid claim against others to act in favorable ways toward us. Consider the second possibility. The only likely candidate for a justifying principle is a moral one, but Gewirth cannot refer to one in trying to derive the ultimate moral principle. As a last resort, we could refrain from interpreting A's rights-claim in the usual way and strip it of any suggestion that B has a reason for acting in the appropriate ways, but then Gewirth will not have the conclusion he wants.

But there is an alternative interpretation of Gewirth's argument that A *must* make the rights-claim against B. Perhaps it is not the justifiability of the claim that is rooted in prudential considerations, but the *action* of A's making the claim against others that is so rooted. If A makes the claim against B, B may take it at face value and accord A rights to freedom and well-being. As a prudent, purposive agent, A surely has nothing to lose and everything to gain from making the claim. But A might have something to lose. There are places in the world where claiming one's rights would not only be silly and beside the point but dangerous to one's health. The prudent thing to do may be to keep silent and makes plans for escape or for overthrowing the authorities. On either interpretation of Gewirth's crucial step, therefore, he has failed to derive his ultimate moral principle from standards of practical reasoning.

His argument illustrates a common failing of the Kantian tradition—an illegitimate transition from premises that are indeed requirements on practical reasoning to substantive moral principles. There is another, complementary common failing of arguments designed to prove the Kantian thesis: there is a legitimate transition to substantive moral principles from premises that are dubious as standards of rationality for practical reasoning. In my opinion, Thomas Nagel's interesting argument for altruistic moral principles displays this failing.

7.3 Nagel's Kantianism

To understand Nagel's argument, let us begin with his claim that first-person, present-tense, practical judgments about what one has reason to do are judgments with "motivational content." If a practical judgment has motivational content for a person p, p accepts a justification for doing what the judgment prescribes. To accept a justification is to have a tendency to act. Nagel gives a complex and rewarding argument that this tendency to action need not be derived from some preexisting desire. Instead, this tendency may be provided by pure practical reason, and the fact that p has accepted a justification of performing an action is sufficient in itself to explain p's performance of an action (without reference to a desire of p). For example, suppose G. E. Moore is standing in the path of an oncoming truck and makes the judgment that he has reason to get out of the way. If he accepts this judgment and jumps aside, we would take as a sufficient explanation of his action that he accepted the judgment. There is no need to refer to a preexisting desire to jump or even to a desire to live.

Next, Nagel argues that in making such a judgment, p is committing him- or herself to an *impersonal* judgment about the same situation, and a statement specifying who, in the impersonally described scene, p is. In making the judgment that he has reason to get out of the way, therefore, G. E. Moore is committed to the judgment that the person standing in front of the truck has reason to get out of the way and to the statement that he is that person. He is committed to the impersonal perspective because it is rational to have a conception of oneself as a single person among others. To lack this conception is to fall into the irrationality of solipsism.

Nagel goes on to argue that one's impersonal judgment must have motivational content, as well as one's first-person judgment. For example, if Moore makes the judgment that someone in the path of the truck has reason to get out of the way, this in itself should be accompanied by a tendency to act. If the person in question is not Moore, the relevant action would be something like shouting a warning, if one is in a position to do so. If Moore's impersonal judgment lacks such motivational content, while his personal judgment has it, he is committed to a *practical* equivalent of solipsism, a kind of practical irrationality. He is not recognizing the reality of other people in his tendencies to action.

This implies that the reasons one refers to when one makes practical judgments are "objective reasons." A *prima facie* reason to promote an act X is an objective reason when it is a reason for the occurrence of X and not merely a reason for a particular individual to promote X.

If G. E. Moore is to avoid practical solipsism in making the judgment that he has reason to get out of the way, his reason must be objective in the sense that everyone has a reason to promote his life or someone's life. In contrast, a subjective reason is a reason for each person to promote his or her own life. If *this* was the reason Moore had, he would not be recognizing in his actions the reality of others.

From the requirement that reasons be objective, Nagel derives a principle of altruism. As soon as one recognizes that a thing is of value for someone else, one must recognize an objective reason for oneself to promote the having of that thing for the other. Also, if one recognizes that pleasure or a degree of material well-being is of value to oneself, one must recognize that they are of value to everyone, and thus one must recognize an objective reason to promote the having of those things by everyone. The conclusion, then, is that failing to act altruistically is to fail to recognize in a practical sense others as equally real. Of course, Nagel is a long way from showing that there is a single true morality, since more than one morality embodies an altruistic principle. His argument, however, could be regarded as the beginning of a larger argument for absolutism, and he seems to regard it in that way.[3]

The conclusion of his argument is intuitively appealing. To sit in front of a television set, calmly viewing the dead bodies of those who were opposing a repressive government that one's own government is supporting, and to do nothing about it, is in an important respect to view those people as less real than oneself. The question, however, is whether this is a failure of rationality. It is not clear that one manifests irrationality merely because one's first person practical judgments have motivational content while one's impersonal judgments do not. What *is* clearly irrational is the failure to take into account the existence of others when one is deliberating about what to do. But an egoist could avoid such irrationality, merely by paying close attention to the needs and desires of others and calculating the best way to take advantage of them. Surely, the egoist would be recognizing the existence of others in his or her tendencies to action, and there is a perfectly good sense in which he is recognizing these others to be as real as him- or herself.

Why is Nagel's conclusion so intuitively appealing if his argument is faulty? There is a sense of "more real" in which people become more real to us when we are able to understand their internal workings as similar to our own. We understand people by using ourselves as models. When we see that their happiness and misery is of the same nature as our own and have the same general causes and effects, they become more vivid to us. And — Hume was right about this — in general, the more others appear like us, the more sympathetic we are to them (there are exceptions: the more people are like us in ways we dislike about ourselves, the less sympathetic we may be). So it is generally true that the more real people are to us, the more we are moved to act in their welfare; but this is made true by the way we understand others and by sympathy, not by the existence of objective reasons.

I should note, however, that Nagel's argument is reinforced by analogy with another argument he gives for the rationality of prudential motivation. The argument may be summarized in the following manner: (1) to conceive of oneself as a unity over time, one must be able to adopt a tenseless standpoint (to regard all temporal stages of one's life as equally real); (2) for any tensed judgment there is a corresponding tenseless judgment with the same content except specification of the present time (e.g., an agent's judgment that he will have reason to learn Italian is equivalent in this way to the tenseless judgment that he has reason to learn Italian); (3) if one's tensed judgments about what one now has reason to do have motivational content, but if one's tenseless judgments do not, then one fails to regard all stages of one's life as equally real and is guilty of practical irrationality. The point is that if one finds this argument persuasive, one is more likely to find the argument for altruism persuasive, since the structures are parallel.[4]

The argument for prudential motivation depends on the claim that one is not regarding the temporal stages of one's life as equally real if one's tenseless judgments lack motivational content. This claim has a great deal of plausibility, but the reason for its plausibility cannot be transferred to the argument for altruism. We do not think of ourselves as collections of temporal stages, but as single entities persisting through time and passing through these stages. Hence we would be irrational in not being motivated to provide for our future desires and interests, for these are desires and interests of the entity for which we have a great deal of concern in the present. It is the common belief in the metaphysical identity of persons over time that confers plausibility on Nagel's argument. No analogue of this belief, however, helps the argument for altruism. Most of us are not monists. We believe we are metaphysically distinct from others, and it is not clear that all people form some kind of unity that would be analogous to the unity of an individual over time. That is why we can recognize the reality of other persons without being motivated to provide for their desires and interests.

This is how Nagel's argument demonstrates a failing that is complementary to the one that Gewirth's demonstrates. He does not show that a standard (that one's impersonal practical judgments must have motivational content when the corresponding first-person judgment does) from which a substantive moral principle legitimately follows, is a genuine standard of rationality. It is a challenge for any such theory to avoid both ways of failing, for any theory that clearly avoids one way is liable to fall into the other.[5]

7.4 Kantian analyses of moral language

Now that we have an idea of the general thrust of Kantian arguments for absolutism, and of their characteristic problems, we are ready to discuss the kind of analysis of moral language that would be compatible with them. A "reasons" analysis of "A ought to do X" statements would seem to fit most naturally. In previous chapters, it was noted that A's admission of the truth of "A ought to do X" is usually interpreted as an admission of a reason for A to do X.

The connection between admission of truth and admission of reasons to act is so close that it has motivated some philosophers to analyze "A ought to do X" statements as ones about reasons to act. Mackie presented such an analysis, and Kantians might give an analysis of "A ought to do X" statements as follows:

Under actual conditions C, A has a conclusive and overriding reason to do X that satisfies standards of rationality for practical reasoning.

Standards could have the canonical expression specified in the last chapter: "R is to be F," where 'R' is a place holder for the description of a reason to act. The reason must be conclusive and overriding in order to be a "categorical imperative."

For moral "X is a good Y" statements such as "X is a good person," Kantians could adopt the following analysis in terms of standards:

Under actual conditions C, X satisfies those adequate moral standards for Y's applying to X.

The "conditions C" and "applying to X" clauses serve the same functions as in the recommended relativist analyses. What is an "adequate moral standard for Y's" depends partly on what Y's are (a certain set of standards would apply to persons as such, another set to fathers, another set to actions, and so on), and partly on what ought to be done (a good person intends to follow certain moral principles of right action; fathers perform the duties of fathers; citizens the duties of citizens; good actions are what ought to be done; and so on). Presumably, Kantians would say that the adequacy of standards applying to a given class of Y's is determined by their derivability from standards of rationality for practical reasoning.

Since the plausibility of the Kantian analyses of moral statements ultimately depends on the identification of certain standards as standards of rationality, the analyses should be accompanied by a theory of how the extension of the term 'standards of rationality' is determined. Kantians have not said much about this matter. Gewirth's argument, however, is easily combined with a descriptive theory of reference. One premise of his argument is a standard of rationality—that an agent is not to logically contradict him- or herself in making practical judgments—and this standard certainly seems to be part of our common concept of rationality. If we have any beliefs about what it is to be rational, this would be one of them. Nagel's argument also could be combined with a descriptive theory of reference. A crucial premise of his argument—that it would be a practical equivalent of solipsism to deny the reality of others in one's actions—could be supported by the claim that it is irrational to deny in one's actions an obvious truth. And this claim could be said to follow from our concept of rationality. Of course, I have argued that the standard Nagel derives from the above premise—that impersonal practical judgments must have motivational content—is not a legitimate part of the concept of rationality.

If Kantians do adopt a descriptive theory of reference, the challenge they face may be redescribed as follows: to find a reference-fixing description for 'standards of rationality' that genuinely implies substantive moral principles that could form the core of a single true morality. Gewirth failed to find a description that genuinely implied moral principles. Nagel failed to find an appropriate description that was a part of our concept of rationality.

Another possibility is something like a causal theory for 'standards of rationality'. Alan Donagan is the Kantian who comes closest to making such a suggestion.[6] He claims that reason has a certain nature or essence and that there are true propositions attributing properties to reason in virtue of its nature. Donagan shows that "essence" talk is respectable in philosophy once more by pointing to Kripke's claim that natural kinds necessarily have certain properties in virtue of their structure. Next, he argues that not all truths about necessities *de re* need by established by a priori demonstrations, whereby a property is shown to be presupposed in any description by which the reference of 'reason' is fixed, or by the *a posteriori* methods of natural science. The propositions that temporal priority is transitive (if event A precedes B, and if B precedes C, A precedes C) is neither experimentally testable nor a priori demonstrable, but, says Donagan, "most of us are convinced that it is necessarily so, because we seem to ourselves to have sufficient insight into the nature of time for anything else to be unthinkable."

Donagan believes that Kant had sufficient insight into the nature of practical reason to affirm that "rational creatures have a negative freedom in virtue of which their actions are not determined to any end by their physical or biological nature, and to affirm that because of such freedom, they are creatures of a higher kind than any others in nature." In other words, we intuit the essence of practical reason, and in virtue of this intuition we know that practical reason enables us to transcend the causal laws that determine the behavior of other creatures. The substantive moral principle that follows is that rational beings are to respect their own natures.

Donagan seems to be suggesting that there is some possible relation between human beings and the nature of practical reasoning, in virtue of which we come to intuit standards of rationality and derive moral principles from them. The reference of 'standards of rationality' is not fixed according to description, but through some process of direct insight into the nature of practical reason. Thus Donagan is adopting something like a causal theory of reference, though I hesitate to call it 'causal', since we are supposed to be creatures who transcend the laws of cause and effect. The problem that faces Donagan's version of Kantianism is somewhat different from the one I described above. Donagan does not need to find an appropriate description that is part of the concept of rationality. Instead, he needs to make plausible the existence of intuitive insight into the nature of practical reason. Donagan does not do that. He merely asserts its existence. And the problem is that the mere assertion amounts to saying, "If you don't agree with my fundamental moral beliefs, you just fail to have sufficient insight into the nature of practical reason."

Claims for the existence of intuitive knowledge are the most plausible when two conditions are fulfilled. First, the claims concern basic truths about our world, such that it would be extremely difficult or even impossible to conceive of a world in which they were false. An example is the truth that temporal priority is transitive. Or take a general truth about physical objects, such as "Physical objects exist in space and time." Second, it is plausible to assert that adults of normal intelligence are capable of having such an intuition, at least when they are given some prompting. Why are claims for intuitive knowledge most plausible under these conditions? I suspect that we are most willing to believe we have intuitive knowledge when we can think of it as resulting from some innate cognitive equipment. Why should we have such equipment? Perhaps it enabled relatively puny creatures like us to survive and is thus acquired through evolution. This evolutionary story allows us to conceive how the facts of which we have knowledge had a role in the production of that knowledge. Permutations of the species which developed the cognitive equipment to apprehend these facts survived and reproduced. The point is that when the two conditions are fulfilled, they enable us to tell some halfway plausible story about the reasons why we should have intuitive knowledge.

But Donagan's claim for intuitive knowledge of practical reason does not meet the two conditions. It is certainly possible for me to conceive of a world in which the nature of practical reason does not enable us to transcend determinism. Donagan has given us no reason to think otherwise. And many normal adults of extremely high intelligence (and some with philosophical sophistication besides) do not seem able to have

Donagan's intuition. Of course, I have not proven that Donagan's claim is false if the two conditions are not fulfilled. But his claim seems arbitrary unless he can explain why many people don't have the intuition, and in general, he must provide some kind of explanation of why we should be so fortunate to have the intuition, assuming that we have it. This explanation would have to include a characterization of the relation between certain facts about practical reason and our intuitive knowledge of these facts. The characterization need not be of the sort of causal, evolutionary relation mentioned above, but we do need some sort of characterization.

7.5 McDowell's Aristotelianism and corresponding analyses of moral language

Instead of attempting to ground the single true morality in standards of rationality, some absolutist philosophers have followed Aristotle and attempted to ground it in human nature and in the ideal of a single (though complex) way of life that constitutes the right balance among human interests and thus the greatest fulfillment of that nature. Under this ideal, each of the virtues could be realized within a single complete life. It may be extremely difficult to achieve the ideal balance, however. Circumstances may force a person to choose justice at the expense of friendship. There are no hard and fast rules that will give an unambiguous answer as to which virtue to honor in such a situation, or an answer as to how to compromise between the conflicting virtues. A person must be guided by judgment, informed by knowledge of the particular circumstances and by a conception of the single most fulfilling way of life.

Aristotle likened to a perceptual capacity the virtuous person's capacity to discern what the particular circumstances demand, and it is on this doctrine that John McDowell places a great deal of emphasis. His theory may be summarized in five claims. First, a virtue is a "reliable sensitivity to a certain sort of requirement which situations impose on behavior." Kindness, for instance, is a kind of "perceptual capacity," the deliverances of which are cases of knowledge of what it is like to be confronted with a requirement of kindness. Second, the requirement imposed on a situation exhausts the kind person's reason for acting in the way he or she does. Third, "no one virtue can be fully possessed except by a possessor of all of them." Virtue is, in general, a single sensibility to requirements imposed by a situation. If kindness is a genuine virtue, it must issue in nothing but right conduct. Thus in a situation in which A's feelings will be upset by a projected action, but in which the same action would constitute honoring a right of B's, the truly kind agent will know what to do. Fourth, an agent who fails to act virtuously may perceive the situation in somewhat the same way as the virtuous person would, but the former's appreciation of what he perceives is clouded or unfocused by the impact of the desire to do otherwise. Finally, the sensitivity is informed by a conception of the way of life a human being should lead. This conception, though uncodifiable in exceptionless, universal rules, interacts with particular knowledge of the situation at hand to enable the virtuous agent to pick out "this particular fact rather than that one as the salient fact."[7]

Now I do not want to attribute to McDowell a belief in absolutism. This would follow from his theory only if it were claimed that the moral reality that the virtuous person detects is itself not relative, that its nature is not dependent on how it is perceived, and I am not sure that McDowell is willing to claim this. It is worth considering his theory as a possible version of absolutism, however, so let me do so, without attributing that view to McDowell.

His theory may be combined naturally with a "reasons" analysis of moral "A ought to do X" statements:

Under actual conditions C, A has a moral reason to do X.

A moral reason is revealed through the virtuous person's perceptual sensitivity to the requirements of the situation identified through the "conditions C" clause. McDowell believes that we need not manifest irrationality in failing to see that one has reason to act as morality requires, but he also believes that a moral reason detected by the virtuous person's sensitivity may motivate action independently of any desire he or she possesses.[8]

Moral "X is a good Y" statements could be analyzed as in the last section, as statements about X meeting adequate moral standards for Y's under conditions C.

When 'Y' is replaced by 'person', the adequate standards refer to the virtues. When 'Y' is a role term such as 'father', the adequate standards could refer to virtues appropriate to persons assuming the relevant role. Presumably, the good father is sensitive to the requirements of the situations in which he acts as a father. When 'Y' is replaced by the description of an action, and we are talking about a good thing to do, the speaker could be invoking standards for actions that constitute the fulfillment of requirements as the virtuous person detects them in the situation at hand.

The crucial terms in the above analyses of moral statements are 'moral reasons' and 'adequate moral standards'. However, the extensions of these terms are determined by the extension of an even more crucial term: 'requirements of a situation'. It would seem that a causal theory would be most appropriate for explaining how the extension of the latter is determined. McDowell speaks of a "moral reality" with which we interact and of which we have glimpses. He does not place much faith in our ability to describe which requirements obtain in a given kind of situation, but the virtuous person can "see" what they are in a *particular* situation.

The major problem with McDowell's theory lies in making good on this claim of the virtuous person's interaction with a moral reality. There is a lack of persuasive detail surrounding the claim. One wants to know what the ontological status of McDowell's "requirements" is. Those who believe morality is a social creation could say that any moral requirements are conceived and developed by people as ways of resolving internal conflicts between needs, desires, and goals of the individual, and as ways of resolving interpersonal conflicts of interest. McDowell does not believe this, but then, where do requirements come from? Are they part of the furniture of the world?

He anticipates such questions, asserting that moral reality *is* part of the world. He suspects, furthermore, that the origin of doubt about the perception of requirements is a "philistine scientism," a refusal to admit into our conception of reality anything that science does not admit.[9] And surely, he is right in objecting to any dogmatic, a priori dismissal of moral reality. It need not be scientism, however, that would motivate the person who is not aware of perceiving any moral reality to ask for more explanation of what that reality is like. To this latter request, I believe McDowell would say that one must have a perception of the kind in question. For instance, when one perceives that a friend is in trouble and open to being comforted, and when one sees it as the salient fact of the situation, as a reason for acting that silences all other considerations, one has a glimpse of moral reality.

But isn't it possible that all virtues arise not from some unique perceptual capacity but from desires such as not wishing to see one's fellow human beings suffer (such a desire could give rise to the virtue of charity, for instance)? To this question McDowell denies that

any purely natural fellow-feeling or benevolence, unmediated by the special ways of seeing situations which are characteristic of charity as it is thought of above, would issue in behavior which exactly matched that of a charitable person . . . [10]

McDowell gives no further explanation of what he has in mind. Perhaps he is referring to the complex situations in which there is more than one fact that is potentially salient as a reason for acting, and in which these different facts would call for incompatible actions. Remember the situation in which A's feelings would be hurt by a prospective action of the agent, but the same situation constitutes the honoring of a right of B's. Under McDowell's theory, the virtuous person sees one fact as the salient one, silencing all the others.

It is not clear, however, that an explanation of virtue as arising from desires could not also cover such situations in a plausible way. Under this theory, a virtuous person may have conflicting desires. He or she may not only have the desire appropriate to charity, but a desire to treat others with respect, to accord to them freedoms and opportunities necessary for their self-development. Granted this latter desire does not appear to be a purely "natural" feeling, but could it not be that our concern for others is mediated by rules, developed in the course of social cooperation and arising from the need to have established and public means of showing respect for others? And these rules could give guidelines on resolving conflicts between charity and justice. It seems, therefore, that McDowell has not shown his explanation of virtue to be better than the explanation of virtue as arising from desire.

He is vulnerable, furthermore, to an objection that proponents of the latter explanation could make: why cannot someone use arguments exactly analogous to those McDowell makes to assert that there are other kinds of irreducible normative realities in the world, corresponding to other normative systems of conduct? Someone could say that a person who appreciates the need to refrain from using one's index finger as a knife is a person who perceives a fact in a situation as the salient one, providing a reason to act in the polite manner, and that an outsider who lacks the appreciation simply has not had the perceptions in question. The point is that McDowell's arguments can be used to proliferate irreducible normative facts, and the existence of at least some of these is dubious indeed. My analysis of the general use of "A ought to do X" and "X is a good Y" statements does allow for facts of etiquette, but these reduce to facts about rules and standards. I prefer this to saying that there are irreducible facts of etiquette. Or take another example: why could I not say that those who want the designated hitter rule in baseball are obviously not attuned to irreducible baseball reality?

In the end, his assertion of a perceptual capacity to discern moral requirements is like Donagan's assertion that we can have insight into the nature of reason. To those of us who are not aware of these ways of knowing, both philosophers end up saying, "You fail to see what I see." The fact that McDowell's argument can be used to support the reality of many irreducible normative facts shows the weakness of it. At the very least, McDowell needs to give us an explanation of why we need a theory that commits us to such ontological extravagance. He must do that or find an argument for saying that there is an irreducible moral reality but not an irreducible baseball reality or an irreducible reality of polite table manners.

Perhaps such an argument could be derived from an explanation of the nature of the relation between moral reality and the psychological states corresponding to our perceptions of it. We need not be adherents to a philistine scientism to ask for such an explanation, for how else can we begin to distinguish McDowell's claims for the existence of an irreducible moral reality from claims for the irreducible reality of facts of etiquette or of baseball? Let us heed McDowell's criticism of scientism and not conflate the demand for explanation with the demand for scientific explanation. But then we must insist on the former.

7.6   Foot's Aristotelianism and corresponding analyses of moral statements

Philippa Foot has a theory of moral language that places her squarely in the Aristotelian tradition, but her theory does not rely on the assertion of an irreducible moral reality. Hers is a naturalistic Aristotelianism that identifies virtues as traits of character beneficial to the possessor and to those affected by him or her. Courage, temperance, and wisdom benefit the possessor of them, as well as others. Charity and justice directly benefit others and do not necessarily benefit the possessor.[11]

Foot allows that a person's will, character, and circumstances may be such that he or she has no reason to consistently want to benefit others and thus to be charitable and just. A person who demands that "morality should be brought under the heading of self interest" may not have a reason to be charitable and just. Foot assures us, however, that there are those who care about the suffering of others, who want to help if they can, who care for truth and liberty and want to treat others with respect, and they have reasons to be charitable and just. At the same time, they can make moral judgments about those who have none of these concerns; the latter are not necessarily being irrational; but they are selfish and perhaps evil. They morally ought to care.[12]

The fact that Foot believes a moral 'ought' may apply to a

person even if he or she has no reason to behave morally is relevant to the question of what truth conditions analysis of moral "A ought to do X" statements is best suited to her theory. A "reasons" analysis is ruled out. On the other hand, an analysis in terms of "adequate moral systems" fits with her claim that the moral 'ought' is a term by which "society is apt to voice its demands" on the individual to care about suffering and injustice. The theory behind the analysis recommended in chapters four and five includes the claim that the extension of the term 'adequate moral system' is socially established for a given group of moral language users, and it does not commit one to the claim that each subject of a true "A ought to do X" statement necessarily has reason to do X, no matter what the motivational structure of his or her character.

The analysis becomes an absolutist analysis when combined with the claim that there is only one set of adequate moral systems. Foot never explicitly commits herself to such a view, nor does she deny it. She is opposed to the theories of Hare and Stevenson, which have been associated with relativism, but it would be unfair to attribute to her a categorical denial of all versions of relativism. What we can do is to extend what she has said into a theory claiming the existence of the single true morality, being careful to note that this is not necessarily the view of Foot. We may say, therefore, that an absolutist extension of Foot's theory would include the claim that the single set of adequate moral systems has rules that require the agent to benefit others and him- or herself.

Foot's theory may be combined with an analysis of moral "X is a good Y" statements that refers to standards of adequate moral systems (X satisfies the standards for Y's contained in adequate moral systems applying to X). The standards for persons would require the virtues, while those for actions and states of affairs would require that some benefit result, either for the agent, or for others affected by the action. Now Foot believes that when 'Y' is replaced by some role term such as 'father', the standards for goodness are at least partly determined by the nature of the activities mentioned in the meaning of the term. To be a good father is to raise children well. She also recognizes, however, that opinions may vary as to what is best for children, and that in different communities more or less of a child's care may be assigned to parents.[13] Here she may be allowing for some moral relativity within certain limits, at least, but this could be accommodated by the concept of a *set* of adequate moral systems, a member of which may apply to one community but not to another.

To complete the analyses of moral statements that are compatible with an absolutist extension of Foot's theory, we should provide a theory of reference for 'adequate moral system' that is also compatible with that extension. It would seem that a descriptive theory is most compatible with the way she argues that morality is a matter of benefiting oneself and others, for she does so by appealing to our beliefs on what could count as evidence for or against a moral claim. If Foot were an absolutist, therefore, she would have to argue that there are descriptions that competent moral language users universally associate with the term 'adequate moral system' that uniquely pick out an extension for it. These descriptions would specify that an adequate moral system contains rules conformance to which tends to benefit the agent and those affected by the agent's actions. The challenge for her (as absolutist) is to identify the relevant descriptions and make it plausible that these are sufficient to pick out a unique extension for the term.

It is questionable that this could be done, because of the difficulty of settling on a single interpretation of the virtues. For instance, the virtue of wisdom implies that there is an ideal balance that is to be struck among all the worthwhile human pursuits. Yet Foot admits that it is extremely difficult to present a true account of the ideal balance in any detail.[14] So if there is a set of descriptions implicitly embodied in the beliefs of moral language users that determines the nature of that ideal balance, we have not found it yet. There is reason to believe it will never be found. For one thing, important desires for various pursuits vary in intensity from person to person, depending on genetics and personal history. The development of certain of these desires, furthermore, may be encouraged in one society while being discouraged in others. For instance, it is probably true that in American society, the desire for the kind of personal achievement that is not necessarily related to the welfare of others is encouraged to a greater degree than in other societies that may place greater emphasis on individual fulfillment in a life lived with others. Of course, it may be wise or unwise to encourage these desires beyond a certain point, but I only want to argue here that no one has ever given any detailed account of the ideal balance. This difficulty raises the question of whether human nature is sufficiently determinate so that there exists a single, ideal balance to be struck among worthwhile pursuits. If not, what may truly count as wisdom for one group or society may not count as such for another (I discuss this question in sections 10.5 and 10.6 and give reasons for thinking this relativity does indeed exist).

Other virtues are open to various interpretations. The primary example is justice. To be just is, of course, to benefit others (and perhaps oneself, if there are occasions when one could be just to oneself), but it will not do to benefit *any* set of people in *any* way. To be just is to accord to others what they are entitled to, and the question is how to determine what people are entitled to. Are they entitled to a distribution of goods in accordance with Rawls's two principles of justice, or are they entitled to the freedom to exclusive control over the fruits of their labor and what has been freely and knowingly transferred to them, as in Nozick's theory? I see no way to extend Foot's naturalism to answer these questions. Foot's problems lead us to suspect that an explication of the virtues in terms of what benefits people is not enough to justify the claim that there is a single true morality. If there is such a morality, there must be constraints on what counts as an adequate moral system other than the descriptions concerning benefit Foot has in mind.

To summarize, a naturalistic version of Aristotelianism that bases its conception of the truth conditions of moral statements on what satisfies our desires and interests runs into the problem of plasticity of our desires and interests and the problem that these desires and interests provide insufficient grounds for the interpretation of crucial virtues. McDowell's version of Aristotelianism avoids these problems because his concept of moral reality promises to contain within itself the correct balance to be struck among worthwhile pursuits and the correct interpretation of all the virtues. But doubt as to whether this promise could be kept led us to Foot in the first place. Here again, absolutists must steer their way between two hazards, and there's a good chance there is no space between them. Of course, I do not pretend to have refuted these theories by pointing out their characteristic problems. What I am doing is pointing out the problems that will affect the capacity of such theories to furnish adequate explanations of our moral experience. In chapters nine, ten, and eleven, we will see how seriously these problems affect the capacity.

7.7 Moore's Platonism

Today, few moral philosophers would subscribe to Moore's theory of moral language. Yet he presents the clearest, most straightforward, and detailed theory of how moral terms refer to irreducible moral properties, and all philosophers who find such a *general* view appealing must find a way of incorporating these virtues of Moore's theory while avoiding its problems.

The core of his theory is the notion of intrinsic goodness. That which is intrinsically good possesses a property that is simple in the sense that it cannot be analyzed into component parts, and it cannot be identified with any other simple property. This property is detected through a special faculty of perception — a moral intuition. The extrinsically good is good as a means. It is involved in the production of an intrinsically good object. An action that results in at least as much good as any other alternative action that could have been performed under the circumstances is the right action to perform.[15] This teleological doctrine of right action may be incorporated into a truth conditions analysis of moral "A ought to do X" statements in terms of "adequate moral systems." An adequate moral system would contain rules to which conformance will result in at least as much intrinsic goodness as would result from conformance to any other system of rules.

It is not so easy to see, however, how Moore's theory could be expressed by the kinds of analyses of "X is a good Y" statements that I have discussed in this book so far. His talk of intrinsic and extrinsic goodness does not square with talk of X's satisfying standards for Y's. There is an explanation for this that Peter Geach first pointed out.[16] The kind of analysis discussed so far was partly founded in the recognition of 'good' as an attributive adjective, while Moore's theory is better expressed by treating 'good' as a predicative adjective. That is, Moore's theory is incompatible with the view that 'good' is logically 'glued' to the noun phrase for which 'Y' stands in, that it functions as an operator on the noun phrase, picking out a subset (under a description) of the extension of that phrase. Moore's theory of intrinsic and extrinsic goodness as two kinds of properties leads us to the view that 'good' is detachable from the noun phrases it modifies: "X is a good friendship" implies that X has a certain simple property (Moore thought friendship to be intrinsically good) and X is a friendship; or "X is a good book" implies that X is involved in the production of intrinsic goodness and X is a book. A truth conditions analysis of "X is a good Y" statements that is consistent with Moore's theory, therefore, would make the truth of such statements dependent on the possession of the relevant properties by X and on X belonging to the class of Y's.

Now we could go on to discuss which theory of reference is most appropriate for 'good' as Moore conceives the term, but there is not much point in doing so, for Moore's analysis simply does not conform to the logical behavior of the term. 'Good' does behave like an attributive rather than a predicative adjective. It seems impossible to handle statements like "X is a good safecracker" or "X is a good assassin" in a plausible way except as statements containing an attributive adjective. These statements are not susceptible to plausible analysis in terms of the production of intrinsic goodness. In order to save Moore's theory, it would be necessary to limit it to the treatment of a certain class of "X is a good Y" statements, a class for which it is not obviously fallacious to detach the 'good' from the noun phrase it modifies. Perhaps Moore could say that he is analyzing *moral* "X is a good Y" statements. This is how John Mackie interprets him.[17] But as Mackie points out, it would be implausible to give the word 'good' a sense (or way of contributing to the truth conditions of "X is a good Y" statements) quite unconnected with its sense or senses (its way or ways of contributing to truth conditions) in other contexts. Different uses of 'good' do not seem to involve homonyms, for languages other than English have counterparts to 'good' (a general adjective of commendation that modifies noun phrases) that have a similar range of moral and nonmoral uses.

7.8   Platts' Platonism and corresponding analyses of moral language

Not all theories within the Platonic tradition need to founder on the logical form of "X is a good Y" statements. An interesting alternative to Moore is suggested by Mark Platts. He limits his theory to moral evaluations of the kind "X is courageous," "X is kind," and "X is loyal," where X can be (at least) a person, an action, or an attitude. He describes his theory as "austerely realistic." It is realistic because it assumes that the statements in question are factual claims about the world. It is austere because a truth conditions analysis of such statements will specify the systematic contribution of evaluative terms such as 'courageous', 'kind', 'loyal' to the truth conditions of statements containing them, but there is no attempt at decompositional analysis. That is, a statement of truth conditions will look like this:

An object a satisfies 'is courageous' if and only if a is courageous

in the homophonic case.[18]

The combination of austerity and realism implies for Platts that there are many distinct moral properties—courage, loyalty, honesty, and so on. Platts supplements his denial that these properties can be given informative definitions by the notion of "semantic depth." The features of the world that correspond to moral terms possess infinite complexity. The process of investigating these features has no end, and a complete understanding of them is beyond our powers.[19]

Even though Platts does not extend his theory to 'ought' and 'good', I would like to suggest a way of doing so, without implying that he would at all approve of it. To give an analysis of moral "A ought to do X" statements, we adopt a "reasons" analysis that is the same in form as the one adopted on

McDowell's behalf (under actual conditions C, A has a moral reason to do X). Like McDowell and Nagel, Platts believes that not all action need be motivated by some desire. In particular, he believes that the perception of a moral fact may provide a reason for an agent to act. An example he gives of a moral fact that could serve as a reason for action is "I did it because it was the loyal thing to do."[20] Presumably, the fact that motivated the agent at the time he or she performed it is that the action *would* be the loyal thing to do. Of situations in which action X would be the loyal thing to do, while Y would be the fair thing to do, Platts may say with McDowell that one fact may silence the other, or he may say that one may appear more salient than the other.

If we were to extend Platts' theory to moral "X is a good Y" statements, we could use the analysis that under actual conditions C, X satisfies adequate moral standards for Y's. The adequate moral standards would be derived from the particular evaluative expressions for which Platts gives an analysis. For instance, the standards for a person may include "X is to be courageous," while the standards for actions may stipulate that the action is to exemplify one of a number of possible properties (courageousness, loyalty, and so on).

Now it should be obvious that Platts would not believe that moral reasons to act and adequate moral standards are fixed by descriptions embedded in beliefs of speakers about these things. Rather, they are ultimately constituted by the plurality of moral properties that we perceive, however obscurely. It would seem, therefore, that if we were to try to identify the extensions of 'loyalty', 'courage', and so on, we would have to identify them as the properties with which speakers interact and about which the speakers can most plausibly be said to have certain beliefs—those expressed with the use of the terms. Perhaps Platts would agree to a causal theory like Evans'.

The problems with Platts' analysis are similar to the ones that beset McDowell's theory of virtuous sensitivity to the moral requirements of a situation and Donagan's theory of intuitive insight into practical reason. There is no persuasive argument for the claim that we interact with moral properties and no explanation of the relation between ourselves and moral properties, in virtue of which we perceive them.[21] Again, the theory seems to amount to the flat assertion, "You doubters fail to see what I see," to which a doubter could reply, "Perhaps what you see is overly influenced by what you want to see; give me a good reason for believing you." And like McDowell's theory, Platts opens the door for a proliferation of irreducible normative facts. His austere realism makes this vulnerability obvious. In fact, McDowell and Platts have very similar theories, despite the fact that I have placed them in different traditions. Platts' moral facts are close to McDowell's requirements imposed by a situation; I placed McDowell's theory in the Aristotelian tradition because he does center his theory around the virtues and the notion of a most fulfilling way of life; however, the way he explains the virtuous person's sensitivity to the requirements imposed by a situation brings him close to the Platonic tradition.

8 The Method for Explaining Diversity and Disagreement in Moral Belief

8.1 *Why we need a principle of translation*

Having set out the most plausible relativist and absolutist truth conditions analyses, it is time to set out the way to make a decision between the two types of analyses. In translating the truth conditions of the moral language of different societies and groups, we encounter what I will call "apparent variation" in moral belief after we have (1) tentatively identified a sentence type of the language to be translated as corresponding to "A ought to do X" or "X is a good Y," by tentatively identifying the kinds of speech acts it is used to perform and the way it functions in inferences, arguments, and other conversational contexts, (2) tentatively translated enough of other parts of the language to have a good idea of what terms of the metalanguage to match with the terms in the object language for which 'A', 'X', and 'Y' are place holders, and (3) gotten an idea of what sorts of actions are required or prohibited and what sorts of objects, persons, and actions are evaluated negatively and positively. When we find a difference between two groups or societies with respect to (3), we have a case of apparent variation in moral belief. Of course, it is only apparent until we have settled on a truth conditions analysis of the moral statements used to express these beliefs. The question is how to translate in the light of such apparent variation. In chapter two, I briefly stated my guiding maxim for translation — the principle of the best explanation. It is now time to argue for and to clarify it.

8.2   *Quine's principle of charity*

Any argument for a principle of translation must begin with consideration of Quine, who was the pioneer in translation theory. The part of his theory most relevant to our purposes is his guiding maxim of translation: that one should maximize agreement, at least with respect to obvious truths (those to which speakers readily assent), between oneself and native speakers. The agreement is an agreement in belief, which is for Quine a disposition to assent to a sentence under query given appropriate stimulation. When we translate indicative sentences we fix our interpretation of the beliefs of native speakers because (for Quine) their beliefs are simply dispositions to assent to the sentences under query given appropriate stimulation. Quine's "principle of charity" tells us that

the more absurd or exotic the beliefs imputed to a people, the more suspicious we are entitled to be of the translations... For translation theory, banal messages are the breath of life.[1]

The problem is that the principle of charity does not yield the correct results in certain situations. For instance, what is obvious to a linguist may not be obvious to a speaker. Richard Grandy points out that the speaker's past history of learning may influence the way he or she focuses attention on the environment, so that it is substantially different from the way the linguist focuses attention on the same environment.[2] Placed in the deep woods, a lifelong New Yorker would fail to perceive things that would be obvious to a hunting guide. Also, there are situations in which being charitable to a speaker is to misinterpret him or her. To make this point, Grandy adapts Donellan's example of the man who arrives at a party and asserts, "The man with a martini is a philosopher." Standing in front of him is a man drinking water from a martini glass and who is not a philosopher; while we know that in the garden, out of sight, is a philosopher drinking a martini. The charitable thing to do is to interpret him as referring to the philosopher; but clearly the best translation of his remarks has him asserting something false about the man in front of him.

In this latter case, what makes the less charitable translation the better one is the fact that it renders the speaker's beliefs intelligible to us. We understand how he could have acquired such a belief, since we can plausibly hypothesize causal interaction between him and the object we interpret his utterance to be about. Under the charitable interpretation, the object that would be the reference cannot be understood as interacting with the speaker. More generally, less charitable translations are better when they make for plausible explanations of the speaker's linguistic behavior and of his or her nonlinguistic behavior insofar as such behavior is related to the propositional attitudes expressed through his or her utterances.

8.3 Grandy's principle of humanity

These considerations should move us to consider other possible constraints on translation. Grandy has proposed that we translate a speaker's utterances in such a way "that the imputed pattern of relations among beliefs, desires, [and all other propositional attitudes] and the world be as similar to our own as possible."[3] This principle should be of particular interest to us because Grandy derives it from the assumption that the ultimate purpose of translation is to enable the translator to make the best possible predictions and to offer the best explanations of the speaker's behavior. We predict and explain behavior by translating verbal behavior into our own language, using the translation to fix the content of the speaker's beliefs, desires, and other propositional attitudes. Then we combine this information with a psychological model of the speaker to turn out predictions and explanations. Grandy suggests, plausibly enough, that we use *ourselves* as models. That is, we consider what we would do if we had the relevant beliefs, desires, and so on. The success of the simulation depends on the similarity of the speaker's belief and desire network to our own.

Should we accept this principle? It is plausible that we could not understand a speaker unless he or she displayed the ability to perform basic forms of practical reasoning. The speaker should be able to reason from a desire for a state of affairs to

obtain and a belief that a certain action is the necessary means
to that end to an intention to perform the action, or as Aristotle would have it, the action itself. The same holds for simple
forms of reasoning from beliefs to beliefs. We should be ready
to impute to the speaker the ability to stay away from contradictions when they are quite obvious and there is nothing in
the speaker's present situation or past history to indicate that
he or she is aware of them as contradictions.

Grandy pointed out a relation between beliefs and the world
that should be imputed to the speaker: that beliefs about
objects are formed through causal interaction with them. This
"causal theory of belief" is plausible, but must be qualified.
There is a sense in which I could have a belief about the first
man to land on Mars even though I could not have any causal
interaction with him. I could believe he will be an American,
for instance. The sort of belief about an object that requires
causal interaction with it is one that appears in "transparent"
contexts. The object of such a belief can be identified by any
applicable descriptions. If in Grandy's example the man drinking water from the martini glass is a plumber, we could say
that someone had a mistaken belief about that plumber: that
he was a philosopher. On the other hand, suppose that the first
man to land on Mars turns out to be the first man of Lithuanian descent to be pictured on the cover of *Time*. I do not
have the belief that the first man of Lithuanian descent to be
pictured on the cover of *Time* will be an American.

Grandy's principle also allows for plausible attributions of
erroneous reasoning to the speaker. There is a good reason why
fallacies such as affirming the consequent are regular features
of introductory texts to logic: many people commit them in
certain circumstances. We know ourselves as beings capable of
mistakes in certain kinds of circumstances and with certain
past histories of learning. We, therefore, should be prepared
to attribute error to the speaker should the same kinds of circumstances and histories apply.

Beyond a certain point, however, it is unwise to duplicate
ourselves, whether we view ourselves as possessors of the truth
or as eminently fallible beings. There are special problems in
interpreting people from societies that are significantly differ-

ent from our own with respect to prevalent modes of social, political, and economic organization. These different modes of organization are often accompanied by different patterns of relations among propositional attitudes and the world.

Within anthropology, for instance, there is a debate over the interpretation of the magical rites practiced by some "primitive" peoples. Frazer put forward the view of magic as a kind of rival to science, as an attempt to predict and control nature through the supernatural.[4] Under his view, people who practice magic are not so different from us, just misguided. Another view is that magic has a purpose different from any one we might use it for — that of expressing or symbolizing social values. Beattie asserts that Trobriand canoe magic expresses the importance of canoe building for Trobrianders and that blood pact ritual emphasizes the need for mutual support between parties to it.[5] Under his view, we should be prepared to impute patterns among beliefs and the world that would be different from those appropriate to the task of prediction and control, and these different patterns may become intelligible if we recognize a symbolic or expressive purpose for magic.

Peter Winch has argued that Zande magical rites are not only a misguided attempt to produce crops but a "form of expression" that provides an Azande the opportunity to reflect on how "the life he lives, his relations with his fellows, his chances for acting decently or doing evil, may all spring from his relation to his crops."[6] More specifically, Winch suggests that Zande rites express a recognition that

one's life is subject to contingencies, rather than an attempt to control these ... We have a drama of resentments, evil-doing, revenge, expiation, in which there are ways of dealing (symbolically) with misfortunes and their disruptive effect on a man's relations with his fellows, with ways in which life can go on despite such disruptions.[7]

It is quite possible that magic does play an expressive role, instead of, or in addition to, the role of prediction and control. The success of the interpretations of Beattie and Winch depends on whether it can be shown that magic is indeed *given* such a role by the people who believe in it. Are they, or at least some of them, conscious of magical rites as expressing social values? If not, can a case be made for their unreflective or unconscious acceptance of such rites as expressing values?

We cannot answer these questions here. It suffices to note that the interpretations of Beattie and Winch are coherent and could be better explanations than Frazer's under some circumstances. Suppose that a people such as the Azande are offered Western technology with the power to accomplish all the goals related to prediction and control that they could hope to accomplish with their magical rites. If they choose to go on performing their rites, then we might have evidence for explanations such as Beattie's or Winch's. We would have to say that this group is not as similar to us as Frazer thought. Their desire to express social values through ritual and ceremony is much greater than ours. The moral is that explaining the behavior of a group of people may require that we make them different from ourselves. Three immediate qualifications are in order, though.

First, we do rely on elements of self-knowledge even when we do make people different from ourselves. We can understand a practice as expressive of certain values because we have or had practices with analogous functions. Winch refers to the Judaeo-Christian conception of "If it be thy Will," as developed in the story of Job, to illuminate the attitude toward contingencies he sees expressed in Zande rites. He does not say that the rites and Christian prayers of supplication are much alike with respect to the content of attitudes expressed, only with respect to the fact that they do express such attitudes. Second, it is not clear we have to ascribe different criteria of *rationality* (fundamentally different forms of reasoning) to people even when we make them different from ourselves. The Azande accept magic because it fulfills certain of their purposes, which we don't have. No fundamentally different forms of reasoning need be attributed to them (here I disagree with Winch; see appendix B for a critical discussion of his view).

Third, we may gain an understanding of a different way of life by construing it as a response to certain conditions that human beings commonly face. We can understand the logic of making such a response, even if our own way of life may have arisen from a different response to similar conditions. For instance, Winch interprets Zande rites as a response to "misfortunes and their disruptive effect on a man's relations with his fellows." Surely, we can recognize that condition as one we face, and even though we did not respond to it in the way the Azande did, we can understand their response as one that is possible for human beings to make (here we make use of our experience of practices in our own way of life that have analogous functions).

Another example of the point I want to make is a possible explanation of the Chinese emphasis on the theme that the individual finds his or her fulfillment in service to the group. This theme is pervasive in Chinese social practices, from the supreme importance of filial piety as a duty children must fulfill throughout the lifetimes of their parents, to the modeling of all levels of government in pre-Communist China after the structure of the family. The sinologist Richard Solomon traces the origin of this theme to the requirements for survival in a social economy of subsistence agriculture:

The great stress on family interdependence is a clear response to the needs of production and security in this type of society. Adults had to rely on the life-long commitment of their children to the family group for both labor and, eventually, for their material needs in old age . . . The dominant forms of authority and social sanction which characterized traditional Chinese society reflect this basic logic of social interdependence.[8]

Solomon goes on to note that the theme of social interdependence was to gain a life of its own: urban Chinese of the upper- and middle-income levels accepted and lived this theme. He explains this phenomenon partially by sketching the socialization process through which the theme of social interdependence is incorporated into the developing personality.

It is relevant that other societies have faced conditions of material scarcity and have relied on subsistence agriculture. Yet some have not developed the culture of social interdependence to any degree approximating the Chinese. So acceptance of the theme of social interdependence is just one possible response to these conditions. My point is that Americans with no experience of this way of life can understand it at least to some extent as a possible response to a common human condition, as a road that was not taken in the formation of their culture. They can understand it, perhaps, by analogy with and extension of experiences they have had, situations in which people had to pull together to accomplish what was important to them. The ultimate point of all three qualifications I have made is that when we put together a picture of why a group behaves in the way it does, its members may come out looking rather different from us in important respects, but we rely on bits and pieces of our own experience in arriving at the picture. From the way we are, we form a picture of what we could have been.

My intention has been to clarify the scope of application of the principle of humanity. We do use ourselves as psychological models to explain the behavior of others, but we can explain how others could differ from ourselves by seeing how basic needs, desires, and forms of reasoning, all of them familiar to us, could be accompanied by different needs, desires, goals, ways of understanding and dealing with the world. The principle of humanity is simply a guide to translation, and our most basic goal is to make native speakers intelligible to ourselves.

8.4   *The principle of the best explanation*

In fact, it is better to make the most basic goal explicit in the principle of the best explanation: a translation of a group's language should be such that the content of imputed propositional attitudes, and the relations among them and the world, can be included within the best explanation of the group's linguistic and nonlinguistic behavior.

Let me make some clarifying points. First, the principle implies that the content of imputed propositional attitudes should be such that their acquisition is explicable. This makes explicit what was implicit in Grandy's discussion of the causal theory of belief and the man with the martini. Second, let it be understood that the "best explanation" will satisfy the principle of humanity with respect to basic forms of practical reasoning and logical inference. As the discussion of magic illustrates, however, we cannot assume that people are like us with respect to needs, desires, and purposes that may influence the formation of patterns of relations among propositional attitudes and the world. We must allow for a certain plasticity in human nature, a responsiveness to shaping by social and physical environment. We must allow for different needs, desires, and purposes when we can see them arising from a possible response to certain conditions. As I noted in the last section, we can rely on self-knowledge in understanding a response as one that is possible for human beings to make, but the resulting picture, when all the pieces are put together, may expand our conception of the variety to be found in humanity.

Third, the principle permits us to use every bit of knowledge that could help in the effort to produce the best explanation. This includes not only our psychological self-knowledge, but relevant parts of neurophysiology, sociology, and anthropology. If we have two translations, and if one commits us to an explanation of a group's behavior that conflicts with an important generalization about the way groups function, while the other doesn't, then we have a reason to prefer the latter. Of course, the surrounding body of knowledge should not be treated as fixed. If a translation of a group's language leads us to a conflict with a psychological generalization, we may have to give up the generalization instead of the translation; it depends on how much evidence we have for the translation and on the adjustments we would have to make in our explanation of the group's behavior if we were to give other translations.

Fourth, let me note that there need not be a single best explanation. We may have a number of them that are better than the rest and that are equally good, given the available evidence. The main question I want to answer in this book is whether the best explanation or explanations of moral language users must be consistent with moral relativity. When I mention "*the* best explanation" in later parts of this book, I am implicitly allowing for the possibility of there being more than one. My argument will be that the best explanation, or all of them, must be consistent with moral relativity.

Fifth, the "best explanation" required by the principle is not necessarily the ideal extracted from the natural sciences. We are not required to have a set of laws that enable us to deduce the behavior of members of a natural kind, given the values of various parameters that involve the members of the kind, and of those parameters defining initial and boundary conditions. In the very distant future, such an explanation may be possible. Perhaps it will never be achieved, as Hilary Putnam and Alasdair MacIntyre have recently argued.[9] At present and for the forseeable future, the kind of explanation that works for us includes reference to goals, desires, interests, beliefs, and the reasons for action that stem from them. We may explain the relations among these items for a given individual or group by subsuming the particular case under a generalization. But the generalizations available to us do not include well-defined sets of counterfactual conditions; that is, they cannot be systematically extended to unobserved or hypothetical instances and are not universally quantified over the individuals whose propositional attitudes and behavior are the subjects of generalization. MacIntyre suggests that they must be prefaced by a phrase such as "characteristically and for the most part."[10]

8.5   *Charity versus the best explanation in translation of moral language*

To shed further light on the character of a translation governed by the principle of the best explanation, let us compare it with an approach to translation governed by the principle of charity. David Cooper has attempted to resolve the issue of absolutism versus relativism using the latter approach. His rationale for applying the principle of charity to the translation of a group's moral language is that "We can only identify another's beliefs as moral beliefs about X if there is a massive degree of agreement between his and our beliefs."[11] He takes his cue from Davidson, who argues that "a belief is identified by its location in a pattern of beliefs; it is this pattern that determines the subject matter of the belief, what the belief is about . . . False beliefs tend to undermine the identification of the subject matter; to undermine, therefore, the validity of the belief as being about that subject."[12] It is even unclear that the ancients believed the earth was flat. If they believed none of the things we believe about the earth, how do we know that they had any beliefs about the earth? Similarly, Cooper argues that those who do not believe what we believe about good, evil, right, and wrong do not have beliefs we could count as moral beliefs. A moral belief must have for its subject matter something connected with "welfare, happiness, suffering, security, and the life."[13] Hence moral relativists are refuted.

Now Cooper's argument is vulnerable even if his general approach to translation is taken as a given. Others may have beliefs about how to act that are connected to welfare, happiness, and so on, and there may be sufficient resemblance between their beliefs and ours that we must admit they have a morality, but this does not rule out significant differences between their morality and ours. For instance, they may have different beliefs about the extent to which an individual should contribute to the welfare of others. The difference may not be radical, but it still raises the issue of relativity in moral truth.

The main problem with Cooper's argument, however, is his general approach to translation. A group's beliefs don't have to be the same as ours for us to identify their beliefs as being *about* the same thing as some of our beliefs. We can take the object that stands in an appropriate causal relation to that group and say that they have beliefs about it, even though their beliefs may conflict with ours. This certainly seems to be the right consequence with respect to the ancients and their belief that the earth was flat. Of course, the object about which they had the belief is the same object we believe is round (actually, it is pear-shaped). We apply the causal theory of belief to the ancients because it makes for a good explanation of their behavior. We can understand why they would say the earth was flat because we can understand how the earth would appear flat to them. True, if the ancients had *all* false beliefs about the "earth," we would wonder if we are talking about the same object as they were. That is because it is doubtful we could explain how any intelligent person could manage to have all false beliefs about an object that presents some of its aspects so directly to him or her.

The conclusion is that moral relativism cannot be dismissed as easily as Cooper argues, and in the course of criticizing his argument, we have seen one example of the difference between the principle of the best explanation and the principle of charity when they are applied to the translation of moral language.

8.6   *A possible objection to the principle of the best explanation*

It might be questioned whether it is necessary for a translation to cohere with the best explanation of moral language users. If we demand this, and if the best explanation includes scientific facts about moral language users, aren't we falling into a version of scientism?

The first point of reply is that our project does not require us to *reduce* moral language to nonmoral language, though I have developed what I consider to be an enlightening analysis of moral language that does not contain moral terms.

The point is the argument is not premised on any general doctrine that a nonreductive translation is by its very nature unacceptable. The second point of reply is that the explanation need not be a scientific explanation, as has already been pointed out. There is a difference between a scientific explanation and an explanation that fits with scientific facts. I understand scientism as demanding a reduction of the moral to the nonmoral and a *scientific* explanation of moral experience, not just an explanation that fits with scientific facts. The third point of reply is a question: what is wrong with requiring the latter kind of explanation? The principle of the best explanation requires us to translate moral language in such a way that the resulting explanation of behavior connected with the use of this language be coherent with our total explanation of what human beings are like and the way they deal with the world. If science helps us with the total explanation, then we *should* require that a translation of moral language fit with the relevant scientific facts. In any case, the reader will see that no truth conditions analyses of moral statements that are seriously entertained in this book will be rejected solely because they are inconsistent with scientific theory. One of my primary arguments against absolutism is that it leaves *gaps* in our theory of moral language users, not that it conflicts with scientific claims in that theory. I see no way for the absolutist to avoid the need for giving explanations of apparently irresolvable disagreements and apparent variations in moral belief.

8.7   *Absolutist methods of accounting for diversity and disagreement*

At this point, it will be useful to enumerate the different methods of explanation that are consistent with absolutism and with the principle of the best explanation. Then we will see whether these methods work in particular cases. The most obvious way to explain diversity in moral belief among different groups or societies is to claim that the difference is caused by an error in perception or reasoning made by at least one group, or by the group being ignorant of some crucial fact. This method of explanation is open to all absolutists, though the kind of error or ignorance absolutists will claim is likely to be made will depend on the kind of theory they have. Suppose that Gewirth's theory is true. Then an important fact of which many people are likely to be ignorant is that the PGC follows from standards of rationality for reasons to act. Because the reasoning that allows one to see the logical connection is complex, it is understandable why many have not seen it. They, therefore, may not hold to the PGC or not hold to it in quite the form it must have if it is to follow from standards of rationality.

Even if a group knows that the PGC holds for itself (and for all people), it still has the complex task of translating this broad and abstract principle into a set of concrete duties, practices, and institutions. In particular, it is possible to have much disagreement over what sets of political and economic institutions are best suited to promote equal rights to freedom and well-being. In such complex matters, there is room for error rooted in fallacious inference, misinterpretation of evidence, wishful thinking, thinking distorted by one's vital self-interests or strong emotion, and so on.

If we assume Foot's theory is true, then we have a different kind of error or ignorance that is likely to be the source of moral diversity. This kind would concern mistakes about the proper interpretation of virtues such as wisdom and justice. Since the questions of what balance is to be struck among one's pursuits and of how to benefit others in a just manner are likely to be complex, requiring much knowledge of human needs and desires, and again, of the relation of various kinds of economic and political institutions to human welfare, we could expect our fallibility and limitations of knowledge to show up. If an absolutist theory such as (my extension of) McDowell's or Platts' is true, then we would expect the relevant kind of error and ignorance to be misperceptions of a complex situation caused by lack of experience in perceiving that kind of situation or by self-interest or emotion.

Besides error or ignorance, another way of explaining moral diversity is to refer to environmental relativity. For instance, when different groups or societies operate under different conditions relating to the availability of human and material resources, it may be appropriate for them to have different duties and virtues as well as practices and institutions. This, however, does not mean that there are essentially different moralities that are equally true. Different moralities may have a common core, in terms of which the differences are justified because of the varying conditions. Aristotelians such as Foot could say that two societies may have different virtues because a trait that is beneficial to the possessor in one society is not beneficial to the possessor in another. We would not expect thrift to be listed as a virtue in a society where there is an abundance of material resources and wealth. In a warlike society where there is constant struggle for the resources necessary for existence, one would not expect gentlemanly virtues such as Aristotle's wittiness, agreeableness in company, and gentleness or good temper. McDowell could say that what the virtuous person sees to be the requirements of a given kind of situation may vary with the conditions of the society. When conditions are such that all are struggling for mere survival, the virtuous man may see more of a requirement than he would under different conditions to reserve his time, energy, and material goods for the sake of protecting his family, as opposed to strangers.

Kantians such as Gewirth could assert that the PGC justifies different practices and institutions according to the conditions of a society. Where resources are few and relatively undeveloped, the PGC may justify a lesser freedom for all for the sake of raising the level of material well-being to the point where freedom becomes more meaningful. Under a theory such as Platts', the moral facts are fixed by nonmoral facts (or in any case, facts not clearly moral), and these latter facts include the availability of human and material resources in a society. Where there is variation in the latter, there is variation in the former.

Now what about apparently irresolvable disagreement in which all sides seem to possess all relevant nonmoral facts and in which none seems to have made an error in reasoning? Absolutists who hold to theories such as those of McDowell and Platts could assert that at least one side fails to perceive the relevant moral facts. There is, however, another method of explanation available to all absolutists, and that is to say that some moral questions are simply beyond human powers to resolve one way or another, at least as these powers exist in their present state. Why? McDowell and Platts could stress the extreme difficulty of perceiving moral reality clearly; Foot could say that questions of which balance among worthwhile pursuits is the most beneficial to human beings are simply beyond our ability to answer given our present knowledge of human nature and of the relation of various kinds of social structure to human welfare. Gewirth could make an analogous claim about certain questions in application of the PGC. On this method of explanation, the diversity of moral belief and existence of apparently irresolvable disagreements simply indicate our limitations. No one can prove the other wrong, but there is a right and a wrong nevertheless.

These are, I believe, the major methods of explanation available to absolutists. We are now ready to pose the crucial question: are these methods going to be sufficient to explain actual cases of moral diversity and apparently irresolvable disagreement? In the next three chapters, we will see that these methods fail, when applied to disagreements and differences in belief concerning virtue-centered and rights-centered moralities, and that the reason for their failure is intimately connected with what I have identified in chapter seven as the serious problems besetting the theories of each of the three absolutist traditions. The conclusion I will advance is that we should adopt the relativist analyses, those that preserve a good deal of moral objectivity while making possible an explanation of why some of us would think there is a single true morality that everyone has reason to follow, even if there is not.

9 Virtue-Centered and Rights-Centered Moralities

9.1 *The claims to be made for moral relativity*

In chapter one, I briefly characterized a virtue-centered morality as one concerned with a good common to all members of a community (this characterization will have to be qualified later when we come to Aristotle). The common good is partially constituted by a shared life, defined by a system of roles specifying the contribution of each member of the community to the sustenance of that life. Virtues are the qualities necessary for the role performance and for successful contribution to the common good. Notions of a common good and shared life are not central to a rights-centered morality. In their place, we find an emphasis on what each member of the community is entitled to claim from other members. The rights belonging to each person — such as those to freedom, property, and well-being — must be recognized.

In this chapter, I will discuss the work of Alasdair MacIntyre. He has done the most to illuminate the difference between virtue-centered and rights-centered moralities, and I want to take advantage of that work. At the same time, he makes the striking and controversial claim that only the principles of virtue-centered moralities can be genuinely objective in the sense of having truth values and being confirmable or disconfirmable by facts. I will criticize the arguments for his claim and will use it as a counterpoint to the ones I will make in the next two chapters. In chapter ten, I will claim that the principles of *both* types of moralities can be genuinely objective (in MacIntyre's sense) but that there is indeterminacy and variation in the truth conditions of moral statements made by speakers who subscribe to each type. In chapter eleven, I claim that there are differences between the truth conditions assignable to moral statements made on the basis of virtue-centered moralities and those assignable to moral statements made on the basis of rights-centered moralities. In other words, I claim that we find moral relativity when we look *within* each type of morality and when we *compare* the two types.

9.2   *MacIntyre's theory of moral catastrophe*

Let us begin with MacIntyre's explanation of the way virtue-centered moralities begin. In his view, these were the moralities of the heroic societies, as pictured in the Homeric poems, the Icelandic sagas, and the stories of Ulster. He admits that it is questionable how much the narratives provide an accurate account of these societies as opposed to an idealization, an abstraction from which the discordant elements were removed. What matters to his argument, however, is that the narratives provided the historical memory of the heroic societies and that they provided a moral background to contemporary debate in classical societies.

As pictured in the narratives, the heroic societies of Homer, Iceland, and Ireland were such that an individual had a role and status within a "well-defined and highly determinate system of roles and statuses," of which the key structures were the kinship and the household. One defines one's identity in terms of certain roles in these structures. Attached to these roles are duties and privileges so that one knows what one owes and what is owed to one by the occupant of every other role. There is a clear understanding, moreover, of what it is to perform one's duties and privileges. To the extent, therefore, to which 'ought' plays a role in the morality of these societies, its meaning is fixed by what is required of people as they occupy roles. But *virtue* is the key concept of heroic moralities, for it refers to the qualities that sustain one in one's role and that manifest themselves in actions required by the role. The virtues, moreover, are qualities needed in members of the community to sustain the common good of the shared life as it is defined by the total system of roles and statuses. Courage, for instance, allows an individual to sustain household and community. The correct applications of 'ought', 'owe', and 'virtue' are fixed by the total system. For members of heroic society, the application of these terms was as much an objective matter as anything was.

The situation becomes more complex as we move to classical society. In Athens, the primary moral community is no longer the household or kinship group, but the Athenian democracy. Household and kinship groups still exist, and the values stemming from them, but they are now parts of larger units. The Homeric values compete with others for acceptance. When small and cohesive moral communities are combined into larger units, knowledge of the variety of possible human practices becomes common. It is now possible to ask what it is to be a good *man,* or a good citizen, because one's moral horizon has expanded beyond the smaller units. In Homer, to be just is to do what the established order required, but in fifth-century Athens, one is aware of many possible orders and so it is possible to ask whether it is just to do what the established order requires. There is a received set of virtues: friendship, courage, self-restraint, wisdom, and justice, but the interpretation of them is open to extended disagreement. Still, there is a shared context in which debates over the virtues take place: the *polis.* Being a good man is intimately related to being a good citizen. Friendship, company, and the city state are essential components of humanity, and any account of the virtues must pass the test of explaining how the virtues are necessary to sustain this common good. There were, furthermore, shared communal modes for uniting Greeks in their conflicts with each other. These shared modes, which MacIntyre takes to be manifestations of *agôn* (the contest), include the Olympics, for which a truce between warring city states was declared every four years, debates in the assemblies and law courts of Athenian democracy, dramatic forms of tragedy and comedy, and philosophical dialogue.

The point is that, even though there is less agreement on the interpretation of the virtues, and even different lists of the virtues, the Greeks, or more exactly, the Athenians, still assume the existence of a common good that all members of the community strive to realize. Debates over lists of virtues and their interpretation take place against this unifying context and are given form in the communal modes of *agôn*. The *polis* and the *agôn* make fifth-century Athens a moral community, in spite of the extensive political and moral conflict. To enter into the debates within this context and in these modes is to take part in a moral tradition, and in MacIntyre's view Aristotle was the greatest representative of that tradition. He assumes that the city-state is the only political form in which the virtues of human life can be fully realized. The virtues are still those excellences of mind and character that contribute to the sustenance of that community and to the realization of the common good. That is why Aristotle places the highest form of friendship at the foundations of community. That form is not constituted by the mere liking of friends for one another, nor by mutual advantage, but by a shared commitment to the realization of goods.[1] Justice is the virtue that includes knowledge of how to apply those laws that prohibit wrongs destructive of the relationships that make common pursuit of the good possible.

Virtue-centered moralities are undermined when a community can no longer envisage its life as a shared project. It is explainable, therefore, why such moralities faded with the replacement of the city-state by the Macedonian kingdom and then the Roman Empire. The common good of a shared life becomes fragmented into individual goods, and to be moral reduces to obeying the laws regulating the conflicts of private goods. At home in such an environment is the Stoic view of man, not as a contributor to the life of a particular community, but a cosmopolitan citizen of the world. Virtue becomes conformity to the cosmic law, and its interpretation as a set of related qualities necessary for the sustenance of the shared life disappears.

The Middle Ages, however, saw the evolution of a new social context for virtue-centered moralities. Medieval society was a synthesis, or rather a combination of several syntheses, of the older paganism, Aristotelianism, and Christianity and Judaism. Here again, it was possible to view oneself as part of an ordered community seeking the common human good. As in the ancient world, the individual is "identified and constituted in and through certain of his or her roles, those roles that bind the individual to the communities in and through which specifically human goods are to be attained."[2] The common good is now conceived as divine, and human life as a quest or journey in which a variety of evils are encountered and to be overcome. The virtues are those qualities enabling the evils to be overcome. Christian purity, for instance, enables one to strive for the supreme good in the face of worldly distraction while patience is endurance in the face of evil. With Aristotle, Maimonides recognized the virtue of friendship as an essential bond of community, and explained that God in the Torah provided so many holidays in order to make opportunities for the growth of friendship.

A useful part of MacIntyre's theory of virtue-centered moralities in his analysis of their common, underlying structures. The core concept of such moralities is of course that of virtue, and the logical development of this concept has three stages. In the first stage, virtue is defined in terms of practices. By 'practice', MacIntyre does not merely mean any "coherent and complex socially established cooperative human activity," but one "through which goods internal to that form of activity are realised in the course of trying to achieve those standards of excellence which are appropriate to, and partially definitive of, that form of activity, with the result that human powers to achieve excellence, and human conceptions of the ends and goods involved, are systematically extended."[3] Practices in this special sense include the arts, sciences, games, politics under Aristotle's conception of it, family life, and, in the ancient and medieval worlds, the creation and sustenance of human communities.

Internal goods are those that are constituted at least partly by the rules and standards of excellence of the practice in question. They only reliably can be identified by the experience of participating in the practice. They are to be contrasted with goods externally and contingently attached to the practice, e.g., prestige, status, and money. In fact, part of the American public's disaffection with the professional athlete may be its perception, probably justified, that the athlete is increasingly enamored of the external goods of the sport, rather than the goods internally constituted by the achievement of excellence. To enter into a practice is to accept the authority of its rules and standards of excellence. "It is to subject my own attitudes, choices, preferences and tastes" to those standards and rules. A young baseball pitcher may get into the major leagues on the strength of his arm, but he will not last long if he does not, as MacIntyre suggests, accept the authority of those more experienced than he, and learn when to throw a fastball and when not to. The achievement, furthermore, of standards of excellence by an individual is a good for the whole community of those participating in the practice. For instance, after the sixth game of the 1975 World Series between the Boston Red Sox and the Cincinnati Reds, some of the players on both teams remarked that they had felt proud and privileged to have played in that game (in so many words).

Given this conception of a practice, MacIntyre roughly defines a virtue as an acquired human quality the possession and exercise of which tends to enable us to achieve those goods internal to practices and the lack of which effectively prevents us from achieving any such goods.[4] Justice requires that we treat others with merit or desert according to the uniform and impersonal standards of the practice, and those who have authority in the practice must be just to legitimate their authority and teach newcomers effectively. Courage is a virtue because the care and concern it embodies is necessary for the achievement of goods internal to practices.

MacIntyre points out that the conception of virtue in terms of practices is incomplete in three ways. First, the conception does not address the problems of conflicting practices. A man may find himself unable to fulfill the demands of sustaining the human community in which he lives and at the same time devote himself to the arts. Unless more can be said about how such conflicts are to be resolved, a "subversive arbitrariness" will pervade the moral life. Second, the conception of particular virtues remains incomplete. For example, to be just is to give to each what he or she deserves. But what is due a person depends on what he or she has contributed to the achievement of those internal goods, "the sharing of which and the common pursuit of which provide the foundations of human community."[5] These goods need to be ordered and evaluated if we are to assess the relative desert of persons. Third, there is one virtue that must be defined with reference not to a practice but to the whole of a human life, and that is integrity or constancy. These ways in which the practice conception of virtue is incomplete point to the need to conceive of each human life as a unity, as a life in which conflicts between the requirements of practices are resolved or at least dealt with in better or worse ways, in which the various goods are ordered in some hierarchy, and in which the virtue of integrity is exercised.

The second stage of the development of the concept of virtue, therefore, is to characterize what constitutes the unity of human life, the good for human beings, not just the goods of practices. Unity is provided by narrative, says MacIntyre. We are "story-telling" animals who must ask ourselves, "Of what story or stories do I find myself a part?" in order to answer the question, "What am I to do?"[6] The unity of a human life, therefore, is the unity of a narrative embodied in a single life. Is there something that can be common to the narratives embodied in all lives? Yes, answers MacIntyre; the good for man as such is a narrative quest for the good itself that provides a unity for each and every life. It is in looking for the good that we will find the answers to the questions that the practice conception of virtue leaves unanswered. We cannot characterize the final goal of the quest ahead of time, for a quest by its very nature is an education in the character of what is sought. Now I know this is obscure; MacIntyre seems to be saying both that we cannot know what the good for man is before engaging in a quest for it *and* that the search itself *is* the good. Perhaps he means to characterize the quest as a partial constituent of the good for man, which provides some unity, but the quest is not and cannot be the whole good. The virtues are now reinterpreted as those dispositions that will not only sustain practices and allow us to achieve their internal goods, but that will also sustain us in the quest for the good, which will allow us to understand what more and what else the good life for man is.

The third stage of the development of the concept of virtue

involves tradition. An individual seeks the good within a context defined by traditions of which his or her life is a part. The practices we engage in have a history, one through which the practice in its present form was conveyed to us. Thus the history of each of our individual lives must be understood in terms of the larger and longer histories of traditions. Living traditions are always partially constituted by an agreement on the internal goods of the practices embedded in them. And the virtues are necessary to keep traditions alive in this sense, as lack of justice, courage, and truthfulness corrupt them.

The turn to rights-centered morality can now be understood at least partly in terms of the undermining of this basic structure of virtue-centered moralities. With modern science came the rejection of Aristotelian teleology with its conception of the good for man lying in the performance of a biologically-determined function. There was the secular rejection of theological conceptions of the good for man. The cultural place of a narrative was diminished and is no longer seen by many theorists of art as connected with human life. The concept of a practice with internal goods also has been removed from the lives of most of us:

So long as productive work occurs within the structure of households, it is easy and right to understand that work as part of the sustaining of the community of the household and of those wider forms of community which the household in turn sustains. As, and to the extent that, work moves outside the household and is put to the service of impersonal capital, the realm of work tends to become separated from everything but the service of biological survival and the reproduction of the labor force, on the one hand, and that of institutionalized acquisitiveness, on the other hand.[7]

Most modern individuals can no longer see themselves as members of a community with a tradition, as people with roles of son or daughter, citizen, member of profession, and hence with certain duties, debts, and inheritances that define their social identities. From the standpoint of the modern individualism that underlies rights-centered moralities, one is what one chooses to be. One cannot help being a son or a daughter, but one does not have to assume the corresponding duties unless one chooses to. That is why, as MacIntyre perceptively points out, modern Americans think they can disclaim any responsibility for the effects of slavery by claiming, "I never owned any slaves."[8]

The process that culminated in this contemporary manifestation of individualism started in the Middle Ages. By the end of the seventeenth century, Hume was faced with the problem of giving an account and justification of virtues that had their source in moral traditions (Christian, for Hume) the structural foundations of which had been undermined. He attempted to construct an argument with premises characterizing some features of human nature and with the conclusion that rules of morality would be those we could be expected to accept, given human nature as characterized. The relevant features of human nature for Hume are long-term self-interest and sympathy. But self-interest, long-term or not, will not justify unconditional adherence to general and unconditional rules of promise-keeping and justice; and sympathy, if it is supposed to motivate such adherence, is a philosophical fiction, says MacIntyre. I would suppose that he would regard as one reason for this failure of justification the institutionalized acquisitiveness that followed disintegration of the common good. At best, the combination of self-interest and acquisitiveness would motivate one to appear trustworthy and just. MacIntyre is not explicit on why he believes sympathy to be insufficient, but we could say on his behalf that if sympathy must compete with acquisitiveness and self-interest, it cannot constitute a very strong, consistent moral motivation. MacIntyre also may have the view that sympathy is a somewhat capricious emotion. The rest of the Enlightenment thinkers attempted a similar project with different features of human nature — Kant, Diderot, Smith — but all failed, as could be expected if the morality they were trying to justify was rooted in a vanishing culture.

In the twentieth century, we are in an even worse position than Hume. We cannot, as he did, matter-of-factly take the prevailing morality as the one to be justified. We have inherited bits and pieces of conflicting moralities: different tables of virtues, different interpretations of single virtues, mixed in with the talk of rights and utility. The result is moral debate that is apparently interminable. Each side can give logically valid arguments for its position, but the rival premises are such that there is no rational way of weighing the claims of one against the other. One example is the debate over justice, in which Rawls and Nozick are the philosophical representatives of the opposing sides.

Rawls represents those who are impressed with the arbitrariness of inequality in the distribution of income, wealth, and opportunity in our society. His second principle of justice requires that these goods be distributed so that they are to the greatest benefit of the least advantaged and attached to positions and offices open to all under conditions of fair equality of opportunity. His first principle of justice — that each is to have an equal right to the most extensive total system of equal basic liberties compatible with a similar system of liberty for all — has priority over the second; we cannot sacrifice satisfaction of the first for the sake of satisfying the second. Nozick represents those who want to defend what they have acquired. For him, a distribution is just if everyone is entitled to what he or she has acquired legitimately, through honest toil or transfer from others, without force or fraud.

MacIntyre points out that Rawls makes primary what is effectively a principle of equality with respect to needs while Nozick makes primary a principle of equality with respect to entitlement. Their positions are incommensurable with each another, "For how can a claim that gives priority to equality of needs be rationally weighed against one which gives priority to entitlements?" And yet they have much in common. The notion of desert plays no important role in their accounts of justice. Why? In both accounts, society is composed of individuals with their own interests who come together and formulate common rules of life. The identification of individual interests is prior to the construction of any moral bonds among them. The notion of desert belongs to "the context of a community whose primary bond is a shared understanding both of the good for man and of the good of that community and where individuals identify their primary interests with reference to these goods."[9] What an individual deserves is measured by his or her contribution to these goods.

Let us now turn to the implications for the issue of absolutism versus relativism of this pessimistic view of the turn from virtue-centered to rights-centered moralities. MacIntyre does not identify any explicit implications. He certainly is not a relativist in the sense of believing that virtue-centered and rights-centered moralities may be equally *true*. What is more, he seems to subscribe to the Aristotelian view that there is a good for man as such. What is that good? Well, it is not possible to say, except that it partly consists of the quest for it. We have abandoned that quest, but MacIntyre's book constitutes an eloquent plea to construct "local forms of community within which civility and the intellectual and moral life can be sustained through the new dark ages which are already upon us."[10]

9.3   Are rights-centered moralities less objective than virtue-centered moralities?

The problem with MacIntyre's theory of moral catastrophe is that its arguments are based on dubious claims about the nature of rights-centered moralities, or they are insufficient to support the sharp distinction between virtue-centered moralities as at least potentially objective and rights-centered moralities as nonobjective.

One argument MacIntyre uses to persuade us that we have lost moral objectivity is to give examples of the conceptual incommensurability of the rival sides in contemporary moral debates. The supposed incommensurability between Rawls' emphasis on equality of need and Nozick's emphasis on equality of entitlement is an example. Let us look more closely at the grounds for calling the two positions incommensurable. MacIntyre defines two positions as incommensurable when the arguments for them each contain premises with "quite different" normative or evaluative concepts; the claims made upon us are of quite different kinds, and we possess no rational way of weighing them against each other.[11]

Now it is true that need and entitlement are different concepts, but false that they are entirely unrelated. Nozick does not take the emphasis on entitlement as a brute fact. Underlying the emphasis is his notion of side constraints that prevent us from using others as a means to our own ends, even if among these ends is the promotion of some social good.[12] His objection to Rawls' principles is that they require continuous interference (or at least periodic interference, if we are thinking of taxation) with people's lives and thus violation of moral side constraints in order to realize a certain favored distributional pattern. One way of putting this is that Nozick is concerned with *freedom*, with each individual's right to noninterference. Rawls is also concerned with *freedom*, as is obvious from consideration of his first principle. It is true that in *A Theory of Justice* he is concerned with defining an ideal end state in which a certain distribution of freedom and other goods is realized, but he certainly recognizes the existence of side constraints on any endeavor to achieve an ideal end state, and the value of freedom would have to enter into the characterization of the content of at least some of those constraints. The point is not that Rawls and Nozick agree in the end but that the motivations behind their respective emphases on need and entitlement overlap. Both recognize freedom from interference as a fundamental value, but Nozick elevates one *kind* of freedom from interference into an absolute.

Still, it is open to MacIntyre to say that Nozick's claim for entitlement as a moral absolute is so different from Rawls' claim for the priority of need that we possess no rational way of weighing the claims. Now, if a rational way of weighing the claims is a way that all rational and informed people will agree is valid, I believe there is no rational way, though I do not, as will be seen below, base this conclusion on any view of the two claims as somehow too "different" from one another. In any case, my point here is that once we remove the talk of premises being incommensurable because they contain different normative concepts, and simply look for the lack of rational ways of weighing conflicting claims, the sharp contrast between the virtue-centered and rights-centered traditions disappears. We can realize that we have no reason to suspect that there is always a rational way to settle conflicting claims made within a *virtue-centered* moral tradition. Indeed, MacIntyre correctly observes that a living virtue-centered tradition is marked by arguments about the goods internal to practices encompassed by the tradition. He has admitted that practices may make incompatible demands on participants that force them to make choices between internal goods. He has given us no reason to believe there is always a rational way to make these choices.

Perhaps MacIntyre anticipates this objection when he asserts:

One way in which the choice between rival goods in a tragic situation differs from the modern choice between incommensurable moral premises is that *both* of the alternative courses of action which confront the individual have to be recognised as leading to some authentic and substantial good. By choosing one I do nothing to diminish or derogate from the claims upon me of the other, and therefore, whatever I do, I shall have left undone what I ought to have done.[13]

He goes on to claim that the tragic protagonist is unlike the modern moral agent depicted by Sartre because the former is not choosing one moral principle over another, nor is he or she deciding upon some principle of priority between moral principles. And even though the tragic protagonist has no one *right* choice to make, he or she may behave well or ill in making a choice and carrying it out heroically, unheroically, generously, ungenerously, and so on. The existence of such dilemmas casts no doubt upon and provides no counter-examples to the thesis that "Assertions of the form 'To do this in this way would be better for X and/or his or her family, city or profession' are susceptible of objective truth or falsity."[14]

But this attempt to separate the dilemmas of the virtue-centered tradition from those of modern morality is not successful. The most famous of Sartre's moral agents is the boy in the occupied France of World War II, who must choose to join the Free French or stay with his mother and care for her. The choice is between resistance to tyranny and family loyalty. To be sure, we can view this as a choice between moral principles or some principle of priority between them, or as a choice between two ways of life, as Stuart Hampshire does,[15] but these views are compatible with saying that the choice is between two "authentic and substantial" goods.

Similarly, we can view as authentic and substantial goods the sort of freedom that Nozick is so concerned to protect, and the fulfillment of need that Rawls is so concerned to achieve. True, many of us, perhaps most, have strong inclinations to accept either Rawls' or Nozick's claims for the priority of one or the other good, and this may be so even though we are unable to refute the claim we do *not* accept. In this respect, the debate between them differs from the choice between MacIntyre's tragic protagonist and Sartre's moral agent. But MacIntyre does not show us that the choice between rival goods for an adherent to a virtue-centered morality cannot sometimes be like the choice facing Sartre's agent and at other times like the choice between Rawls and Nozick. Within a virtue-centered morality, two philosophers may propose incompatible ways of ordering rival goods, and other adherents may have strong inclinations for one or the other of these ways, without there being a commonly-agreed-upon way of deciding the issue between them. MacIntyre himself emphasizes a common ambiguity in the medieval vision of the moral life. On the one hand, life is idealized as an integrated order. On the other, that integrated order is imposed on the reality of the heterogeneity of medieval thought about the virtues, caused by the heterogeneity of its sources — the heroic, Aristotelian, and Biblical. Aquinas held that all other virtues come from the four cardinal ones of prudence, justice, temperance, and courage. This means that patience and humility are contained within the former virtues. But Aristotle mentioned humility as a vice and patience not at all.

Or take the conflict that Aristotle himself seems to have experienced in trying to answer the question of what balance to strike between the intellectual virtue of contemplation of truth on the one hand and the social life lived in accordance with the moral virtues on the other. In most of the *Eudemian* and *Nichomachean Ethics,* Aristotle makes both intellectual and social excellences parts of *eudaimonia.* Moral requirements are in no case to be sacrificed to or made dependent on intellectual goods. They must be provided for first. In cases where moral requirements are already fully met or do not apply, however, theoretical activity is to be promoted, if necessary, to the exclusion of all else. It is well-known, however, that in parts of the *Nichomachean Ethics,* and perhaps the *Eudemian* as well, a different conception of the relation between the intellectual and the social emerges, one in which *eudaimonia* is activity in accordance with the *highest* virtue. That virtue is of the best, the most noble and divine thing in us, and Aristotle goes on to identify the activity as contemplation.[16] What is more, he observes that

for deeds many things are needed, and more, the greater and nobler the deeds are. But the man who is contemplating the truth needs no such thing, at least with a view to the exercise of his activity; indeed they are, one may say, even hindrances, at all events to his contemplation; but in so far as he is a man and lives with a number of people, he chooses to do virtuous acts; he will therefore need such aids to living a human life.[17]

Here virtuous acts are viewed as concessions to one's existence as a mortal; one does one's best to keep them from distracting one in contemplation. It seems that Aristotle, at least some times, was willing to put aside the ideal of a moderate, even balance between the intellectual and the social, for the sake of a single-minded intellectualist perfectionism. That is why I said in section 9.1 that the definition of virtue-centered moralities would have to be qualified when we came to Aristotle. Even though he is the inheritor of a tradition that is centered on the common good of the shared life, he sometimes diverges from the tradition on this one point. His ethics threaten to turn into a perfectionism purged of any concept of the common good. In fact, some moral philosophers take this strain in Aristotle to be representative of virtue-centered moralities as a whole; they contrast rights-centered moralities with "perfectionism" and throw philosophers like Nietzsche into the same net with Aristotle. I believe this is mistaken because it ignores the nature of the moral tradition from which Aristotle's ethics emerged, and it causes us to miss broad similarities between Greek virtue-centered moralities and those virtue-centered moralities of other cultures that display no strong perfectionist strain.

Returning to the main issue, is there a rational way of

weighing one conception of *eudaimonia* against the other? If there is, MacIntyre has not shown that the same way is not applicable to Sartre's dilemma or to the debate between Rawls and Nozick. Nor has he shown that the two conceptions are commensurable in a manner that is absent in the pairs of family loyalty and resistance to tyranny or the priority of entitlement and the priority of need. I will argue below that there is no neutral, rational way of weighing the two conceptions.

Sometimes MacIntyre seems to rest the case for the "catastrophe" theory on the observation that modern morality consists of fragments of inherited moralities that have lost the contexts giving them significance. To be sure, we have inherited such fragments. And it is probable that they have lost the contexts giving them the significance they *once* had. But that does not mean that they have not acquired other contexts. In the Middle Ages, the virtues were supplied in a context that was different from the one they had in heroic society or in fifth-century Athens.

MacIntyre could reply that morality needs a certain *kind* of context to acquire the significance that confers objectivity. The required context is one that makes it possible to recognize a *telos* for man. His argument for this claim begins with the premise that a morality is objective (has genuine truth values) when it is possible to derive moral conclusions from factual premises, in a manner similar to the one in which it is possible to derive "This is a bad watch" from "This watch is grossly inaccurate and irregular in its time-keeping" and "This watch is too heavy to carry about comfortably." The argument is valid because 'watch' is a functional concept in that the set of criteria of being a watch and that of being a good one are factual and interdependent. In the Greek or medieval Aristotelian tradition, it is possible to derive moral conclusions from factual premises in a similar manner. Man is understood to have an essential nature or function; and it is possible to derive moral conclusions about the virtues and what is required of human beings from factual statements and a characterization of man's function. Since a pervasive theme of modern moral philosophy is the is/ought dichotomy, and since modern moral philosophy has rejected the Aristotelian tradition with its concept of a *telos* for man, it is plausible to conclude that the loss of moral objectivity is intimately connected with a rejection of the Aristotelian tradition, that the kind of context that makes recognition of a human *telos* possible is the only kind of context that confers objectivity on morality. What is this context? It is a form of social life in which one's identity is defined by a set of roles each of which has its own point and purpose: "member of a family, citizen, soldier, philosopher, servant of God."[18]

I believe MacIntyre would admit that this is not an airtight argument. After all, from the fact that rejection of moral objectivity has accompanied rejection of the Aristotelian tradition, it does not logically follow that moral objectivity requires the Aristotelian tradition. But MacIntyre's argument does shift the burden of proof on those who would like to resist the conclusion, for they need to identify a way in which a moral 'ought' could be derived from an 'is' without reference to a human *telos*. But such a way is identified in the recommended relativist analysis of moral "A ought to do X" statements. It can be as much a factual matter as anything else that in not doing X under conditions C, A would be breaking a rule of an adequate moral system applying to him or her. Now it could be objected that there is simply not enough agreement on what constitutes an adequate moral system, at least in modern, complex, heterogeneous societies. Such a challenge cannot be brushed aside, at least by me, since I have argued that a descriptive-causal theory does apply to the extension of 'adequate moral system'. This challenge, however, is not as effective as it first may seem, for a number of reasons.

For one thing, it is a double-edged sword for someone like MacIntyre to wield. We have already seen that the extent and nature of disagreement among adherents to a virtue-centered morality is not qualitatively different from the extent and nature of disagreement in a virtue-centered morality. Even if adherents to a virtue-centered morality believe there is a human *telos* that is the objective reality that makes their disagreements ones to which there is an objective answer, we have to question the correctness of that assumption. In the end, MacIntyre can only characterize the good for man as, in part, the quest for that good. Such a characterization will not convert any heretics who believe there is no single good for man.

More important, there is a way of admitting to the existence of genuinely irresolvable disagreements within either the virtue-centered or rights-centered traditions, while at the same time preserving the possibility of objectivity for moral statements in the sense that they have truth values and are derivable from factual statements. This way, furthermore, preserves the possibility that most of the moral issues that confront us in our daily lives *are* capable of rational resolution by reference to facts. This way is based on the recommended relativist analyses.

10 Moral Relativity Within Virtue-Centered and Rights-Centered Moralities

10.1 *A statement of the hypothesis that there are indeterminacies and variations in truth conditions within rights-centered moralities*

The basic strategy is to interpret irresolvable disagreements as resulting from indeterminacies or variations in the extension of 'adequate moral system'. Let us begin by discussing the nature and origin of indeterminacy in the extension. I claim that the indeterminacy is not such that the term fails to refer at all. Rather, it fails to pick out a set of moral systems that is well-defined with respect to certain important rules and standards. That is, there may be no fact of the matter determining whether a potentially important rule or standard is included within the extension or not. Such indeterminacy results in irresolvable disagreement in the sense that a moral issue may turn on the question of whether the rule or standard is included in the extension. Both sides would be equally right and equally wrong.

How could such indeterminacy come about? Within a moral tradition there may be agreement on standards for moral systems, such as the one requiring that a morality be consistent with the treatment of humanity never as a means only but always as an end in itself. In the application of such a standard, there may be agreement on a large number of moral rules, but with respect to certain areas of conduct it may be quite unclear which rules satisfy the standard. To treat each person as an end may be to distribute goods such as freedom,

income, and wealth on an egalitarian basis, in the ways that a
Rawls suggests, or it may be to accord the individual exclusive
control over the fruits of his or her honest toil, as a Nozick suggests. In American society, many people simply seem to have
no coherent, determinate set of thoughts on this issue. We
have recently witnessed increasing complaints about excessive
taxation and the money wasted by government bureaucrats,
but it is extremely unclear whether the complainants are willing to dismantle the vast liberal welfare state in favor of anything like Nozick's minimal state. There has certainly been no
significant movement for dismantling the greater part of the
vast infrastructure created by government that supports the
modern capitalist system—from subsidies to farmers and to
other individuals and businesses to the Federal Reserve System
—and that is more pervasively redistributive in its effects than
all the social welfare programs put together. In other words,
Americans show the very human trait of picking up a fragment
of ideology when it suits their interests but letting it fade into
the background when it does not.

Given the relativist analyses of moral "A ought to do X" and
"X is a good Y" statements, and the accompanying descriptive-
causal theory of the extension of 'adequate moral system', the
most plausible translation of the truth conditions of these statements as made by the vast majority of American speakers will
allow for indeterminacy in the extension with respect to rules
of distributive justice. This conclusion could be avoided only if
the vast majority of speakers who have the confused and vague
set of beliefs regarding distributive justice also had an overriding intention when using a term such as 'adequate moral system' to refer to what others refer to when using the term, and
only if these others have a definite and coherent set of beliefs
on distributive justice. In other words, they may intend to refer
to what certain people in the past referred to, or they may
intend to refer to what others in the present refer to (moral
authorities). A descriptive theory allows for such possibilities
(see section 5.3), but I see no evidence to indicate that Americans defer to anyone in these matters.

For most Americans, therefore, disagreements over distributive justice are likely to have no rational resolution, if such resolution depends on the discovery of which distributive rules are included in the adequate moral system applying to this society. Now it is possible that there is some standard for the adequacy of moral systems from which certain rules of distributive justice follow. But if (as I argue below in 10.4) there do not seem to be other constraints on the adequacy of moral systems that are restrictive enough to eliminate the systems of Rawls or Nozick, not constraints derived from practical reasoning, nor from the human potentials for various kinds of fulfillment or satisfaction, nor from some moral reality that is entirely independent of human will and purpose, then the interpretations of Rawls and Nozick may simply be different ways of performing the function of morality that have to do with reconciling interpersonal conflicts of interest.

At the same time, we must recognize that Rawls and Nozick articulate the beliefs of *some* people who do have definite and coherent thoughts on justice. If there is no standard for the adequacy of moral systems that will allow adjudication between the theories of Rawls and Nozick, then we will have to assign different extensions for 'adequate moral system' to those who adhere to one or the other theory. Hence there is variation in the truth conditions of moral "A ought to do X" and "X is a good Y" statements.[1] It is open to the absolutist to claim that the disagreement between Rawls and Nozick is an irresolvable disagreement about the *same* extension of 'adequate moral system', but I will explain below (10.4) why this move is unsatisfactory.

To say that the extension of 'adequate moral system' is indeterminate or varies within a society with respect to matters of distributive justice is not to say, however, that it is indeterminate or varies with respect to other areas of conduct. A morality as a whole does not lose its objectivity simply because of that. Hence it is possible to account for the existence of genuinely irresolvable moral disagreement within a moral tradition without falling into a wholesale moral skepticism about that tradition. Absolutists may regard this result as half a loaf, but I am arguing that they are not entitled to any more than that.

10.2   *A statement of the hypothesis that there are indetermi-*
       nacies and variations in truth conditions within virtue-
       centered moralities

A similar phenomenon can be found within the virtue-
centered tradition. When a group of moral language users is
vague or indecisive about what sort of balance to strike between "authentic and substantial" goods, there may be indeterminacy in the extension of 'adequate moral system', with
respect to certain priority rankings among the virtues to be
required of moral agents. This is because the importance of a
good relative to others will affect the ranking of a virtue that is
more intimately related to the achievement of that good than
the other virtues. Thus Aristotle's ambivalence over the relative importance of contemplation of truth over the goods of the
social life results in ambivalence in the ranking of *sophia* relative to the moral virtues. Unless we can plausibly ascribe some
belief in a standard of adequacy for moral systems to the relevant group that will help us to select one priority ranking over
another, it looks like we will have to admit to indeterminacy in
the extension of 'adequate moral system' for those speakers
who do not have a coherent or determinate set of beliefs on the
subject and to variation in the extension among those speakers
who do have such sets but different ones.

A way to avoid this conclusion is suggested by Stuart Hampshire. He distinguishes between the abstract ideal of the good
for man, which takes no account of the contingent circumstances of individuals, groups and societies, and the way of life
chosen by an individual under such contingent circumstances.
Within the abstract ideal, all the virtues are compatible, "with
some more central than the others." The virtues form a coherent set of simultaneously realizable possibilities "if one at the
same time imagines a society ideally adapted to protect and
promote man's development and a population ideally adapted
to the social roles imagined." The incompatibilities arise, says
Hampshire, "as soon as the contingencies of actual societies
enter into the situation and the contingencies also of individual's temperaments and abilities."[2] These contingencies force
an individual to choose between two virtues, in the light of his

or her social position, skills, gifts, and education. A man who chooses the life of a solitary artist may argue that in the modern era art has taken over the functions of religion for him, that the virtues of family and of citizenship are beyond his reach, that his talents suit him for the artistic life and not for the "practical care of humanity." Put in terms of the recommended relativist analysis, we may summarize Hampshire's argument by saying that the extension of 'adequate moral system' is well-defined but ranges over a number of moral systems with varying emphases on different virtues depending on the individual circumstances of the agent in question (these circumstances could be stated under the "conditions C" clause of "X is a good Y" statements, for instance) and the conditions of the agent's society.

Hampshire gives us an appealing picture, but it will not account for the ambivalence that Aristotle felt. When he was espousing the intellectualist conception of flourishing, he did not appeal to his historical situation nor to his individual temperament. Rather, his argument was that one of the intellectual virtues should be the dominant element in the *ideal* of the good for man. He would allow that some were not capable of fulfilling that ideal, given their innate potential, but he hardly allows for the kind of flexibility in application of the ideal that Hampshire has in mind. Note also that his argument for the superiority of contemplation over all other goods pointed to qualities of that activity that were not supposed to be relative to historical situation or to temperament, e.g., that it is the most continuous of activities, that it is self-sufficient (to be morally virtuous, one needs others and a contingent combination of conditions), that it has a quality of leisureliness.

It is true that Aristotle uses some eminently disputable arguments for the superiority of contemplation: that *theoria* is best because its objects are best, that reason is the part of man that is divine. As Kathleen Wilkes points out, it is fallacious to conclude that a type of knowledge is best because its objects are best. And the second argument depends on a theological premise.[3] The other arguments of Aristotle remain, however, and in any case, it seems a mistake to identify his belief in *theoria* as the highest good as depending on the particular argu-

ments he gave. There is a strong inclination toward intellec-
tualism in Greek philosophy and culture that does not seem
explainable on the basis of such arguments (more on this in the
next section).

The main point is that even an abstract ideal of the good for
man is likely to have some priority rankings, and Aristotle's
ambivalence about the proper ones is indicative of the sort of
fundamental incoherence or conflict between well-defined sets
of beliefs that can result in indeterminacy in the extension of
'adequate moral system'. When a person opts for a conception
of the good for man that serves some entirely dominant interest, whether it be aesthetic, intellectual, or religious, he or she
may reason in the manner Hampshire describes; but that person may also identify that conception with the abstract, time-
less ideal of the good for man.

But surely, it may be replied, we should call such single-
mindedness unreasonable, for how can one reasonably recommend such an unbalanced conception of the virtues and of the
goods of human life to *all* people, regardless of their potentials
and temperaments? The problem is to cash in this talk of rea-
sonableness so that we are not merely affirming our belief in a
more balanced and flexible conception of *eudaimonia*. The
single-minded perfectionist would certainly admit that his or
her conception does neglect the development of interests other
than the dominating one, but that is because, he or she could
say, the other interests are not as worthy of development. And
if certain people are less capable of developing the most worthy
interest, they are simply less capable of living worthy lives,
which is certainly not logically absurd nor evidently irrational.
In fact, this is what Aristotle thought of barbarians.

Still, what about the ideal in which all important virtues are
simultaneously realized? Isn't it possible that there is some society that would be ideally adapted to provide the opportunities
for a human existence that allowed the full development of *all*
the important human virtues, so that an individual need not
make the choice of "amputating" his or her existence for the
sake of developing one virtue to the fullest? Richard Miller
makes a similar point in discussing utilitarian theories of justice and nonutilitarian theories such as those of Rawls and

Nozick; he claims that none of these make a plausible case for certain moral considerations as absolutes—not Nozick's right to acquire and transfer property, not Rawls' right to be treated in accordance with the two principles of justice, not the utilitarian goal of maximizing utility. He concludes that the best strategy is to search for ways to reconcile these diverse moral considerations, so that each consideration is honored without the cost of ignoring the others. Miller does not conclude that there *is* such a way and that it will solve all important questions of justice. He only claims that it is best to look for such a way.[4]

It would certainly be reasonable to look for ways of reconciling diverse moral considerations of justice or of reconciling the different virtues. The problem is that the more we refrain from ranking diverse moral considerations or virtues and the more weight we place on the ideal of harmonizing these considerations or virtues, the less we have to say about important moral issues that confront us *now*. At this moment and for the forseeable future, we are far from having the foggiest notion of how to harmonize the considerations that motivate Rawls and Nozick. And we are faced with the problem of preserving or extending the liberal welfare state, which seems close to Rawls' ideal, or of dismantling it and heading in the direction of Nozick's minimal state. If we add considerations motivating socialist theories of justice, the idea of harmonization recedes further into the mist. Similarly, we have very little idea as to how we could harmonize Aristotle's desire to "strain every nerve to live in accordance with the *best* thing in us" with the virtues of the life lived with others. In fact, the demands of excellence in a given field of intellectual endeavor have grown stronger in terms of the time and energy we have to devote to meeting them. An ideal of morality, if it is to retain its action-guiding function, must have something to say about the conflicts we are in fact burdened with, and so there seems to be no getting away from the need to rank various moral considerations and virtues, and no getting away from the kind of indeterminacy in the extension of 'adequate moral system' that sometimes results from ambivalence or disagreement about these rankings.

The subject that originally motivated this discussion of the

extension of 'adequate moral system' was MacIntyre's argument that rights-centered moralities lack objectivity. He
pointed out the existence of irresolvable disagreements within
that morality. I responded by showing how the recommended
relativist analyses of moral "A ought to do X" and "X is a good
Y" statements could allow for the irresolvability of some disagreements and yet preserve the possibility of genuine truth
values for most of these statements and of sound arguments
from factual premises to these statements. In the process of
showing this, I made a case for the existence of some indeterminacy and variation in the extension of 'adequate moral system' as used within virtue-centered and rights-centered moralities, and thus for the existence of some indeterminacy and
variation in the truth conditions of moral statements. Note,
however, that the case was made on the assumption that something like the recommended relativist analyses were correct,
along with the descriptive-causal theory of the extension of
'adequate moral system'. The time has come to compare relativist and absolutist methods of explaining apparently irresolvable moral disagreement.

10.3   *An explanation of the Rawls-Nozick disagreement that
        is consistent with the relativist hypothesis*

As we saw in the eighth chapter, one way in which absolutists could attempt to explain the existence of apparently irresolvable disagreement is to say that at least one side in the disagreement has made an error in reasoning or observation or is
ignorant of crucial facts. Relativists may admit that there *are*
errors or ignorance to be found in many of these disagreements, but would claim that the errors or ignorance are not
the fundamental cause of at least some of them. Instead, they
would claim that some of the disagreements would occur
simply because the two sides have opposing interests and
desires that lead them to adopt opposing moral positions. Let
us compare the methods of explanation in the case of the disagreement between Rawls and Nozick. I shall limit discussion
to this disagreement because the absolutist methods for
explaining apparently irresolvable disagreement within virtue-

centered moralities are basically the same and so is my argument that the relativist method is better.

The way in which Rawls and Nozick argue for their principles can be criticized, and indeed, I believe that some of the criticism is well-founded. But even if we grant the force of these criticisms, the rules of Rawls and Nozick on distributive justice remain viable as candidates for inclusion in the extension of 'adequate moral system'.

Take Rawls' argument that his two principles would be chosen in a hypothetical contract situation called the original position. Since the original position is constructed to yield a fair choice, says Rawls, any principles that would be chosen in that situation have a claim to be valid principles of justice. For instance, one of the features of the original position is that the parties must choose under a veil of ignorance that renders them ignorant of their talents and places in society, so that they cannot hold out for principles giving them an advantage over others. Rawls argues that each party, who does not necessarily take an interest in the welfare of other parties, would choose principles of justice in accordance with a conservative strategy called "maximin"—assuming that the worst will happen and choosing principles that will minimize the worst outcome. Each will assume, therefore, that he or she will be at the bottom end of inequalities and will choose Rawls' two principles as making for the best "worst" outcome for the least advantaged.

I am not at all convinced that "maximin" is necessarily the only rational strategy to take in the original position. There are people who enjoy taking risks or at least don't mind taking them if the possible rewards are large enough and even if the possible result of losing is also quite large. Such people could choose according to maximax—assuming the best will happen and maximizing the best outcome. To head off this objection, Rawls stipulates that the parties have no knowledge of special attitudes toward risk they may have. The trouble with this move is that it makes one wonder how one could choose at all if one has *no* knowledge of one's attitude toward risk. Perhaps one could assume in the original position a "nonspecial" attitude, but Rawls needs to characterize such an attitude and explain why it is entitled to such a privileged place in the heads of the parties of the original position. He characterizes the prohibited special attitudes as "peculiar individual preferences," but what does this mean except "unusual" in our culture and in our time?[5]

To convince us that maximin is the only rational strategy, Rawls points out the seriousness of the worst outcomes under other principles of justice, e.g., slavery, and the "satisfactory minimum" his two principles provides. He also points out that one's descendants will be affected by one's choice and that one should be more reluctant to take great risks for them, as well as for oneself. These are all substantial considerations, but it is hard to know what to do with them unless one has some sort of attitude toward risk, and Rawls obviously believes that it is wise to have a fairly conservative attitude. We are back to the question of why this attitude. After all, if one turns out to be among those who are best endowed to take advantage of inegalitarian principles of justice, one may have the gratitude of one's descendants if one chooses them. And if one turns out to be a gambler by nature when the veil is lifted, one surely will be dissatisfied with the "satisfactory minimum" provided by Rawls' two principles and will have been willing to live with the losses of a big gamble.

Even if Rawls' argument from the original position were persuasive, it is open to someone like Nozick to object that we have no business adopting principles that would be chosen in such a situation, because such a procedure ignores the (alleged) fact that past circumstances or actions of people can create differential entitlements to things. In Nozick's view, we cannot restrict the liberty to acquire and transfer holdings through legitimate means. This is an absolute constraint on action in his theory, and it is precisely what the original position eliminates.

This sort of criticism, however, does not eliminate Rawls' two principles as candidates in the extension of 'adequate moral system'. It is doubtful that all who find his principles appealing would do so simply *because* of a belief that they would be chosen in the original position. Egalitarian theories of distributive justice that emphasize the priority of need have held an appeal to some throughout the history of rights-centered morality, even though the justification given for them has varied in nature, from the Christian doctrine that all are the children of God to the requirements of rationality on practical reasoning. It is quite probable that this appeal is founded on a strong desire on the part of at least some people to live in a society where there is mutual support and cooperation between individuals. For them, a Nozickian society has unacceptable costs in terms of the isolation of individuals, insecurity, and the class warfare between those who have acquired large holdings through luck or skill or inheritance and those who have little.

The positive arguments that Nozick gives for the entitlement theory rest ultimately on intuitions that one either has or doesn't. For instance, in giving an example of how nonentitlement principles of distributive justice require an unacceptable and continuous interference with liberty, Nozick asks us to suppose that we have now achieved a desired distribution D_1 and that a great basketball player is in demand by many teams. He signs a contract with one team that gives him a quarter—let us say two dollars, allowing for inflation since the time Nozick wrote his book—from the price of each ticket of admission. Fans flock to see the player. He makes (allowing again for inflation) a million a year. Nozick asks us whether there is anything wrong with this new distribution D_2 in which the player has a much larger sum than the average income. Each of the fans freely chose to give two dollars to the player. To maintain the desired distribution D_1, one must wrongly interfere with the transfer of resources (forbid the player and owner to make the kind of deal they made) or wrongly interfere to take from some the resources that others chose to transfer to them (tax the player at a much higher rate than others).[6]

One problem with such an argument is that it gives us *one* person who is reaping the rewards of his talent and hard work. Many of us would feel uncomfortable in denying him all the dollar bills the fans freely chose to give to him to see him play. And from this feeling of discomfort, we may be tempted to conclude that we are *never* justified in interfering with such voluntary transferences of resources. Let us make the example more like real life. Assume that there is not just one person who can take advantage of his or her talents to offer what people would pay money to buy but a significant segment of

the population. Some of them pool their resources and are able
to dominate the market for essential goods. They are able to
set wages of people who make these goods at an extremely low
level, and over an extended period of time we have a situation
in which a small segment of the population has an enormously
disproportionate portion of the wealth and income, while
others are living in poverty and find it extremely difficult to
escape that situation because it limits the development of their
potentials. Having pictured such a state of affairs, it is certainly no longer so clear that the sort of interference Nozick so
quickly dismisses as wrong is in fact wrong. Now I would not
claim that everyone would see such interference as permissible,
but Nozick cannot assume that we all share with him the moral
intuitions that form the base of his theory.

As in the case of Rawls, the appeal of the entitlement theory
is to a great extent independent of the success or failure of
arguments for it. It certainly is no mystery why it should appeal
to those who feel they have worked hard for their homes, and
their childrens' educations, and now see it all threatened by
taxes and inflation, both connected in political rhetoric with
government spending, especially on social welfare programs.
Of course, these people could consider alternatives to the present system, which place less of a burden on middle-income
people and more on the small percentage controlling most of
the wealth, but the competitive attitudes that modern capital-
ism depends on and encourages keep most people from seriously considering such a major restructuring of distributive
mechanisms. More positively, Americans have valued the character traits of self-reliance and *self*-fulfillment. Often, these
motivations for adherence to Nozick's theory exist along side
the desire for mutual support and cooperation. No wonder
many people have no coherent, determinate set of thoughts on
the subject of distributive justice.

10.4   *Will the absolutist explanations of the Rawls-Nozick disagreement work?*

Now, if errors in reasoning could be attributed to such
major participants in the disagreement over distributive justice

without destroying the appeal of their basic views, we may wonder how absolutists are going to explain the existence of the disagreement by referring to some error or ignorance of crucial facts on the part of at least one side. Those in the Kantian tradition could claim that at least one side is making an error with respect to which rules of distributive justice satisfy standards of rationality on practical reasoning, or that at least one side is ignorant of crucial facts that would reveal what the appropriate rules are. But this claim must be made good by solving the problem of identifying the relevant standards of rationality, and this has not been done nor do the prospects look good for the achievement of this task in the future (as I argued in chapter seven).

Absolutists in the Aristotelian tradition who hold a theory such as Foot's could claim that the disagreement is a result of error or ignorance on the matter of which rules of distributive justice are to be followed if the just person is to benefit others. But the lack of determinacy in Foot's conception of the virtues (which I discussed in chapter seven) weakens the support for this claim. It is not just a matter of making an error or being ignorant of *how* to benefit others; it is a lack of determinacy in the very conception of what it is for the just person to benefit others. Do we give emphasis to the priority of meeting their needs, or are we required to refrain from interfering with their liberty to acquire and transfer property? What is the proper interpretation of benefiting others in this context? To such a question, Foot's theory gives no hint of an answer and so fails to convince us that there is any fact of the matter about which we can be in error or ignorant. Or take McDowell's Aristotelianism, which places emphasis on the virtuous person's capacity to perceive what is required in a situation, and on our inability to codify in exceptionless rules the way the virtuous person acts. Absolutists who adhered to this theory might say that it is extremely hard to see moral reality clearly, especially when our own interests are so vitally affected by questions of distributive justice. But, as I argued in chapter seven, they fail to persuade that an irreducible moral reality exists.

Absolutists who adopted the theory of Platts would say much the same thing as McDowellian absolutists. They would say that we perceive the moral property of justness: we perceive that in certain situations an action would be the just thing to do, and Rawls' and Nozick's theories are attempts to generalize to rules of justice from the individual perceptions we have of that property in these situations. Platts recognizes the need to explain how a person acquires a false moral belief if our theory of moral language results in the imputation of such a belief to that person, but he waves his hand in the direction of an explanation—to the difficulty of perceiving moral reality clearly given human fallibility and self-interest. This story suffers from a lack of any detail about how we perceive this property, clearly or unclearly (as I suggested in chapter seven). The story need not be scientific, but it needs to be a story with some real content. Without such a story, we have no real explanation of how some people come to have erroneous or incomplete beliefs about justice, for we cannot begin to know in any real detail how some people have more distorted or more incomplete perceptions than others unless we know what relations underlie those perceptions.

The other absolutist method of explaining an apparently irresolvable disagreement is to say that the disagreement is presently beyond human powers to resolve. But in order to make this more than a cover for there being no fact-of-the-matter for the disagreement to be about, absolutists must tell us more about why the truth is beyond our reach in this particular case and not others. What is it about this disagreement that makes it impossible to resolve at this time? To tell us more, absolutists would need to have more of an idea of the general relations between moral facts, whatever their constitution may be, and our beliefs about it. In science and in our everyday knowledge of the world, we certainly may have disagreements that seem irresolvable at the moment, but we are able to understand why these disagreements occur when they do. If we have a raging dispute between scientists A and B over the evolutionary course that led to homo sapiens, we have an idea of how A and B could disagree and why they are not able to settle the dispute. We can construct scenarios in which what A says is true and how the present evidence could have been a result of that state of affairs so long ago. We can do the same for what

B says. It is possible to fill in the scenarios with quite a bit of detail. Can we do the same for Rawls and Nozick? The same problems that hindered the previous absolutist method of explaining the disagreement also hinder this one. Absolutists cannot begin to tell the required stories until they have identified the relevant standards of rationality, or have made more determinate their conceptions of benefit, or have characterized the nature of the relations between irreducible moral reality and those who perceive it and thus make more plausible the existence of such a reality.

The general failing of the absolutist methods is not meeting the principle of the best explanation. We are left with gaping holes in our theory of the speakers of moral language. By contrast, the recommended relativist analyses afford a more complete explanation. By rooting morality in rules and standards intended to fulfill the human needs for the resolution of internal and interpersonal conflict, by allowing for indeterminacies and variations in the extension of 'adequate moral system' with respect to certain rules and standards, and by explaining the existence of these indeterminacies and variations by reference to conflicting human needs and interests (such as those which support the theories of Rawls and Nozick), they help us explain apparently irresolvable disagreements while preserving much moral objectivity and helping us to explain why some may think there is more of such objectivity than there really is.

10.5 Cross-cultural differences between virtue-centered moralities

The dominant morality of ancient Chinese culture is virtue-centered. I shall identify some striking similarities between this morality and those of ancient Greek culture and then discuss apparent variations in belief about the good for man between the moralities of the two cultures. My claim is that the best explanation of these apparent variations includes the admission of a cross-cultural variation in truth conditions.

One of the main features of the Greek moralities is that their moral rules and standards were developed for the purpose of defining or making explicit social roles in the family, kinship groups, and tribes or villages, with well-defined sets of privileges and duties attaching to these roles. In the dominant morality of ancient China—Confucianism—this was also the case. The ideal relationships defined for the family were taken as the model for all other social relationships. For instance, the ruler was to act as father to all the people; he was charged with protecting and promoting their welfare.

Confucianism also contains the themes that there is a common good shared by all members of the community, that the common good is the shared life as defined by the total system of roles and statuses, and that the virtues are qualities that sustain members in their roles, enabling them to sustain the common good. The best way to illustrate this is to explain the central concept of *li* in this tradition. The root meaning of this word is translatable as "holy ritual." In its broader meanings, it covers rules of propriety and the authentic traditions and conventions of Chinese society. *Li* forms the structure of the shared life of the community.[7] To conform effectively to *li*, therefore, is to contribute to the shared life, and this in turn is to realize one's distinctively human characteristics. This theme is the key to understanding how two other themes can coexist in the *Lun-yü* (*Analects*) of Confucius: the importance of ancestor worship as defined by *li* and the consistent refusal by Confucius to affirm or deny the existence of spirits, ancestral or otherwise.[8] What Confucius values in ancestor worship is not any possible favors granted to the living by their ancestral spirits but the unifying effect it has on the living who are able to see themselves as part of a tradition reaching back through the past and forward into the future.[9]

Not surprisingly, filial piety is a primary virtue. This virtue, and that of brotherly respect, are said to be the root of *jen,* the general virtue that embraces all others. The Chinese character for *jen* consists of both the word for man and the word for two—signifying a group—meaning man in the group or society. *Jen* is that social nature that enables people to live together in some reasonable approximation of harmony. *Jen* also refers to a particular virtue that is variously translated as love or benevolence. The practice of filial piety and brotherly respect, therefore, encourages the development of one's social nature, which leads to the further development of other particular virtues, including love or benevolence, as practiced toward all. *Li* provides the form through which one expresses one's social nature.

Despite these similarities between ancient Greek and Chinese moralities, there is an important difference in the conceptions of the good for man that are at the heart of the moralities. We have noted the struggle that Aristotle had over the place of contemplation in the total good for man. The fact that Aristotle seriously considered a life devoted to contemplation indicates the strong intellectualist leanings of Greek culture. Of course, we must not take Aristotle's work as representative of the popular culture, but there are elements in that culture that formed a home for that work. In his study of Greek popular morality based on comedy and forensic oratory, Dover remarks on the striking number of passages "which refer to intellectual competence [as an object of praise] where we would have expected a reference to good will."[10] There was a tendency to oppose the rational element in human nature to the emotions, and when the Greeks spoke of a person as being "forced," "conquered," "worsted," "overcome" or enslaved by desire or emotion, they identified the self with reason.[11]

When we turn to Confucianism, we find no comparable intellectualist leanings. Wisdom is given a central place, but it is clearly *practical* wisdom that is regarded as a virtue. In that tradition, *jen* and wisdom are "like two wings, one supporting the other."[12] There is no tradition of recognizing knowledge as a good for its own sake. Reason does play an essential role in the good for man; it makes a distinctive *human* good; but it does this by making human relationships distinctively *human* —relationships of an "essentially symbolic kind, defined by tradition and convention and rooted in respect and obligation."[13] Correspondingly, there is little tendency in Chinese culture to contrast or oppose reason and feeling. When Mencius identifies the four features of man's innately good nature, he calls them four "feelings (*ch'ing*): commiseration (the beginning of *jen*), shame and dislike (the beginning of righteousness), respect and reverence (the beginning of *li*), and right and wrong (the beginning of wisdom)."[14]

10.6   *Do the cross-cultural differences correspond to differ-
       ences in truth conditions?*

We have here a contrast between two virtue-centered traditions: one in which the good of *theoria* and the corresponding
virtue of *sophia* play important roles as constituents of the
good for man (if not the dominant constituent, as in Aristotle),
and one in which those goods do not play important roles at
all. What implications does this apparent difference in moral
belief have for the question of whether the truth conditions for
moral statements are the same? Is this a case of environmental
relativity: What conditions were present in Greek society and
absent in Chinese society that could make appropriate a high
value for *theoria*? As far as we know, there aren't any. In both
societies there was a class with the leisure and the capacity to
engage in contemplation. This does not mean that there are no
causal explanations of the difference. We are looking, however, for a moral justification of the difference. Is this a case of
a disagreement for which there is an objective solution but that
is beyond human powers to resolve? We have already pointed
out that to make good on this claim absolutists would have to
explain why this disagreement is resolvable and others are not.
It would seem, then, that error or ignorance of some crucial
fact would have to be the absolutist explanation of the difference in moral belief.

But under the principle of the best explanation, we are
required to explain how the error was made or how the ignorance was caused. Suppose that the Confucians were wrong.
How did they miss the value of *theoria*? Here the usual explanations of moral misperception through self-interest or self-
deception do not even have *prima facie* application. Did the
Confucians *never* experience it? That seems most unlikely. Perhaps it will be maintained that they implicitly recognized the
value of *theoria* but believed that it would be inappropriate to
indulge themselves while most Chinese were trying to achieve a
comfortable level of material well-being. But sainthood and
self-denial belong to another culture. Confucians managed to
enjoy fine art and beautiful ceramics, although these had little

direct connection with improving the material well-being of others.

What about the Greeks? Remember that a relatively weak claim about the importance of *theoria* is at issue here: the claim that *theoria* is an *important* constituent of the good for man, not Aristotle's occasional claim that it is the dominant constituent of the good for man, and not even his claim that it is the *highest* good (if not the dominant one). Perhaps some would be willing to claim that even the weak claim is a mistake; but, as was pointed out above, some of the reasons that Aristotle gives for claiming *theoria* to be the highest good are at least comprehensible as grounds for assessing highly the worth of an activity: its continuity, that it is the purest and most enduring of pleasures, that it is the most self-sufficient. These grounds seem to embody perfectly eligible criteria for evaluating the worth of activities. We should be able to imagine perfectly rational and relevantly informed people who do not have such criteria, but it is difficult to accuse those who have them of error.

Perhaps it can be said that Aristotle took what were proper criteria for *him,* given his preferences and interests, and mistook them as appropriate criteria for all people, some of whom did not share the relevant preferences and interests. But it is difficult to attribute to Aristotle the obvious error of assuming that all people's preferences and interests are such that *theoria* would give them the greatest satisfaction. He sometimes expresses a low regard for the actual preferences and interests of most people. He does not regard an activity as good because it satisfies actual preferences and interests. Rather, he regards it as good for people if he believes their preferences and interests *ought* to be cultivated toward an appreciation of *theoria.* Why? Because once they are able to appreciate it, they will see that it is the purest and most enduring, the most self sufficient, and so on. Aristotle, therefore, cannot be convicted of misreading people's actual preferences and interests.

I conclude that there is a genuine variation in the truth conditions of value statements between ancient Greek and Chinese morality—in the standards for the goodness of activities and thus for what counts as a virtue. Each culture sets out an ideal of the best person and the best activities. This is a way of resolving the internal conflicts in requirements between needs, desires, and goals that is one of the functions of morality. There seem to be, however, at least two ways of resolving those conflicts that seem equally valid. When absolutists assert that there is only one valid ideal of the good for man, they believe that validity is grounded in determinate features of human nature, such as reason or distinctive human potentials for satisfying activities. If I am right, however, there is no feature or set of features that eliminates all but one ideal as valid. And this should not be so surprising in the light of two plausible hypotheses that could form part of the best explanation of moral language users.

First, a social and cultural environment can influence the degree to which a person experiences an activity as rewarding. Here I am talking about the degree to which a person finds rewarding the achievement of "internal goods" of the activity, goods that are not contingently attached to the activity but that necessarily accompany its successful performance. On a small scale, we can experience this whenever we notice that our own valuing of an activity may be influenced by the degree to which other people value that activity. Furthermore, the rewards internal to some complex and demanding activities may only be experienced to the extent that a person is willing to apply him- or herself to the project of becoming good at them. A person's social and cultural environment may encourage him or her in some of these projects but not others. It may sustain a person in the risks and pain that accompany these projects, or it may tell a person that he or she must go it alone. Second, insofar as there is such a thing as a fixed human nature, remaining invariant from social environment to social environment, it is not sufficiently determinate to justify the claim that there is a determinate good for man, a complex of activities arranged in an ideal balance, which any rational and informed person would find the most rewarding.

In light of these two hypotheses, we can say that a moral ideal of the good for man expresses the collective judgment of a group or society on which of an individual's many potentials for different activities are to be encouraged and which discouraged. This judgment fulfills the need to have a direction and an identity for oneself. It also may make it more probable that people will attempt to develop themselves in ways that are compatible with the particular structure of social cooperation of the group or society in question. But there is no neutral standpoint from which to eliminate all but one ideal as the most rewarding life for human beings.

11 Comparing the Truth of Virtue-Centered and Rights-Centered Moralities

11.1 *Identifying the differences*

I have noted the general differences between the two types of morality. It is time to establish differences between the truth conditions of moral statements based on virtue-centered moralities and truth conditions of moral statements based on rights-centered moralities. To begin the case, we must be more specific about the differences between virtue-centered and rights-centered moralities.

The first point I want to make has been made by others in connection with Greek moralities—that nothing in these moralities corresponds to the modern moral 'ought' as it evolved since the Middle Ages. In Greek, remarks MacIntyre, there is originally no clear distinction between 'ought' and 'owe' (*dein*).[1] The word was used to identify the duties of social roles, originally those in the household and kinship groups, and then the duties of a citizen in the city-state. The word was used, therefore, to designate duties tied to the practices of a particular social and political structure. The same was true of the Chinese 'ought' (*ying*). The modern moral 'ought' of Western Europe and America, on the contrary, is a word often used to designate duties that transcend any particular social and political structure. Kant's categorical imperative epitomizes what the word has become. In fact, Kant's moral 'ought' designates duties for all *rational* beings, not just us human beings in this corner of the universe.

It has been noted also that 'ought' does not play such an

important role in virtue-centered moralities as compared to the value terms—'good' and more specific evaluative expressions designating virtues—while the modern 'ought' has become the primary word for communicating the requirements of morality. This is something we might expect if one of the major differences between virtue-centered and rights-centered moralities is the presence in the former and absence in the latter of a common good shared by all members of the community. Where the common good is present, the focus of moral concern will be the characterization of that common good and the identification of those qualities in people that would be necessary for sustaining the common good. In rights-centered moralities, we would expect those moral terms directly tied with action to be the most frequently used.

But do such differences really result in variations in truth conditions for moral "A ought to do X" statements? Let us focus on what has been thought to be an important conflict between the two kinds of moralities. Take the well-known distinction between liberty of the ancients and liberty of the moderns. In Benjamin Constant's view, the ancients were not concerned with defending the modern liberties of religion, opinion, expression, and property. Rather, they were concerned with the political liberties to participate in ruling as well as being ruled. Isaiah Berlin observes that there was scarcely any discussion of individual liberty "as a conscious political ideal" in the ancient world—the Greeks, the Jewish, and the Chinese. He identifies the liberty of the ancients as "positive" liberty in the sense of self-direction and self-mastery —hence the emphasis on political liberties to participate in ruling. He identifies the liberty of the moderns as "negative"— liberty to do as one wishes, unobstructed by the deliberate interference of others. Berlin notes that the two concepts are at no great logical difference from each other but claims that they have developed in logically different directions until they finally came into direct conflict.

The emphasis on positive liberty is supposed to be accompanied by the doctrine that some part of the self—the rational, deliberative element, most often—is the "true" self that ought to have mastery over the lower parts of the self—the appetites, uncontrolled desires or emotions, for instance. This doctrine allows suppression of negative liberty on the grounds that the lower self must be restrained for the true self to gain mastery. The assumption is made that the rational ends of all true selves must coincide and that it is right to suppress the conflicting ends of the lower selves. Emphasis on positive liberty also may become associated with the demand for status or recognition or independence for one's class, nation, or race. Berlin identifies this demand as underlying the protest of colonized peoples against outside administrators, no matter how benevolent or enlightened. The demand is more closely connected with such values as solidarity, fraternity, and equality, but not with liberation of the individual self, with which both positive and negative liberty are concerned. Berlin concludes that a hybrid form of freedom is involved here — born of the intermingling of positive liberty and values such as fraternity and solidarity. It is self-direction for the *group* with which individuals identify. In the name of this hybrid freedom, some may be willing to sacrifice their individual negative freedoms.

In the tradition of "negative" liberty, as developed by Constant, Mill, and Tocqueville, a society is truly free only if there is recognition of the inviolability of a minimum extent of individual "negative" liberty. The demand is to curb authority, no matter who wields it, while those who believe in positive liberty want it placed in certain hands — the people, the philosopher kings, the proletariat, the rational self.

11.2   *Are there differences over the value of freedom?*

Will these distinctions between the liberties of the ancients and of the moderns and between positive and negative liberty help us locate a difference in truth conditions between rights-centered and virtue-centered moralities? It is true that civil liberties are not an important moral concern for virtue-centered moralities. In debating with his friends and followers on the matter of whether he ought to submit to the death penalty, Socrates shows no great concern for anything like a general right to freedom of expression. Neither does Plato. And Aristotle identifies the functions of a citizen as serving on juries and in the assembly. He does not define any area of conduct within which the citizen is free to act "as he wishes." Berlin seems to have put his finger on an important difference between the two moralities.

On the contrary, contrasting two kinds of liberties does not seem the appropriate way to identify the difference between Chinese Confucian and rights-centered moralities, for there is not even great moral concern for the political liberties. Confucius offered his teaching to those who held and those who aspired to political office, but he did not hold that all those who met certain qualifications were in any way *entitled* or *owed* the opportunity to participate. That opportunity was a privilege, even for those who could do the most good with it. In fact, Confucius said, "A person not in a particular government position does not discuss its policies."[2] The Chinese modeled ideal political relations after the hierarchical structure of the family. Rulers and ministers were to act as fathers would act for their families. Paternalism was the prevailing philosophy of government. The primary duties of rulers and ministers were to give the people security and peace and to ensure a sufficiently equal distribution of wealth so that there would be harmony and no poverty.[3] Now Mencius advocates that a ruler listen to the people. He even advocates a right of revolution for the people.[4] His philosophy of government for normal times, however, when a ruler is not so oppressive as to merit revolution, is that he should be the "parent of the people."[5] Perhaps, then, the way to describe a major and general difference between virtue-centered and rights-centered moralities is to say that there is an emphasis on civil liberties in the latter but nothing comparable in the former.

Berlin's distinction between negative and positive liberty is not as helpful as it could be because it is not a clear one. Since he admits that the two concepts of liberty were not originally at such a great distance from each other, the cogency of his distinction depends on his characterization of how the two concepts developed in divergent directions. But the characterization does not sort out the proponents of negative and positive liberty as neatly as a clear distinction would require. Berlin sometimes chastises individuals listed as proponents of negative

liberty for wandering into the other camp.[6] He has trouble
finding a clear basis for putting major philosophers into one
camp or another. He puts Kant in the camp of positive liberty,
despite the latter's "severe individualism" and condemnation
of paternalism.[7] But after noting that Kant says things that are
not so different from orthodox liberalism, Berlin says that the
real distinction between Kant and modern liberals is that the
latter

> want a situation in which as many individuals as possible can realize
> as many of their ends as possible, without assessment of the value of
> these ends as such, save in so far as they may frustrate the purposes of
> others. Kant, and the rationalists of his type, do not regard all ends
> as of equal value. For them the limits of liberty are determined by
> applying the rules of 'reason' . . . In the name of reason anything that
> is non-rational may be condemned, so that the various personal aims
> which their individual imagination and idiosyncrasies lead men to
> pursue — for example aesthetic and other non-rational kinds of self-
> fulfillment — may, at least in theory, be ruthlessly suppressed to make
> way for the demands of reason.[8]

The problem with this way of making the distinction is that
in modern Western societies we can count on the purposes of
men to collide in many different ways, and it would hardly be
liberal to prevent all such collisions through the limitation of
freedom for the area of personal freedom would shrink to the
size of a pea. What, for instance, about those who desire to
practice "abnormal" sexual preferences in private with consenting adults versus those who see it as their duty to God to
prevent the fulfillment of such preferences? The orthodox liberal will have to make some discriminations among legitimate
purposes that must be preserved, whether or not they collide
with others, or he or she will have to decide what to do when
two legitimate purposes conflict. Berlin, furthermore, does not
accurately characterize the logical implications of Kant's
theory with regard to "non-rational" ends. It is only immoral
ends that are *contrary* to rationality that are condemned by
Kant. Not all "non-rational" ends — ends not among those all
rational beings would adopt insofar as they are rational — fall
into the former category. The fulfillment of many of these

"non-rational" ends constitutes the happiness of human beings, and Kant's formula of humanity as an end in itself implies that we have a duty to promote the happiness of others. It seems, therefore, that Berlin has not given a solid argument for placing Kant in one camp rather than another.

Instead of trying to sort out disagreements over freedom by correlating them with two concepts of freedom, it is better to adopts MacCallum's suggestion that any genuine disagreements over freedom may be discussed and analyzed with the use of but one concept of freedom. He suggests that the relevant concept is of the freedom of an agent X from conditions Y that prevent X from doing, not doing, becoming or not becoming, Z (an action or condition of character). When one of the three terms in the triadic relation is missing, it should be treated as implicit in the context of discussion. Disagreements over freedom are to be understood as disagreements over the ranges of the term variables — over the 'true' identities of the agents in question (rational selves or natural persons), over what counts as a preventing condition (arrangements that are intended by others to be obstacles, or arrangements that constitute obstacles whether they be intentional or not), and over the range of what such agents might or might not be free to do or become (expressing criticism of the state, or doing as one wishes, or participating in ruling).[9]

Given such a schema, we may say that in ancient Greek morality, emphasis is placed on the freedom to perform a certain range of actions — those falling under the heading of participation in ruling. The protected range of actions does not include the range protected by the modern civil liberties — expression, religion, and so on. Ancient Greek morality, furthermore, restricts the range of agents who have the protected freedom. It belongs to agents who have the capacity to make wise decisions on how to sustain the common good of the community. In Plato's ideal state, these agents composed the class of Guardians. Aristotle excludes from citizenship the mechanic class because its members lack the leisure to participate and because manual labor makes the soul unfit for enlightened virtue.[10]

In Chinese Confucianism, there is no emphasis on the established Western categories of political and civil liberties. This does not mean, however, that Confucians were not concerned with removing barriers to certain actions or to acquiring certain character traits. They were most concerned with removing the barriers to becoming a person of *jen,* to becoming a person with a fully realized social nature who could act in accordance with filial piety and brotherly respect. It is a gross simplification to call this a freedom to conform to moral constraints (filial piety and brotherly respect), for Confucians viewed a life of *jen* as the most rewarding life a person could have. The stereotype of Eastern morality as subordinating the individual to society is not accurate for the reason that individual fulfillment is seen as lying in society.[11]

At the same time, those who respond to the stereotype by replying that there is *no* difference between Western, rights-centered moralities and Chinese morality on the matter of freedom are also wrong. Hsieh Yu-wei argues that Confucianism does value freedom, the freedom to do good and not freedom from constraints of any kind. This includes freedom to choose which prince to serve, which friends, the place where one lives, and to speak when it is right to do so. And, he asks, which morality allows the individual to do what is wrong?[12] The problem with this reply is that it does not take into account how the range of free choice may be widened or narrowed by the definition of the good and the right. Consider the "freedom to speak when it is right to do so." Clearly the range of verbal behavior allowed depends on the range of actions regarded as permissible. We saw that Confucius was not inclined to allow much latitude for those who did not participate in a government.

We see, therefore, a significant difference between virtue-centered and rights-centered moralities on the protected range of actions, and that virtue-centered moralities do not display a uniform position on the matter either. To understand the basis of these differences, we must go back to the notion of a common good that occupies the center of virtue-centered moralities and that is absent or subordinated to other values in rights-centered moralities. In Confucianism, the common good is a life of *jen* for all in accordance with righteousness, *li,* filial piety and brotherly respect. In ancient Greek morality, it is the public order, including the political life. In both kinds of virtue-centered moralities, a shared life is seen as the fulfillment of human nature, and thus they do not provide a congenial home for the notion that the individual needs to be protected *against* interference by the group. There is, however, a difference in the conception of the shared life between Chinese and Greek morality. For the Chinese, the family and kinship group remained the centers of man's social existence. For the Greeks, to say that man is a social animal is to say that he is a political one. It is not surprising, then, that the latter were concerned with the political liberties, while the former were not.

We are now in a position to return to Berlin's characterization of "positive liberty" and explain the trends he associates with the development of the concept. He says that the proponents of positive liberty tend to distinguish between the true selves and lower selves of individuals and are willing to sanction repression of the lower selves. This characterization did not seem to yield a clear distinction, but there is another distinction between those who believe in a common good, the sharing of which constitutes the fulfillment of each individual, and those who believe that many of an individual's important and *legitimate* purposes are not necessarily compatible with any common good. When Aristotle wanders away from the notion of a common good to his intellectualist perfectionism, he is still far from a rights-centered morality for the question of what freedoms to grant to the individual would have to be decided on the basis of what promotes *theoria*. I believe that such differences may have been what Berlin was attempting to identify, but he conflated the latter differences with the distinction between those who believe in true selves and lower selves and those who do not — a distinction that does not perform the desired job of sorting out libertarians from nonlibertarians.

Now Berlin also associates positive liberty with the desire for the autonomy of one's group. This desire becomes more comprehensible when placed in the context of a virtue-centered morality in which the primary moral end is to sustain the shared life of one's community. The movement of colonized

peoples for autonomy may be seen as a protest against the
destruction of a shared life. The desire to sustain a shared life
explains why, in Swaziland, tribal members who are doctors,
lawyers, and engineers still perform the rituals their ancestors
performed in the ceremonial dress their ancestors wore and
why they still have a king who wields genuine political power.

11.3   *The case for variation in truth conditions*

We now come to the crucial question: given the difference
between rights-centered and virtue-centered moralities on the
questions of freedom and of the existence of a common good,
the sharing of which constitutes each individual's fulfillment,
is there a variation in truth conditions between moral statements made on the basis of two kinds of moralities? Consider
what absolutists could say about this case. Perhaps this is a case
of environmental relativity in which a virtue-centered morality
is applicable to some groups or societies, given their conditions, but inapplicable to others, given different conditions.

May and Abraham Edel apply this method of explanation to
the Zuni Indians, who have a virtue-centered morality that is
focused on a shared life, structured around religious ritual, in
much the same way that Chinese social life was structured
around the rituals of ancestor worship. In both cultures, performance of these rituals was an occasion for affirmation of
one's place in the community. By performing a role that others
in the tradition performed far into the past and that others
would perform in the future, one gains a vivid sense of the continuity of community. By performing a role that is coordinated
in complex ways with the roles of others to produce a kind of
drama symbolizing certain collective attitudes (reverence for
the past, acceptance of the contingencies of nature) of the
community, one gains a vivid sense of the present unity of the
community. The Zuni center their lives around such ritual,
and, as is appropriate under a virtue-centered morality, they
praise and encourage the development of qualities that enable
them to sustain the ritual life. Here is the description of an
anthropologist:

In practically all his activities, the individual must conform to the patterns established by a number of social groupings: matriarchal household [which in the sharing of food is communally organized], the matrilineal clan, and religious societies and esoteric cults . . . It is rather the cooperative person, ready to share his food with his relatives and needy friends, ready to assist his neighbor or religious or clan colleague in agricultural labor, who is most respected in the community. Ideally, wealth that has been accumulated is redistributed among the members of the village . . . the aggressive, competitive, noncooperative individual is regarded as the aberrant type.[13]

In fact, the Edels note that among the Zuni

the only purpose to which wealth accumulation could be put with any meaning, was to help finance a religious ceremony. In so doing, a man redistributed his entire surplus — giving help and support to the less fortunate in the community. But that was not the purpose of the undertaking; rather it was participation in the appropriate fashion in the religious rituals which was the good end desired.[14]

We see in Zuni culture, therefore, the same emphasis on the common good of the shared life and the same absence of emphasis on the civil freedoms. There is great moral concern over the removal of barriers to participation in the religious life of the community.

Now the Edels suggest that at least part of the explanation for the emphasis on cooperation and on the value of a close-knit community life is that the Zuni live in an "isolated desert environment, quite permanent, and subject to attack from without."[15] This method of explanation for the adoption of virtue-centered moralities is also exemplified by Richard Solomon's explanation of why the Chinese adopted Confucianism (see 8.3). As I noted in discussion of Solomon's explanation, however, other cultures have operated under hard material conditions that might motivate a group to adopt a virtue-centered morality, but they have not. The Eskimos of Greenland are an example. Furthermore, Solomon himself notes that in traditional China, urban Chinese of upper- and middle-income levels also adopted Confucianism.

This method of explanation, therefore, will not tell us why
virtue-centered moralities are appropriate to a certain set
of conditions, while rights-centered moralities are appropriate
to another set of conditions. This is the result that would support the subsumption of the differences between the two moralities as a case of environmental relativity. This result is also
undermined by comparative studies of different tribal cultures. Margaret Mead devised a classification of social systems
as cooperative, competitive, and individualistic on the basis of
the proportions of time and energy devoted by groups to ends
that were shared, competitive, or individual. The Zuni social
system was classified as cooperative because success in that system was intimately tied to the good of the group and one's status did not go up or down with one's own success. In competitive cultures, one's status does go up or down with one's own
efforts, and individual achievement tends to be compared on a
single scale of success. In the competitive social system of the
Manus of the Admiralty Islands, the overriding goal of each is
individual success through the accumulation of property. In
individualistic social systems, the individual is not even motivated to achieve status in the eyes of others. Instead, each is
like a sovereign state. For the Eskimos of Greenland, the ideal
man is one who does what he pleases and takes what he wants
without fear. Mead found that such differences did not corre-
late with differences in subsistence level, with classifications of
a system as food-gathering, hunting or agricultural, or with
the state of technology. She concluded that the dictates of the
natural environment were overridden by cultural definition:
"The social conception of success and the structural framework into which individual success is fitted are more determinate than the state of technology or the plentifulness of food."[16]

Absolutists may reply that a virtue-centered morality may *in
fact* be appropriate only under certain material conditions
having to do with material scarcity or threat of attack from the
outside, and that when a group adopts such a morality under
other conditions, it is making a mistake. Absolutists must then
explain, however, what the mistake is, and how a group could
have made it. After all, people do seem to derive certain satisfactions from a way of life embodying a virtue-centered moral-

ity, including a sense of security and acceptance in relation to one's fellow human beings. Absolutists may go on to object that there could be some environmental relativity I have not thought of and that should be built into the acceptance of a virtue-centered morality. This, of course, is always possible. Arguments to the best explanation are always vulnerable to the possibility that there is some relevant explanation that has yet to be given. I offer my argument to the best explanation as the best one that can be given now, with our present fund of knowledge.

If environmental relativity is not the entire explanation of the crucial differences between virtue-centered and rights-centered moralities, what about the possibility that the difference is a disagreement over a question that is beyond human powers to settle at this time? As was noted before, it is incumbent on those who give this method of explanation to tell why this disagreement is unresolvable while others are not. This would involve identifying what would be the case if each side were right and telling how the available evidence is consistent with either possibility. Kantian absolutists would have to say that the irresolvability lies in a failure to identify which position in the disagreement is compatible with standards of rationality on practical reasoning. This in turn could be the result of a failure to identify the relevant standards of rationality, or it could be the result of a failure to identify the relevant implications of relevant standards that have been identified. But as far as we know, practically all moral disagreements are irresolvable in this sense because no standard of rationality has been found that clearly implies a substantive moral principle.

Aristotelians such as Foot would have to say that the (presently irresolvable) disagreement is over which way of life is the most beneficial for people. Perhaps we cannot resolve the disagreement at this time because of the extreme difficulty of determining which way provides the best *balance* of satisfactions that seem to conflict with each other. On the one hand, participating in a shared life provides certain unique satisfactions. It provides one with a sense of security and acceptance in relation to one's fellow human beings. It avoids the isolation and stress that competitive and individualistic social systems place on people. On the other hand, the latter social systems provide complementary satisfactions — those stemming from fulfillment of needs for achievement and creativity that an individual could identify as his or her own. And a morality that stressed rights and individual freedoms might better provide for such needs. Ruth Benedict remarked in her discussion of the extremely competitive and individualistic life of the Kwakiutl that

the pursuit of victory can give vigor and zest to human existence. Kwakiutl life is rich and forceful in its own terms. Its chosen goal has its appropriate virtues... Whatever the social orientation, a society which exemplifies it vigorously will develop certain virtues that are natural to the goals it has chosen...[17]

Now Benedict believes that "it is most unlikely that even the best society will be able to stress in one social order all the virtues we prize in human life"; but Aristotelians would dispute that judgment, and it would seem arbitrary to eliminate such a possibility a priori. We may be able to find social systems that provide a better balance of satisfactions than the Zuni or Kwakiutl. For instance, Bernard Mishkin reported that in the Maori social system of New Zealand, community welfare is the primary end, but that that end is achieved through competition among individuals for approval of the community. Means of production are collectively owned and everyone's important needs are provided for, but the laws of distribution recognize the primacy of participants in production.[18] Perhaps the Maori system provides a better balance of the complementary virtues achieved in the Zuni and Kwakiutl systems. And perhaps such a system is more beneficial to human beings because it does provide a better balance. It remains for us to discover the ideal balance, and perhaps we haven't enough knowledge to do that at present.

This is an interesting reply and it is probably true that some social systems provide a better balance of important, complementary satisfactions. But it must be pointed out that the idea of balance is itself a moral ideal that is not obviously entitled to the title of the only valid ideal. A culture may tend to place much more value on a certain *kind* of satisfaction and may reject the ideal of *balance* between that kind and others, opting to achieve the highest degree of the most important kind (as Aristotle tended to do on occasion with *theoria*). The ideal of balance, furthermore, is in reality a largely formal notion that is compatible with a number of different interpretations and corresponding ways of life. It is not likely that all satisfactions will be given equal value, for instance. Even if we set aside Aristotle's most zealous intellectualist tendencies, we must recognize that he gave *theoria* a relatively high valuation and a prominent place in his ideal of a way of life balanced between the moral and intellectual virtues. In ancient Chinese culture, however, *theoria* was not given such a high valuation, and the corresponding ideal of balance would be different.

Also, one satisfaction upon which ancient Greek culture seems not to have placed any great value is that of being in harmony with the nonhuman world, knowing its rhythms and changes, not to manipulate it but to live with it. In ancient Chinese and in many American Indian cultures, this is an important part of any desirable way of life. Compare the Greek preoccupation in art with the perfect human form to the Chinese landscapes in which human beings are tiny figures tucked into great living mountains. The notion of what is the most beneficial to human beings is too indeterminate to convince us that there is a fact of the matter over which there is a disagreement we cannot resolve at this time. And the question of how to make the notion more determinate is in fact part of the disagreement to be resolved.

A different problem is faced by Aristotelians such as McDowell, who place much weight on Aristotle's likening of moral wisdom to perception. In order to explain why we are presently unable to resolve the disagreement, they must tell a persuasive story about the way we are related to the moral reality that at least some of us allegedly perceive in varying degrees of accuracy. They have not done this. For this reason, they cannot begin to tell us in any detail how those who adhere to virtue-centered moralities could be missing the moral reality that motivates a recognition of rights to certain freedoms, or how those who adhere to rights-centered moralities could be missing the moral reality that motivates the recognition of the desirability of a shared life. The same criticism applies to the moral intuitionism of Platts.

Returning to the final absolutist method of explaining diversity of moral belief, it declares one or the other side to be in error or ignorant of crucial facts. Kantian absolutists would fail to give a convincing explanation for the same reasons they would fail to convince us that the difference between virtue-centered and rights-centered moralities is an irresolvable disagreement over a fact of the matter. Aristotelians such as Foot again could have trouble with the indeterminateness of their conception of benefit, and if they made it more determinate — say they proclaimed that the most beneficial way of life was one that provided a certain balance between important satisfactions, they would have to explain why those who seem to have a different interpretation of the most satisfying way of life are mistaken or ignorant. And those who rely on the concept of an irreducible moral reality would have the problems of specifying the nature of the relation between that reality and perceivers of it in such a way that it could form the base of a plausible and reasonably detailed explanation of how those who adhere to virtue-centered or rights-centered moralities are mistaken.

This is how relativists could argue by elimination to the hypothesis that there is a difference in truth conditions for moral "A ought to do X" statements between virtue-centered and rights-centered moralities. This variation centers on the question of whether one ought to recognize areas of conduct within which the individual does as he or she wishes without moral or legal constraint. Virtue-centered moralities do not protect certain areas that rights-centered moralities do, and to say there is variation in truth conditions is to say that an adherent of virtue-centered morality could truthfully deny a statement to the effect that one ought to recognize these areas of noninterference, while an adherent of rights-centered moralities could truthfully make that statement. Clearly, if this difference in truth conditions for moral "A ought to do X" statements is established, there is going to be an accompanying difference in truth conditions for "X is a good person" statements, for good people will be required to recognize different freedoms and to do different things in support of those freedoms.

Throughout this chapter, I have tried to connect the failure of absolutist theories to explain certain kinds of disagreements and apparent diversity in moral belief with the general difficulties I identified in the seventh and eighth chapters. By making this connection, I am suggesting that the failure is likely to be incurable. Human beings have needs to resolve internal conflicts between requirements and to resolve interpersonal conflicts of interest. Morality is a social creation that evolved in response to these needs. There are constraints on what a morality could be like and still serve those needs. These constraints are derived from the physical environment, from human nature, and from standards of rationality, but they are not enough to eliminate all but one morality as meeting those needs. Moral relativity is an indication of the plasticity of human nature, of the power of ways of life to determine what constitutes a satisfactory resolution of the conflicts morality is intended to resolve.

11.4   *Accepting moral relativity*

Some may regard this hypothesis as a depressing one. But this tendency may itself be a matter of cultural variation. It is not obvious that we need any moral absolutes by which to live. It is not obvious that instead of being depressed by our inability to say who is absolutely right and wrong in every moral disagreement, we cannot instead be exhilarated by the wide range of human possibility to live in different ways and to become different people. And it is not obvious that we cannot learn to accept that what is morally true for us is in part determined by our specific historical and cultural environment.

But whether or not we find moral relativity depressing, we must recognize the consequences of its existence. One such consequence is a new perspective on moral reform and revolution. If we view morality as something that evolves in response to human need, we can allow for further evolution in response to changing need or to greater awareness of certain needs. This change may go beyond the type of change that absolutists would allow: changing the rules to come closer to the truth. We may change the moral truth itself in response to human need. Having recognized this, we can take conscious control of the direction of such change. If we find that a way of life has frustrated certain needs, and if we desire greater satisfaction with respect to them, we ought to be prepared to alter our way of life and its attendant moral constraints. If we are not prepared to accept a Nozickian society in which everyone's primary concern is to control his or her property, as I am convinced we are not, then we ought to at least consider dropping the moral ideology that justifies such a society and to which many people still cling. If we find ourselves longing for greater community and mutual support, but wish to preserve an emphasis on rights, we ought to explore the possibilities of social systems that combine at least some of the satisfactions of virtue-centered and rights-centered moralities. And we can do all this without pretending that we are engaged in a search for the single true morality or that we are absolutely justified in seeking greater satisfaction of needs for more community.

A second consequence of a recognition of moral relativity has to do with the moral implications of that relativity. What is unique about our particular historical situation is that we are now so much more aware than before of the variety of ways of life. And much more than before, we need to interact with those who have been shaped by alien ways of life. It is necessary to ask what our moral stance should be toward the others. Many of us seem to be caught between an attitude of greater toleration for other ways of life and an uneasy feeling that our own values are being eroded the more tolerant we become. In response to this dilemma, some who are sympathetic to moral relativism as a metaethical thesis argue that this thesis has no implications at all for the way we ought to behave toward those with moralities that may be as valid or as true as ours. I believe that this argument is not only incorrect, it prevents us from facing important moral issues. I explain why in the next chapter.

12 Tolerance and Nonintervention as Implications of Moral Relativity

12.1 Does anything follow from moral relativity?

Within the philosophical community, it is not disreputable to hold the sort of view I have argued for in the first eleven chapters. It is disreputable, however, to present arguments from moral relativism to the conclusion that one ought to tolerate those who practice a different morality that is as true as one's own. Moral relativists who are also philosophers take special pains to disown such arguments. Geoffrey Harrison is an example.[1] Bernard Williams, who seems sympathetic to many of the philosophical motivations behind moral relativism, called one relativist argument for tolerance "the anthropologist's heresy, possibly the most absurd view to have been advanced even in moral philosophy."[2] Harrison and Williams correctly criticize relativist arguments for tolerance, given their own interpretations of the arguments. I will argue, however, that they neglect other interpretations of the arguments. These interpretations merit serious consideration and are based on principles central to Kantian and utilitarian ethics.

12.2 Criticisms of relativist arguments for tolerance

To state his belief in moral relativism, Geoffrey Harrison defines a "moral system" to include principles that are used to justify moral judgments of the form "A ought to do X." A "well-established" moral system satisfies the criteria for an acceptable system, an example of a criterion being that a moral system should be internally consistent and not require

incompatible actions of an agent. Harrison believes that there
is more than one well-established moral system and that two
such systems could yield conflicting judgments concerning the
matter of whether an action X ought to be done by A. Each
judgment would be justified by reference to ultimate principles
in one system, but the ultimate principles would have no justification.

Harrison considers how such a belief in moral relativism has
been used to support tolerance. He asks us to suppose that two
persons A and B are disputing what action ought to be taken
on a given occasion. They find that their disagreement rests on
differing ultimate principles of two well-established systems.
The argument is that the "sensible and fair" course is to agree
to differ:

Sensible, since the alternative suggests a Hobbes-like state of moral
nature, with moral interest taking over the role traditionally filled by
self-interest. Fair, because neither side can conclusively prove his
case, or refute the other, and he has no right to impose his own views.
Looked at objectively, one moral system is as good as another.[3]

Harrison claims that these arguments are premised on a confusion between normative ethics and metaethics. Normative
ethics is participating in morality, making moral decisions, following principles. Metaethics is observing the participation,
analyzing the first-order activities of normative ethics. Moral
relativism belongs to metaethics and implies nothing about
which values ought to be adopted. The moment that relativists
advocate the value of tolerance, they cross the border into normative ethics and become participants in morality instead of
observers. Tolerance must be defended from the point of view
of some moral system, not from a morally neutral one.

Harrison adds that a crucial mistake in the first argument
for tolerance is its trading on the ambiguity of the claim that
one moral system is as good as another. It could mean that all
moral systems meet the criteria for acceptability equally well,
in which case it would be a metaethical claim, though it does
not follow from moral relativism. It could mean that there is
no moral reason for preferring any moral system above any

other, in which case it would be neither a metaethical claim nor a moral claim, for neither an observer nor a participant in a particular moral system could make it. Adopting a morality necessarily involves rejecting at least some aspects of any doctrine incompatible with one's own.

Bernard Williams focuses on another relativist argument for tolerance. The "anthropologist's heresy," which he regards as the "most distinctive and influential" of such arguments, consists of three propositions:

That 'right' means (can only be coherently understood as meaning) 'right for a given society'; that 'right for a given society' is to be understood in a functionalist sense; and that (therefore) it is wrong for people in one society to condemn, interfere with, etc., the values of another society.[4]

The argument is inconsistent because it makes a claim in its third proposition about what is right and wrong in one's dealings with other societies that uses a nonrelative sense of 'right' not allowed for in the first proposition.

The central confusion of the argument, says Williams, is to try to derive from the fact that societies have different values some nonrelative principle governing the attitude of one society to another, an impossible task. He goes on to observe that there are features of morality that make it difficult to regard a morality as applying only to a group. Even though a tribal morality may apply only to members of the tribe, it progressively comes to range over persons as such. Values, furthermore, come to be internalized and cannot evaporate when one confronts people in other societies. He mentions by way of example the horrified reactions of the men who went with Cortez to Mexico, when they came upon the sacrificial temples of the Aztecs.

12.3 *A valid relativist argument for tolerance*

The relativist argument stated above are not straw men. When people are reluctant to condemn another's moral position, they will often make remarks very similar to the ones

Harrison states on their behalf. And Williams is not far off in his criticism of at least some anthropologists. Melville Herskovits argued for an "emphasis on the worth of many ways of life" that "seeks to understand and harmonize goals, not to judge and destroy those that do not dovetail with our own," and one of his major premises is that a society's values are in some way functionally necessary.[5]

But the relativist arguments for tolerance that nonphilosophers give are typically vague and incomplete. They are subject to multiple and conflicting interpretations. As Williams and Harrison interpret them, they proceed from the premise of moral relativism directly to tolerance. They have no premise that expresses a particular ethical viewpoint, and thus are, in Harrison's terms, attempts to derive a participant's conclusions from an observer's premises. Harrison and Williams neglect the possibility that the relativist arguments of nonphilosophers also can be interpreted as arguments from moral relativism and one or more ethical premises to tolerance. This interpretation is an expression of the fact that an observer's premises may be relevant to a participant *within the context of his or her ethical viewpoint*. Consider the argument Harrison criticizes: because "neither side can conclusively prove his case," neither has any "right to impose his own views." We can interpret this as containing a suppressed ethical premise, to the effect that it is wrong to impose one's views on another person unless one can justify them to him or her. And when Herskovits argues that we should seek to harmonize goals that do not dovetail with our own, we can interpret him as speaking from an ethic that values interaction between members of different cultures through mutual consent.

To develop an alternative interpretation of these arguments, let us begin with Kant's formula of humanity as an end in itself: that one ought always to treat humanity never simply as a means but always at the same time as an end. In an illustration of how the formula is to be applied, Kant says that the man who makes a false promise to another man is intending to make use of the man merely as a means to an end he does not share. This is so because the man being deceived "cannot possibly agree with . . . [that] way of behaving to him, and so cannot himself share the end of the action."[6]

Thus one implication of the formula is that we should refrain from interfering with the permissible ends of others. The qualification that the ends be permissible is necessary because others may have immoral or unworthy ends that one may justifiably interfere with.

Now the question arises as to how one is able to distinguish permissible from impermissible ends. Kant does not explicitly address this problem, but an answer naturally falls out of his view that the possession of a rational nature is the basis for the status of human beings as ends in themselves.[7] Permissible ends are rational ends—those that accord with the nature of human beings as rational beings.[8] This implies that one should not interfere with the ends of others unless one can justify the interference to be acceptable to them were they fully rational and informed of all relevant circumstances. To do otherwise is to fail to treat them with the respect due rational beings. Let us call this implication of Kant's formula the "justification principle."[9] Kant believes his principle to be objectively valid for all people. Whether or not this is the case, the theme of individual autonomy is a central and pervasive one in the moral traditions of Europe and of cultures descending from Europe. Kant's principle is a plausible expression of that theme.

Let us now consider what follows when his principle is combined with moral relativism. If moral relativism is true, two persons A and B can have conflicting moralities that are equally true and that therefore may be equally justified. Suppose B is required or permitted by his morality to bring about a state of affairs X. A can bring about some other state of affairs Y that precludes the coming about of X.[10] It would be a violation of the justification principle for A to bring about Y, because she could not justify to B the preventing of X. We thus have an argument for A tolerating B's action according to his moral beliefs. This argument is a possible interpretation of the relativist arguments for tolerance given by non-philosophers. In fact, it makes a plausible interpretation of arguments given by people who have come to believe in moral relativism within the context of a culture that emphasizes individual autonomy.

The force of the argument from the justification principle

will vary with the content of A's moral system. Of course, A will not be moved by it at all if her system contains nothing like the justification principle. Suppose it does. Then she must consider whether there is some other principle in it that requires that she prevent B from bringing about X. Assuming that A's moral system is deontological, the existence of such a principle results in a conflict of *prima facie* duties. A would have to weigh the justification principle against the other principle.

Kant did not provide much guidance on these matters. If A places a high priority on the justification principle, something like the Millean principle may occur to her: that one ought not to interfere with B bringing about X unless it prevents harm to others. It is dubious, however, that we can make a clear distinction between self-regarding and other-regarding action. An action that harms the agent has a good chance of adversely affecting those whose interests are in some way dependent on the agent's. Alcoholics, drug addicts, and people who ride motorcycles without helmets may have spouses or children. When we take into account the degree to which people's interests are interdependent, we will probably have a very small sphere of purely self-regarding action that is protected.

It is quite possible that there is no general procedure for drawing neat boundaries of the sphere of actions with which one is not to interfere. A, however, can still weigh conflicting *prima facie* duties, according to the moral significance each duty acquires in the particular situation at hand. For one thing, the weight of the duty to refrain from preventing X (relative to that of the other conflicting duty) varies inversely with the degree to which nonconsenting others are harmed or have their freedom restricted. Consider the difference between B engaging in an unusual sexual act with other consenting adults and B's terrorist act of kidnapping and murder. The relative weight of the duty to refrain, furthermore, varies inversely with the probability of occurrence of possible harm or restriction of freedom, together with the clarity with which the harm or restriction can be defined. For an example of a case in which the relative weight is not diminished, consider the claim by some that homosexual activity between consenting adults could undermine the values of the traditional family over a whole society. There is no hard evidence for the probability of such an effect; the idea of exactly what values would be undermined and why their undermining would be harmful is very fuzzy.

A can also determine whether a compromise could be effected between the conflicting duties. Perhaps she could perform some actions that constitute at least partial performance of one of the duties and at the same time refrain from those actions that would constitute the most serious violations of the other duty. For instance, A might find ways of opposing B's homosexual activity and yet refrain from advocating legal sanctions against that activity. To use the coercive apparatus of the state to prevent X is an especially strong form of intervention in B's affairs that could involve much harm and restriction of freedom.

So far, we have seen how a Kantian ethic could support a relativist argument for tolerance. There is a kind of utilitarianism that supports the justification principle and therefore a relativist argument for tolerance.

Obviously, the relevant kind allows for moral rules other than the principle of utility. Since Mill allows for such rules, let us consider his rationale for them and his conception of their nature. Take his rule that the sole end for which the coercive power of the state can be rightfully exercised over the individual is to prevent harm to others. He thought that the general welfare is best promoted if the state's intervention is restricted to the prevention of harm. Any more interference is ineffective or counterproductive. Given the importance of each individual's autonomy, we ought to lay down the principle never to interfere except for the sake of preventing harm to others. Under David Lyons' persuasive interpretation of Mill, this principle may be regarded as inflexible, though exceptions may be built into it. The point of inflexibility is to "avoid situations that I know will lead to choices that are self-destructive [with respect to promotion of the general welfare or even to the welfare of the individual who is being coerced], though they will not seem such to me at the time."[11] We know, therefore, Mill's brand of utilitarianism is not limited to support of "rules of thumb" that can be set aside whenever the level of general welfare may be raised by doing so. Nor need we think that Mill would set aside the principle to maximize utility, because he never speaks of that end as morally required.

To see how Mill's brand of utilitarianism could support the justification principle, consider his reasons for attaching great importance to individual autonomy. Its importance is not explained merely by the fact that people desire it (if that is even a fact for all or most people). Rather, the desire for it ought to be cultivated because it is a necessary condition for each individual's well-being. Well-being is achieved through exercising control over one's life, through developing the ability to choose one's ends on the basis of rational deliberation and to develop and carry out coherent plans of action designed to realize those ends.[12] That is why Mill emphasized the need for widespread participation in political affairs, not just as a means to protecting one's interest but as an integral part of self-realization. It is a short step from such a view of freedom to the justification principle. When an individual's freedom is restricted in such a way that it cannot be justified to him or her, the kind of growth that Mill thought to be essential to well-being is frustrated. It is reasonable to lay down the justification principle to protect the general welfare.

Given the justification principle, the relativist argument for the utilitarian goes through as before. Of course, the utilitarian will want to limit application of the principle because occasions will arise that necessitate weighing the duty to prevent interference with autonomy against the duty to prevent harm to others and the restriction of their freedom.

12.4 *Problems posed for the argument*

Kantians may raise the following problem for the relativist argument from the justification principle: in arguing for that principle, Kant presupposed that there is a single moral system that is valid for all rational human beings; hence it is highly unlikely that anyone will ever have a good reason to assert the conjunction of moral relativism and the justification principle.

The first point to make in dealing with this problem is that the justification principle is interpretable in such a way that the content of what it prescribes is independent of any proposition entailing the falsity of moral relativism. We don't have to be moral absolutists to resolve to refrain from interfering with the permissible ends of others. Second, it is a fact that many have found Kant's principle appealing while remaining unpersuaded by the arguments for it. Some hold that noncircular arguments valid for all rational beings *cannot* be given for it.[13] Though Kant would think it morally irrelevant, it is a fact that people find satisfaction in treating others and being treated in accordance with the principle. This leads me to a third point.

It is possible for a moral relativist to have a good reason for holding the justification principle, if not all good reasons for holding a moral principle must follow from the nature of practical reason. Historically, it has been non-Kantian philosophers, such as utilitarians, who have stressed the role of desire and instinct in moral motivation. There is no necessary connection, however, between utilitarian principles of right action and this view of moral motivation. Sympathy, compassion, and concern for another for his or her own sake may give rise to reasons for accepting the justification principle. If one desires freedom from the interference of others, one may sympathize with others to whom that freedom is denied, and find satisfaction in helping them to achieve it. Also, the desire to be part of a group in which there is mutual respect and support may motivate adherence to the principles. A person need not be instructed by practical reason to desire to be in a group in which each member acknowledges the worth of every other by intending to promote for him or her the possession of capacities and goods commonly regarded as necessary for a satisfying life. This would include the capacity to make unforced choices.

In general, philosophers doubt the viability of altruistic emotions as a motivating ground for acceptance of a moral principle because they see them as capricious. But people vary in this respect, just as they do in their ability to see the requirements of practical reason and to act on these requirements. There are some people who are able to sympathize with others only under the most propitious of circumstances — when things are going well for them, when they are in an expansive, generous mood—just as there are some who reason correctly only under similar circumstances. Others have sympathy as an enduring and reliable trait of character. They are consistent in their ability to see when another is in trouble and needs help, just as others are strong, reliable practical reasoners. Capriciousness is not an intrinsic feature of the altruistic emotions, any more than inconsistency is an intrinsic feature of practical reason.

Philosophers may be misled into seeing the altruistic emotions as capricious because they confuse these emotions with those of personal liking we have toward certain people. But as Lawrence Blum points out in *Friendship, Altruism, and Morality,* altruistic emotions are "directed towards other people in light of or in regard to their weal and woe, whereas personal feelings are directed towards others in light of their personal features."[14] I may have concern or compassion for someone I personally dislike because he is having a rough time.

Harrison poses other problems for any relativist argument for tolerance. The first problem he poses begins with the claim that almost all significant actions and decisions will be disapproved by someone. If A refrains from preventing X by bringing about Y merely because B disapproves of Y, and if A carries out that policy consistently, she would be paralyzed.[15] This is not a real problem for the relativist argument from the justification principle because it allows for the possibility that the principle may have exceptions or be overridden by another moral principle. The reason presented for tolerance in the argument, furthermore, is not as simple as B's disapproval of Y. The reason is that B is required or permitted by his morality to bring about X, and if A prevents X from occurring this would constitute a violation of the justification principle. Such a reason applies to only a small subset of our significant actions.

Another problem posed by Harrison is that A must weigh her own attitude toward X and Y. If A refrains from preventing X because of B's attitude, and if she believes she is required by her moral system to bring about Y, then isn't she favoring B's over her own? This would be rational, says Harrison, only if A thinks B more liable to be correct in his judgment.[16] If B, however, is persuaded by the relativist argument from the justification principle, she would not be favoring B's attitude over her own. She would be persuaded by her belief in the principle. The conflict is between two principles in A's system, as well as between A and B.

A third problem posed by Harrison is that there is as much reason for B to allow A to override him: "They should both try to allow the other to do what they consider to be wrong."[17] The result would be that no one does anything. In reply, it is relevant to point out an asymmetry between the situations of A and B. A must decide whether to block an anticipated action of B and thus to restrict B's freedom. B must decide whether to offend A's sense of morality by trying to bring about X, but there may be no further result concerning A in particular. Her freedom may not be restricted, and in such a case the justification principle would provide B no reason to allow A's intervention. It is true that if B holds the justification principle, he will have reason to refrain from bringing about X, to the extent that his action will have an adverse effect on A.

But while each may affect the other, one may affect the other in such a way that the justification principle must weigh more heavily in his or her decision-making. For instance, if B engages in homosexual activity with another consenting adult and A must decide whether to prevent such activity through the law, it would seem most likely that the justification principle must weigh more against A's intervention than B's abstinence from homosexual activity. Let us grant, however, that there are possible cases in which the justification principle would weigh as heavily against the latter action as the former. And let us grant that among these possible cases, both B and A decide that the justification principle outweighs the other principle requiring the bringing about of X or its prevention. What we have is not an embarrassment for the relativist argument, but two people who may decide not to act in ways they cannot justify to each other. This is neither absurd nor undesirable.

A fourth problem posed by Harrison is that relativist arguments for tolerance often presuppose an untenable concept of tolerance as the acceptance of decision-assigning rules that specify who has the "legal/moral right to decide what ought to be done."[18] Such a concept rests on the mistaken assumption that the moral question "What ought I to do?" is separate from the question "Who is to make the decision?" and that the latter is prior to the former. The latter is itself a moral question and is part of the former. Unless one can present a cogent argument for observing decision-assigning rules as a *moral* policy, one is simply relinquishing responsibility to decide what ought to be done in each individual situation in which one could intervene. Harrison's objection is sound, but the concept of tolerance presupposed by the argument from the justification principle does not separate the two questions. This is an argument to the effect that one has a responsibility to refrain from intervention in certain kinds of situations; it still leaves to the individual the responsibility of deciding whether any given situation is of a relevant kind. It advocates tolerance as a moral value.

Note that the sort of tolerance supported by the argument is not a partial endorsement of all well-established moralities, but a value of a particular kind of morality. As Williams and Harrison point out, to say that some moralities are as justified as one's own is not to commit oneself to these others, as well as one's own. This would result in moral schizophrenia. Unfortunately, those who make relativist arguments for tolerance tend to succumb to such schizophrenia. When Herskovits argues for an "emphasis on the worth of many ways of life," he tends to use 'worth' in both an epistemological and moral sense. In the moral sense, tolerance becomes partial endorsement of all these ways of life.

A final problem is suggested by one of Williams' criticisms of the "anthropologist's heresy": that its central confusion is to try to derive from the view that moral principles are relative to some nonrelative principle governing the attitude of one society toward another. Does the argument for tolerance presented here make the same error? To answer this question, we need to distinguish different ways in which moral principles can be relative. The form of moral relativism assumed here implies that moral principles can be relative in the sense that they can be true and justified in one society but not in another. It implies nothing about the scope of applying moral principles. It does not imply, for instance, that a moral principle such as "It is wrong to interfere with another society's values" must be implicitly relativized, as "It is wrong for our society (but perhaps not for others) to interfere with another society's values." My version of moral relativism is compatible with Williams' claim that a morality often comes to range over all persons and not just over the members of the society in which it originates. A moral principle can have universal scope; that is, it can apply to all moral agents in the sense of directing them to perform certain actions; and it may be *true of* all agents given a certain set of truth conditions that a group or society assigns to the principle; but since there may be more than one set of truth conditions for the principle, it may not be *universally justifiable* to all agents.

The reader may not be comfortable with my view that a moral principle may be true of all agents but not universally justifiable to them. Keep in mind that when I write that a principle is not universally justifiable, I mean that it is not possible to give every person a reason to act according to the principle, even though it may be shown to be true to every person once its truth conditions are laid out and shown to be relative to a particular referent of 'adequate moral system'. The source of any remaining discomfort the reader may feel probably lies in our tendency to associate A's admission of the truth of a moral statement with an admission of a reason for A to act according to it. Earlier in the book (5.4), I furnish an explanation of why we make this association even if it is not always valid to make it.

The relativist argument from the justification principle concludes with a principle that is nonrelative with respect to the content of truth conditions, not necessarily with respect to justifiability. It is consistent, therefore, with that argument to condemn the intolerant behavior of those in another society even though tolerance may not be justifiable to them. A nice question to raise at this point is whether the argument allows us to try to *prevent* their intolerant behavior. The argument does seem to imply a *prima facie* duty not to interfere with them, but if we are committed to promoting tolerance, then we must ask whether our interference is a lesser evil than letting

them impose their will on others. We would have to weigh conflicting *prima facie* duties, both derived from the value of tolerance. It would not be a contradiction to conclude that our
commitment to that value weighed in favor of interference.

12.5 *Applying the relativist argument to abortion*

I now want to argue that the abortion issue is one to which
the justification principle is applicable. Let us consider the two
positions on opposite ends of the spectrum: the liberal and the
conservative. Liberals hold that abortion should be available
on demand at any stage of development from conception to
birth. Conservatives hold that abortion is impermissible at any
stage except to save the mother's life (there are even more
extreme views, but I don't think they are as defensible as this
one). There is a good case for saying that these positions are
equally justifiable.

Mary Anne Warren presents one of the most fully articu-
lated liberal positions. She argues that a fetus is not entitled to
protection of its life merely because it is a human being in the
sense of possessing the appropriate genetic code. Rather, an
entity is entitled to protection only if it is a person in the sense
of being a full-fledged member of the moral community. Warren lists five criteria for personhood: consciousness and capacity to feel pain, reasoning, self-motivated activity, the capacity
to communicate, and the presence of self concepts. She
believes that a person need not possess all these properties. The
first two or three may be sufficient. She suggests that the first
three may be necessary. Why these criteria? Warren considers
it obvious that an entity satisfying none of the five criteria is
not a person.[19]

This last claim will not persuade a conservative whose criterion for personhood is *potential* to satisfy Warren's criteria.
And it is not at all clear that the conservative is any less a competent user of the term 'person' than Warren is. Liberals who
seek stronger ammunition against conservatives might turn to
Michael Tooley who attempts to connect his criteria for being
entitled to the protection of life with the concept of a right. His
argument is that a being possesses a serious right to life only if

he is capable of desiring to continue existing as a subject of experiences and other mental states and thus has a concept and belief in the self as a continuing entity. The premise of the argument is that to have a right to something a being must be capable of desiring it. Since a fetus has no concept of self, it has no right to life.[20] This argument does not make much of an advance over Warren because Tooley gives no argument for assuming that having a right to something requires the capability of desiring it. L. W. Sumner points out that the right to life is a "welfare right" — a very basic and special case of the general right to a decent and satisfying life. Sumner argues that a person can be harmed by the satisfaction of his or her desires and benefited by their frustration. More importantly, he asks us to imagine a man who is sufficiently retarded as to have no sense of self but who is quite capable of enjoying his life. It makes perfect sense to say he can benefit from efforts to provide a happy life for him.[21]

Is there another way to justify to conservatives a liberal position on the moral status of the fetus? So far, liberals have failed to find one, and I suspect that none can be found. Earlier in this book, I pointed out that there was no logic that compels us from a knowledge of the concept of morality (at least as I characterize that concept) to criteria for determining which persons are entitled to treatment under the rules of morality (though I did argue that once an "in" group cooperates with an "out" group, and applies moral rules to structure that cooperation, there is a compelling reason to extend all moral rules to the "out"s or to give a morally relevant reason for not doing so that goes beyond the fact that the "out"s are members of another group). And if we look at the concept of a system of rules intended to reconcile internal and interpersonal conflicts, we will not find criteria for determining the moral status of the human fetus. The only other possibility for justifying a set of criteria is that some descriptions used to fix the reference of 'adequate moral system' in our society will entail a set. Yet I cannot find a description that would do the job and that would at the same time be a valid reference-fixing description for both liberals and conservatives. What this suggests is that the criteria for determining the moral status of persons, nonpersons, or beings not clearly one or the other, are so fundamental to a morality that they are themselves reference-fixing descriptions of 'adequate moral system'.

It is relevant to consider here, however, a criticism of liberals such as Warren and Tooley by L. W. Sumner. He charges them with not grounding their criteria in some deeper moral theory. In terms of my analyses of moral statements, this seems to translate into the criticism that liberals could connect their criteria for moral status with some other reference-fixing descriptions of 'adequate moral system', and they need to do this in order to confer greater plausibility on their criteria. I am skeptical, however, of the possibility of making a connection in such a way that greater plausibility is conferred. I don't think *anyone* can do this. Consider what Sumner himself does in grounding his own criterion in a deeper moral theory. He grounds the criterion of sentience — the capacity to feel pleasure or pain, satisfaction or dissatisfaction — in the "proto-theory" of utilitarianism.[22]

This proto-theory says that the utilities of all creatures affected by an action are to be included in calculating the social utility of that action. Since all and only sentient beings have utilities, the criterion follows. But this criterion is *too* intimately bound up with Sumner's version of utilitarianism. The criterion is in effect an essential *component* of the proto-theory. What is it to say that the utilities of all creatures must count, except that the criterion for full moral status is sentience? The only way one could dispute the second but accept the first, is to claim that creatures have utilities in virtue of some properties other than sentience, or in addition to it. But Sumner is right in holding that the most plausible interpretation of utilities must connect it with sentience. Now the problem with this intimate connection between criterion and proto-theory is that "grounding" the criterion in the latter does not really provide it much more plausibility than it had in the first place. Someone inclined to reject the criterion would be inclined to reject the proto-theory. Sumner, furthermore, admits that a proto-theory of rights-centered moralities, emphasizing the supremacy of rights to autonomy, could be expected to yield criteria for moral status that require capacity for autonomous behavior. This also indicates that Sumner is not much better off than Warren and Tooley. I think, however, Sumner is right in pointing out that there are different kinds of rights-centered moralities and that some of these might be incompatible with other moral views probably held by liberals on abortion. It is unlikely, for instance, that most liberals on abortion would adhere to Nozick's libertarianism. Hence liberals need to articulate their "base" theory, but I see no reason why they could not do so satisfactorily.

If this is correct, then it is quite possible that while the liberal position is not vulnerable to disconfirmation, it cannot be justified to the conservatives in such a way that they have reason to accept and act on it. Thus Warren was making the only viable move open to liberals, which was in effect to announce that one of her reference-fixing descriptions for 'adequate moral system' is her set of five criteria for personhood. I'm sure that many liberals would be unhappy with this result. Conservatives would too, for a different reason. They want to claim that the liberal position is demonstrably false.

The only plausible conservative criticism that I have run across is the one that points out a conflict between the liberal position and commonsense views on infanticide and adult human beings who are severely retarded or who lack normal faculties of understanding for some other reason. Surely, conservatives say, it's not all right to kill these beings, yet the liberal criteria for moral status rule them out as well as fetuses.[23] This is a serious issue for liberals, but there are at least a couple of possible lines of reply open to them.

First, they could maintain that infants and those severely impaired in understanding do not have moral status, but there are other reasons for protecting their lives. Warren argues that as long as there are people who want children, a mother who does not want her infant cannot kill it but should put it up for adoption. Many in this society, furthermore, value infants and would support orphanages if adoptive parents were not readily available. Similar arguments could apply to severely impaired adults. But the arguments won't work for the prohibition of abortion because preservation of the fetus involves violation of the mother's right to freedom and self-determination.[24] Now this move will not achieve full compatibility with the commonsense view, since it is usually held that when one kills an infant

or severely impaired adult, one has directly wronged the victim, and not just others who have an interest in the victim's
life.[25] It is, however, legitimate to reply that the liberal position is not false just because it collides with common sense, and
this reply may be sufficient if I am right in believing that a set
of criteria for moral status is one of the fundamental reference-
fixing descriptions for 'adequate moral system'.

Second, liberals could make a distinction between those who
have *full* moral status and those who have *some*. Presumably, a
liberal would want to accord equal status and the full panoply
of "natural" or "human" rights to those satisfying criteria such
as those of Warren and Tooley. They may want to give some
consideration to the well-being of infants, the severely impaired in understanding, and even fetuses in the later stages of
development, as long as the important interests of normally
developed human beings took precedence over the important
interests of the others in case of conflict. The criterion for having partial moral status would be sentience. Fetuses in the later
stages of development would be accorded partial moral status
because there is evidence for their sentience at those stages.
But in case the well-being of the fetus collides with that of the
mother who wants an abortion, the mother's would take precedence. This second line of reply would involve some revision of
the liberal position. If the fetus is given any significant moral
status, even a partial one, then not any desire for abortion at
the later stages of development should be satisfied. A woman
who gets pregnant because she decided that it would be fun to
have a child but who in the fifth month decided that childbirth
would disrupt her social calendar would not have a sufficient
reason for abortion. Perhaps many liberals would accept such
a result, and if they do they would move closer to the commonsense view of infanticide.

The liberal position seems fairly secure. What about the
conservative position? The most defensible conservative criterion for full moral status is potentiality. Philip Devine says
that "there is a property, self-consciousness or use of speech for
instance" such that "it endows any organism possessing it with
a serious right to live" and such that "any organism potentially
possessing it has a serious right to life even now." Why this criterion? Devine argues that human beings are special because

they have a "specially rich kind of life." What we must protect for each full-grown adult is life in the future, since his or her present life cannot be taken away. But it is precisely a future, rich life that is possessed by the infant or fetus.[26] This criterion does seem to be an eligible candidate for a reference-fixing description of 'adequate moral system', just as Warren's and Tooley's are. The only way in which it could be undermined is through some inconsistency with other reference-fixing descriptions.

It might be argued that there must be an inconsistency because the conservative view seems to put contraception on a par with abortion. As in the case of the liberal position, there are possible lines of reply. First, the conservative could reply that contraception *is* as wrong as abortion, and that common sense is confused, perhaps because we are psychologically more inclined to identify with a being who is more like us, at least physically. It is harder to think of male and female gametes as like us. What is morally relevant, however, is the potential for a future, rich life, and gametes have that potential. Second, the conservative could try to distinguish morally between contraception and abortion by pointing out that prior to conception, there is nothing that could count as a single being with the potential for life.[27] I believe this second line of reply to be less satisfactory than the first. An ovum has the potential for rich life, since it has the potential to be fertilized by a spermatozoon. True, it is not a genetically complete member of the species, but it is a single entity with the potential. A third possible line of reply is that probabilities of development count. Abortion *is* more seriously wrong than contraception because the probability that a fetus will come to have a rich life is much, much greater than the probability that an ovum will. Should the conservative take this line, he or she must be careful to maintain that the moral status of gametes and fetuses is sufficient to justify the prohibition of abortion except in exceptional circumstances (when the mother's life is in danger, for instance). Taking this line means revision of the original conservative position that potential for a rich life confers equal status on everything possessing it, but some conservatives may find this revision congenial.

Another possible objection to the potentiality criterion is

that rights apply to their bearers in virtue of properties they *presently* possess, not what they *will* possess.[28] The conservative can make two replies. First, the relevant property fetuses possess *is* just their potential for a rich life. Second, much of the moral value of rights lies in their protection of what their bearers can do in the future. This is no less true when the right is liberty and the bearer is an adult. Hence the right to life is appropriately grounded in the *potential* for a rich life in the future.

At this point, it is relevant to mention Judith Thomson's article, "A Defense of Abortion."[29] She points out that even if we accept a conservative criterion for moral status, the fetus' right to life must be weighed against the mother's rights. She asks us to consider a case in which one person is physically connected to the body of another and is dependent for life on the other, and in which the relation is a burden to the nonconsenting host. She argues that even if both have equal rights to life, the host may not be obligated to continue providing life support to the parasite. Thus Thomson's argument leads to a policy permitting abortions in situations other than those in which the mother's life is endangered by pregnancy or childbirth.

The best conservative defense is to admit the principle of Thomson's argument, but to stress the value of the potential life in any conflict of interest between the mother and the fetus. When something less than the mother's life is at stake, the conservative may assert that the cost to the mother, in terms of liberty, setbacks in career plans, and so on, is not sufficient to override the fetus' loss of *all* potential for a rich life. In the end, this amounts to a criticism of Thomson's amount of emphasis on autonomy rights for the woman. Also, the conservative may insist that when the woman has voluntarily incurred pregnancy, she is not permitted to have an abortion unless her own life is at stake. What about pregnancies incurred despite all reasonable efforts to avoid it, such as the careful use of contraceptives? But I have already stated a conservative criterion for moral status that renders contraception wrong, though perhaps not as wrong as abortion. Given this prior result, the conservative could argue that in such a case, the woman may not have an abortion, since she has incurred pregnancy through a voluntary, wrongful act. She is responsible for the consequences.[30]

I hope I've made plausible the conclusion that the conservative and liberal positions are both defensible on the basis of well-established moral systems. Now if conservatives and liberals hold the justification principle, as very many do, then they face a difficult choice. The conservatives must weigh the justification principle against the fetus' right to life. It seems reasonable for them to consider a compromise between their conflicting *prima facie* obligations. They could refrain from the most serious violations of the justification principle — advocating legal sanctions against abortion, for instance — while utilizing other methods of opposition. Some antiabortion organizations strive to reduce the *need* for abortions by advocating public policy making it easier for women to carry a pregnancy to term. This would involve pregnancy disability benefits and better contraceptive research.[31] Liberals could refrain from pressing for public funding of abortions, since this would involve requiring conservatives to actively contribute to the violation of a deep moral belief. Liberals are free to, and should, find other ways to increase the ability of women to have abortions. They could press for health care programs that would decrease the financial impact of having an abortion, even if these programs did not fund it specifically. They might even return to a general attack on poverty.[32]

We now see how the metaethical view of moral relativism does have important implications for normative ethics once it is conjoined with certain ethical premises. And this should not be so surprising, for some of the primary moral issues of our time are raised by deep and irresolvable moral conflict. The question of how to deal with such conflict is necessarily a moral one. Almost all of the previous discussion on such conflict has been devoted to proving one or another side to be right or wrong. In the end, however, we must recognize how much of the conflict remains after articulate and forceful argument from all sides. Such a recognition cannot leave everything as it was before. We cannot find it extremely interesting as metaethicists while remaining in suspended animation as normative ethicists. And relativist arguments for tolerance do not necessarily leave us paralyzed, as Harrison and Williams feared.

13   Moral Relativity and the Problem of Equal Worth

13.1   *Why there is a problem of equal worth*

In the concluding discussion of this book, I will assume that the overwhelming majority of my audience subscribes to the principle that every human being has equal worth. A recognition of moral relativity can help us with the problem of making good on the principle of equal worth. This principle is usually taken as the basis for acknowledging that every person has certain rights (such as those to freedom and well-being) and deserves equal consideration of his or her interests. By equal consideration, I mean the assignment of equal weights in moral deliberation to interests that are equally important to the different people having them. Note that this principle does not imply that we are to treat people equally in all respects. I can't think of anyone who ever really believed such an implication. I do not regard this principle as absolute, furthermore, to be applied in an all-or-nothing fashion. It provides a reason for acting in certain ways, but under some conditions it may be outweighed by other moral principles that provide reasons for acting in other ways.

The problem of making good on the principle is twofold. First, we are very unclear about the ground of equal worth — that quality or qualities that persons possess, in virtue of which they all have value. This is not so surprising in the light of the previous discussion of abortion. Second, in our highly competitive society, where status is gained or lost with individual success or failure (to use Mead's terminology), we have great difficulty in truly believing and acting according to the principle of equal worth, even though we profess belief in it. Let me explain this twofold problem in more detail.

First, there is the problem of articulating the ground of equal worth. Gregory Vlastos has observed that recognizing the human worth of an individual is like loving one's child. Just as we do not turn indifferent or hostile toward our child when his or her achievements slump, we do not need to satisfy ourselves about the moral character of a drowning man before going to his aid. More generally, we recognize the equal worth of all human beings by holding their freedom and well-being to be equally valuable, regardless of their differing merits. Merit is a grading concept, Vlastos points out, and

there is no way of grading individuals as such. We can only grade them with respect to their qualities, hence only by abstracting from their individuality.[1]

Traditionally, it has been assumed that human beings have equal worth in virtue of some quality all possess regardless of differing merits. Most popular is the Kantian view that the quality is rationality. The reason that one ought to treat humanity as an end in itself and never as a means only is that humanity has a worth that is beyond calculation, and it has that worth in virtue of its rational nature.[2] One problem with this view, however, is that rationality is very likely an unequal capacity and cannot be the ground of equal worth. Contemporary philosophers who have worked within the Kantian tradition respond to this problem in common ways. They pick out some aspect of rationality and claim that the possession of this aspect to a certain minimum degree is sufficient or both necessary and sufficient for the possession of human worth. Differences among individuals who fall above the minimum are not relevant to the question of their human worth.

John Rawls, for instance, proposes that the quality of being a moral person is a sufficient condition for being entitled to equal justice. This quality is defined as the capability of having a conception of one's good (as expressed by a rational plan of life) and of having a sense of justice (a normally effective desire to apply and act on principles of justice). He admits that different individuals have the quality in varying degrees, but maintains that having the quality to some minimum degree is sufficient. He does not specify the minimum, except to say that no race or recognized group of human beings lacks it.[3]

A major weakness of this view is that it appears to draw an arbitrary line. If having the capabilities of a moral person to a minimum degree is crucial to one's moral status, why is the question of varying degrees of capability irrelevant once we go beyond the required minimum? If an animal is not entitled to justice because it does not have the requisite capabilities to the minimum degree, why aren't human beings who have these capabilities to a lesser degree than others also less entitled to justice than the others? If it is answered that the gap between human beings and animals is much wider than any of those between individual human beings, it can be replied that differences in moral status between human beings do not have to be wide in order to be differences. So why not have a moral hierarchy in which animals are on the bottom and human beings way above, and in which some human beings are higher than others?

Alan Gewirth tries to head off this sort of objection in defending his view of which aspect of rationality is the ground of human worth. He believes that the basis is "the quality of being a prospective agent who has purposes he wants to fulfill." The quality involves the abilities to control one's behavior by one's unforced choice, to have knowledge of relevant circumstances, and to reflect on one's purposes. He uses the phrase "prospective agent" because he wants to refer to any one who is or *will* in the future take action to fulfill his purposes. Prospective agency is necessary and sufficient for the possession of equal, "generic" rights to freedom and well-being. Gewirth acknowledges that animals largely lack the capabilities necessary for prospective agency, that children have them only potentially, and that mentally deficient persons can only attain them in part. Hence there are "degrees of approach" to full-fledged agency. But, says, Gewirth, this does not imply that there are degrees of being a prospective agent, "at least in the respect in which this quality is relevant to the justification of having the generic rights." The reason why people have rights to freedom and well-being is that they are prospective agents who want to fulfill their own purposes, and wanting to fulfill purposes is not the same as having the ability to fulfill them through action. The fact, therefore, that some have superior abilities cannot justify giving them superior rights.[4]

Gewirth has a point: that there are degrees of approach to being a prospective agent does not imply that there are degrees of wanting purposes fulfilled. But he seems to conclude that there are no degrees of wanting purposes fulfilled that are relevant to the justification of having rights. There are, however, degrees of wanting purposes fulfilled among prospective agents, even if this is not implied by the existence of degrees of approach to being a prospective agent. Part of the reason why children and mentally deficient persons approach but do not attain full-fledged prospective agency is that they have yet to form well-defined desires or are incapable of doing so. They do not yet know or cannot know what they want in many areas of their lives. Prospective agents differ in how well-defined their desires are. Some people know what they want better than others do. That is partly why some succeed in life more than others. It could be argued within the framework of Gewirth's theory that a person can only claim a right to something to the degree that he or she is capable of forming a well-defined desire for it. Gewirth thus fails to explain why differences in prospective agency cease to make a difference once we go beyond the required minimum.

Other views of the ground of human worth suffer the same weakness. Utilitarians say that the capacity to suffer is the ground. But as Joel Feinberg points out, some are naturally more sensitive than others. A more serious weakness, he argues, is that some presumptive violations of human rights may cause no suffering, such as the painless murder of a man with no family or friends.[5]

If all attempts fail to ground human worth in some quality, then we must look for an alternative view of how we come to accord worth to all. Feinberg hints at a promising alternative: human worth is groundless and unconditional. To accord equal worth to people is not to attribute a quality to them but is "a kind of ultimate attitude not itself justifiable in more ultimate terms." I take it that the sort of attitude he has in mind involves a resolution to care for human beings in such a way that one accords certain rights to them and considers their interests equally. Admittedly, the idea of applying this attitude to villains and strangers can be somewhat mysterious to us. Feinberg hopes, however, that most of us are disposed to fall into this attitude when we look at our fellows in a certain way.[6] To characterize that way, he makes use of Bernard Williams' conception of the "human point of view." To look at people from the human point of view is to look at them from *their* point of view, being concerned with what it is for them to have their lives and to do their actions, in their characters.[7] It contrasts with looking at people from a technical or professional point of view, evaluating someone as a failed philosopher, for instance.

Now a possible objection to this proposal is brought to mind by the discussion on abortion. Surely, we must take some position on what qualities a being must have to be worthy of the treatment we accord to normal adult human beings. We would have to do this to take any position on abortion. Doesn't this rule out the sort of attitude Feinberg suggests? A way out of this bind is to regard ourselves as taking a groundless and unconditional attitude toward the class of beings who have full moral status, the boundaries of that class being partially defined by our position on issues such as abortion. For instance, a liberal on abortion need not regard self-awareness and the possession of desire as the ground of human worth in order to take the position that it is only toward beings with such qualities toward whom he or she will take the unconditional attitude. Then why should one draw the boundaries where one does? As we have seen in the discussion on abortion, there seems to be no further justification. This seems to be another ultimate attitude, and that is why the conflict over abortion seems so deep and irreconcilable.

This suggestion may be viewed with alarm. If according equal worth to persons means taking a groundless and unconditional attitude toward them, and if the way one draws the boundaries of the class of persons is ultimately groundless, aren't we vulnerable to those perfectionists and elitists who would draw the boundaries to exclude not only fetuses, but people with IQs below average, or weaklings? But we have this problem whether or not we adopt the suggestion, since we cannot say what it is about human beings that would confer equal worth on them. To adopt the suggestion I have made is to conclude that it is a mistake to look for help in the battle against perfectionists and elitists in some moral fact of the matter that they must accept. Rather than preach against them with rhetoric that will only convince the converted, we had better understand why people are tempted to adopt such positions and what needs are fulfilled by doing so, and we had better find other ways of meeting those needs. Lacking such knowledge, we had better find a way to keep them from power.

13.2   *The costs of according unequal worth*

I now want to argue that consideration of the other aspect of the problem of according equal worth will give us some additional motivation for taking Feinberg's view of what it is to accord equal worth. Sociologists Richard Sennett and Jonathan Cobb have called for something like Feinberg's view, based on their observations of the actual human costs of our present inability to truly believe and act as if every person has equal worth.

One of the costs is illustrated by an interview with a janitor who says self-disparagingly, "You don't need no degrees to clean." He is deeply ashamed because he feels he should have been a better person. They interview other workers with simple, repetitive jobs that make them feel powerless. A natural defense against taking orders all the time is to pretend that one is not there on the job, to daydream. Workers are often ashamed of their need for such a defense. They feel that "If they had more drive and commitment, they wouldn't feel so absent, they would make something of themselves." A senior foreman for an aerospace firm calls the people who work under him "drones"—a homogeneous mass lacking the abilities that would distinguish any of them. He places himself a

little above them, but because he is held responsible to his
superiors for people he disrespects, he disrespects his own
work.[8] These interviews suggest that if the possession of a
valued ability is made the ground of human worth, many people will lack the precious good of self-respect. John Rawls has
correctly characterized self-respect as perhaps the most important "primary social good," without which a person has little
motivation to make life satisfying.

To avoid damage to self-respect, one must perform well,
move on to better jobs. But performing well has costs. It involves doing better than coworkers. Sennett and Cobb describe
the dilemma of one particular worker:

If he demonstrates his ability to the full, he stands out as an individual, not merely losing the affection of his comrades but, by becoming
an example of the unusual person who is hard-working, putting them
in the shade. His sensitivity to the prospect of shaming others leads
him to hold himself back. But holding himself back, he makes himself feel weak . . . he comes to feel that if only he were a more competent person, he could solve the dilemma.[9]

The pursuit of self-respect even distorts what people come to
want for themselves. Studies of career choice among college
students show that they make their decisions in great part on
the basis of what they do well, rather than what they enjoy.
They are afraid of doing things they think they would enjoy for
fear they would not be any better at these things than other
people. A career becomes a means to respect rather than an
end in itself.[10]

Making ability the ground of worth has costs in areas of life
outside of work. Many of the people Sennett and Cobb inter-
viewed moved away from the extended family and the ethnic
neighborhoods in which they grew up, because they wanted to
show upward mobility and because the lack of independence
at work made them feel constricted by the intimate social relationships formed within the extended family and ethnic neighborhoods. The cost is a loss of the support and liveliness provided by these groups. Another common way of compensating
for work that does damage to self-respect is to give that work

meaning by conceiving of it as a sacrifice for loved ones. People who do not think much of themselves because of their jobs can at least tell themselves that they are working so that their children will have better lives. But for them, this sacrifice takes on the painful emotional meaning that if they succeed, their children will not be like them. Sometimes the act of sacrifice gets used as a moral weapon in intergenerational strife. Men demand blind obedience of their wives and children. Anything less would be "ingratitude."[11]

What is to be done about these costs of making ability the ground of worth? One possibility is to increase efforts to give people the opportunity to acquire the ability needed for jobs they are not ashamed of having. Another is to give them more of a voice in production decisions so that they can feel they are making more of a contribution. Sennett and Cobb believe, however, that a more radical change is needed. They call for an "image of human dignity without a face" so that we may accord ourselves dignity as an "act of faith." They argue that "to define what is dignified about mankind . . . sets up the machinery of individualism, for every man enters into the comparative process in order to be rewarded by feeling, and being treated as, a person with dignity."[12]

It is not difficult to see why Sennett and Cobb would think an entirely new view of respect is needed. As long as we have the old one, we will continue to compare ourselves with others and respect ourselves more or less accordingly. If having a valued ability is necessary for respect, having more or less ability will always mean having more or less respect. So even if the people Sennett and Cobb describe are helped to become better competitors in the pursuit of respect, there will still be winners and losers in the competition. In any case, it is arguable that a society in which there is competition for self-respect will not be a place where those who are currently winning will provide substantial and sustained help to those currently losing. Sennett and Cobb believe we must get away from the idea that there must be winners and losers in the pursuit of respect, and this means getting away from the view that respect is deserved in virtue of some quality that can be possessed.

The conclusions of the previous section confirm this reasoning. The qualities that have been proposed by philosophers as the grounds of human worth are possessed by individuals in varying degrees. The view that human worth is grounded in some quality thus provides the opportunity for the kind of comparison and competition for respect that Sennett and Cobb describe.

13.3   *Moral relativity, Taoism, and equal worth*

It is one thing to describe a new view of what it is to accord equal worth to every person. It is quite another thing to truly adopt it. We have a deep tendency to "enter the comparative process" and compete for worth. And yet taking a new view seems the only alternative to having an egalitarian ethic that has inegalitarian consequences, both in philosophical theory and in everyday life. To truly adopt the attitude that human worth is groundless and unconditional, we need to be able to care for people independently of our evaluations of them. We need to be able to "suspend" our evaluative categories and look at them from what Williams called "the human point of view." We will be able to do this more easily if we realize that these categories are not written into the nature of things but in fact are social creations, developed in response to human needs. The recognition of moral relativity helps us to this realization. This line of reasoning is not new, at least in Chinese philosophy. It is a primary theme of Taoism, the other major, native Chinese philosophy besides Confucianism.

According to Taoism, our tendency to evaluate ourselves and each other according to our abilities is part of a larger tendency to order our experience of the world through the use of conceptual categories. We identify objects and persons, distinguishing them from each other by subsuming them under categories. We evaluate objects and persons, comparing them with each other by subsuming them under categories such as "better than." We give ourselves locations and identities within our ordering schemes by subsuming ourselves under categories, including evaluative ones. Confucianism is a philosophical representative of the tendency to order and evaluate. Its vision of the proper social order contains social roles that are well-defined by *i* (righteousness) and *li* (rules of propriety), both of which specify rules and privileges appropriate to the roles.

To help us look at the world without the mediation of *evaluative* categories, Taoism attempts to bring us to a recognition of moral relativity. The Taoist classic *Chuang Tzu* refers to the debate between the Confucians and the Mohists (another philosophical school that in some respects is similar to Western utilitarianism). The Confucians emphasize the importance of filial obligations while the Mohists emphasize the importance of loving all impartially. The former will ask, "Would you really neglect your duties to your parents to aid strangers?" The latter will say, "These strangers are someone's parents or children." According to Taoism, moral theories emphasize one of a pair of opposing values, such as impartial love and love with distinctions. None can claim to have captured the absolute truth, because there is none. The *Chuang Tzu* is full of illustrations of this strategy of shocking us out of our usual perspectives by getting us to assume different ones. For instance, it periodically attacks our anthropocentric, utilitarian perspective. It describes a big, useless, ugly tree, the trunk so distorted and full of knots, the branches so crooked, that no carpenter has a use for it. It is so useless that no one will ever cut it down: "Axes will never shorten its life, nothing can ever harm it. If there's no use for it, how can it come to grief or pain?"[13] We read of men who sing and play music upon the death of loved ones or close friends; the conventional attitudes toward death are dismissed as wrong-headed.

Now it might be charged that if our belief in the objective validity of our categories is undermined, we will fall into nihilism. Taoism replies with an attack on the sacred cow of morality itself. "What is so good about respecting moral rules?" asks the *Chuang Tzu*. Rules are general, vague, ambiguous. If our respect for our fellows comes down to a respect for rules telling us to do so, we can very easily twist the rules to our own advantage:

Fashion benevolence and righteousness to reform people and they will steal with benevolence and righteousness. How do I know this is so? He who steals a belt buckle pays with his life; he who steals a state gets to be a feudal lord — and we all know that benevolence and righteousness are to be found at the gates of the feudal lords. Is this not a case of stealing benevolence and righteousness and the wisdom of the sages?[14]

The *Chuang Tzu* urges us to "forget (*wang*)" morality.[15] This does not mean that we are to lose all awareness of moral categories or that we should not use them in guiding conduct. We must allow for the characteristic hyperbole of Taoism. What it does mean is that we should not make respect for rules the primary foundation of respect for human beings. We should cultivate the part of us that spontaneously identifies with others, the state of consciousness in which the boundaries between self and others fall away. That state is *tz'u,* sometimes translated as "compassion" or "deep love." *Tz'u* gives rise to unpremeditated aid to others when they are in distress, not aid given because it is a moral duty. The idea is that once we are able to suspend looking at people through our evaluative categories, we will be able to accept them for what they are, see them as beings like ourselves, and care for them as we care for ourselves.

13.4 *Social structures conducive to the attitude of according equal worth*

We have been talking on an abstract level about ways to develop our ability to suspend the use of evaluative categories. Staying on this abstract level is inadequate. Even if everyone were educated in the Taoist classics, and for good measure were compelled to study my argument for moral relativity, we would not be assured that the recognition of moral relativity would be sufficiently vivid and sustained to produce the desired effect. What is the answer? We could make confrontation with a diversity of moral perspectives a regular part of our lives and not just a part of the body of our knowledge. We could promote social structures that provide increased opportunities to interact with people whose perspectives are very different from ours. The idea is to switch evaluative lenses with them to lessen our dependence on lenses in general. There have been times and places where opportunities for such interaction have been realities. For instance, the densely-packed American city of the 1920s and '30s was a place where the individual was confronted with many different worlds of ethnicity, social class, and race.

A place to start confronting ourselves with diversity is the school. It is not hard to envision how changes in curriculum could introduce children to the variety of value and custom in their ethnic backgrounds. Also, increased integration of schools would allow students to confront differences not only in their studies but in each other. Confrontation with moral diversity could be encouraged in the larger society by facilitating community participation in the running of schools. Parents, students, teachers, and administrators of a diverse community would confront each other with their different conceptions of excellence and of students' needs, and work together. Ideally, school districts should be structured to be both small and diverse, with significant minority representation. Other suggestions for increasing the diversity of communities come from Richard Sennett in another of his works, *The Uses of Disorder* (his reasons for wanting to increase diversity did not involve the problem of equal worth). He recommends doing away with zoning regulations that determine in advance how an area is to be used and who lives in it. For example, he envisions a neighborhood of young people, blue-collar workers, older people, businesses, and restaurants. There would be tension and conflict, but an individual would be more likely to understand "differences in other people whom he may not like, and who may not like him."[16]

It would be politically unrealistic to recommend doing away with zoning regulations everywhere in the city. Besides, it is contrary to Taoism to force different kinds of people to live with each other. But in certain kinds of neighborhoods, there would be the opportunity for people to live with diversity. An example of such a neighborhood is one in which there is low-income housing, a significant minority population, and people from the middle and upper classes who have bought and upgraded apartments or houses. The recommended policy would be to encourage and maintain the natural mix of housing, businesses, and people in such a neighborhood. To those who fear intolerable conflict and violence, especially between the races, Sennett correctly points out that mixed neighborhoods compare quite favorably with isolated homogeneous ones on that score.[17] He also recommends that we take advantage of high-density living areas, high rises, for instance, by distributing public meeting places throughout. In such areas, there will be so many people that it will be impossible for any majority to pressure anyone into a single pattern of conformity.

When these attempts to encourage diversity are made, it is important at the same time to encourage the decentralization of power and authority. Diversity will do no good unless people actually discover it in one another and *deal* with it. Sennett points out that people can get used to relying upon a centralized, remote authority to settle conflicts within their own neighborhoods. It is encouraging to note, however, that there has been increasing disillusionment with centralized authority, along with a corresponding renewal of interest in such ideas as forming block and neighborhood organizations to deal with common problems, such as crime control, health care, job creation, and housing rehabilitation. In New York City, thousands of such groups appeared from 1975 to 1978.[18] Support could be offered to these groups, especially when they address themselves to problems that previously have been the preserve of governmental bureaucracies.

There are other ways to encourage decentralization of decision-making, even when complex and difficult matters of public policy are involved, matters requiring technical competence or specialized knowledge. Affected groups could decide on parameters that go into the process of decision-making—those that don't require expertise. On a small scale, this idea is illustrated by student evaluations going into a tenure decision. On a larger scale, some social or educational programs have been evaluated for federal funding agencies by a process that includes the participation of the different groups affected by the programs.

To sum up: the problem of according equal worth to every person has led us to the idea of the groundless and unconditional attitude that every person has worth, which led us to the Taoist idea that recognition of moral relativity could be useful in promoting that attitude, which finally led us to the picture of a diverse society in which power and authority is decentralized. The idea is that if we must live with people who have conflicting evaluative standards, we might very well be less likely to let success or failure in meeting our own standards determine our fundamental attitudes toward ourselves and others. There will be fewer who will continue to impose conditions on their acceptance of the worth of others and themselves. Now the society I am picturing also must be conducive to compassion, and I am not as optimistic as the Taoists were when they said that *tz'u* is a natural part of our nature. They may be right if the sociobiologists are right (and altruistic behavior is innately based), but my inclination is to believe that compassion and sympathetic identification must be cultivated by social structure. I do agree that these dispositions, and not a respect for moral rules as such, must form the base of a morality. We, therefore, need to explore ways in which these dispositions are cultivated by social structure.

Now I admit that as a philosopher I am making these claims about what would happen or could very well happen in a diverse, decentralized society with some trepidation. I am not a psychologist or sociologist. On the other hand, I don't think psychologists or sociologists have definitive answers to what could happen in such a society, because we have yet to see such a society fully realized. What I am offering are reasons for engaging in some social experimentation. That is the only way we can gain the kind of knowledge that will generate definitive answers. Social philosophers cannot live on conceptual analysis alone, or if they do, I fear they will not have much to say to others.

It is instructive to see how this picture of society differs from the social ideal of democratic pluralism as it has developed primarily in the United States. According to democratic pluralism, tolerance and mutual acceptance should be exercised between religious, ethnic, and economic groups. It assumes, however, that members of each group are united by their adherence to a common set of values. The society pictured here, on the contrary, will seek to end the isolation of the individual within such uniform groups. It will not deliberately break up uniform groups but will encourage the individual to become a member of other, internally diverse groups. The aim is to have members of internally diverse groups exercise mutual acceptance with respect to each other, even though no set of values is shared.

Because of this difference, the present picture avoids certain objections that have been made against democratic pluralism. Robert Paul Wolff has charged that application of democratic pluralism in American society has resulted in bias—in favor of established and powerful groups at the expense of new and less powerful groups. For instance, organized labor and big business have their interests protected through the law in many ways. Small businessmen and nonunion labor are much less fortunate. The government is supposed to referee conflicts of interest between different groups in a fair and neutral way, but in reality it enforces the preferences of the established and powerful. Wolff also charges that democratic pluralism misleads us into assuming that all fundamental social ills are the result of inequality between conflicting interest groups. There are some problems that affect the good of all alike, such as the despoiling of our environment's natural beauty, the threat to public order caused by increasing crime, and the need to cultivate the arts.[19] The present picture is not liable to these objections, because it does not portray society as an arena of competing groups, each with its own set of common interests. Instead, an individual belongs to at least some groups that contain diverse and often conflicting interests and values. This discourages bias in favor of certain groups at the expense of others, since members of one internally diverse group are liable to have as much in common with members of other groups as they have with members of their own. The internal diversity of such groups would also make it more difficult for a government to enforce the preferences of groups. And finally, if members of each such group learn to work with each other despite their considerable differences, they are more likely to recognize that there are common problems for all.

13.5 *Taoism reconsidered*

By now, many readers familiar with Chinese philosophy will have been surprised to see Taoism pressed into the service of an egalitarian social philosophy. Many see it as the philosophy of the recluse who rejects involvement in human affairs and goes into the wilderness or mountains to commune with the One — the Tao, the ultimate reality that embraces all that is. We are reminded of all the Taoist-inspired landscape paintings of one or two very small human beings gazing at a waterfall or into the far and empty distance while standing on a cliff's edge or on a mountain trail. It is undeniable that Taoism — particularly the *Chuang Tzu* — presents such a face to us at times. This philosophy, however, which purports to be the simplest of all philosophies, has many faces.

The other Taoist classic, the *Tao Te Ching,* is a treatise on the art of ruling. It speaks positively of a spontaneous caring for all the people: *tz'u* helps the ruler to be courageous, to win in the case of attack, and to be firm in the case of defense.[20] It says that the sage does not accumulate for himself, that the more he gives to others the more he possesses, that the Way of Heaven is to benefit others and not to injure.[21] And it warns the ruler that the people starve because he eats too much tax-grain and that they will take death lightly when he strives for life too vigorously.[22] This face of Taoism is compatible with an egalitarian social philosophy.

The Taoist ruler, furthermore, will be aware of the sentiments of his people: "the sage, in the government of his empire, has no subjective viewpoint./His mind forms a harmonious whole with that of his people."[23] While it is true that he governs as little as possible and lets the people take care of their affairs, he will at times find it necessary to take action. When he does, his grasp of the people's sentiments will allow him to act in such a way as to take advantage of the people's energies instead of running up against them: "in order to be ahead of the people,/One must, in one's own person, follow them."[24] This face of Taoism is consistent with a social philosophy in which rulers take positive action to alleviate social ills, or at least as much as is consistent with the theme of decentral-ization whenever possible.

It is understandable how a Taoist may turn away from soci-ety, seeing it to be full of folly. But other people are as much a part of the Tao as waterfalls and mountains. To turn away from them is not to accept all that is. The Taoist may come to realize that a tranquility that can be achieved only at the cost of isolating oneself from fellow human beings is a fragile and false tranquility, that it is as unnatural to place oneself apart from them as it is to place oneself above them. It is plausible, therefore, to say that Taoism forms the core of a social philoso-phy. By outlining the sort of social organization that would be conducive to the attitudes of suspending evaluative categories, of accepting oneself and others, this paper has extended Tao-ism into a more fully realized social philosophy.

In evaluating my use of Taoism here, it is essential for the reader to remember that I am not advocating that we simply forsake evaluative categories. To "forget" morality is not to lose the ability to see self and others in terms of these cate-gories, but it is to acquire the ability to suspend the use of these categories at the appropriate times. The point is best brought out by considering why we cannot take literally one of the most frequently repeated themes of Taoism: that the innocence of one who immediately identifies with others in *tz'u* and who is able to suspend the use of evaluative categories is like the inno-cence of the infant who has no conception of self as distinct from others. Hence the Taoist advice to "forget self." But the innocence of adulthood cannot be identical to the innocence of the infant, because the adult *transcends* the self while never losing it entirely. Nor is a complete loss of self desirable. The categories by which we locate ourselves in the world are neces-sary for function in the everyday world. A Taoist ruler must be able to employ these categories in governing and defending his people. So must the people in governing and defending them-selves. When it is time to recognize and express respect for the worth of all human beings, the categories are suspended. When it is time to pick someone for a difficult and important job, evaluative categories are put to use. The transcendence of self is the fullest adulthood, rather than original infancy.

Let me put it another way. To transcend the self, a self must be formed — a sense of who one is and where one belongs. It is necessary, therefore, to have along with Taoism other philosophies and psychologies that articulate an understanding of how an individual comes to form an identity that he or she is eventually able to transcend, and that compassion of *tz'u* is an important motivation for him or her. To return to Chinese philosophy, some think that when practiced wisely Confucianism will lead to such an identity. That is why there is great significance in the saying that every Chinese is at once a Taoist and a Confucian.

In any case, I hope that I have delivered on the promise of the first chapter and have shown that the recognition of moral relativity can be part of a larger social philosophy. Nothing normative follows from the doctrine alone, but once we recognize it we must integrate it with the rest of our moral concerns. This book is an attempt to argue for its recognition. The last two chapters constitute the beginning of its integration with those concerns.

Appendix A

In my characterization of the reason for moral rules, I am opting for what Frankena calls the "material" conception of morality. This conception identifies morality as an action-guide with a subject matter that pertains to interpersonal relations. Frankena contrasts the material conception with a "formal" conception, which implies that A has a morality if and only if (1) A takes it as prescriptive, (2) A regards it as capable of being universalized, and (3) A regards it as a "definitive, final, overriding, or supremely authoritative."[1] Of course, (1) would be included under a material conception, so the issue is whether (2) and (3) are necessary conditions or sufficient when combined with (1).

Those who believe the formal conditions to be sufficient argue that if we require (1) we would arbitrarily rule out as nonmoral the prevailing action-guides of some cultures. If John Ladd is right in his interpretation of the Navajo, for instance, the closest thing they have to a morality is a form of egoism in which all rules have the ultimate point of advancing the welfare of the agent to which they are addressed.[2] Advocates of the formal conception take (2) and (3) to be necessary because they believe what is commonly regarded as morality is distinguished from other action-guides by these conditions.

Frankena is inclined toward a combination of the material conception and some elements of the formal one. He asks us to make sure that action-guides such as those of the Navajo are truly egoistic and then asserts that if they are they should not be called moral. He also points out that prudential and aesthetic action-guides are usually regarded as nonmoral. He accepts (2) as a necessary condition but rejects (3) on the grounds that it makes sense to ask the question, "Why be moral?" That question wouldn't make sense if to have a morality is to regard it as supremely authoritative.

None of the arguments on either side is conclusive. It is within the realm of possibility to suppose that a group or society could lack a morality, so it is not a strong argument against the material conception that it might imply that the Navajo lack a morality. On the other hand, our common beliefs about morality are not as clear in their implications on this matter as Frankena believes. It is common practice to give "prudential" grounds for conforming to what are commonly regarded moral rules. When parents teach what are commonly regarded moral rules to their children, they often try to convince their children that it is to their ultimate advantage to obey the rules. When morality becomes closely associated with religion, furthermore, the rules are often enforced by divine reward and punishment. Do we want to say that those who are moved to moral behavior by thoughts of the hereafter do not have a morality? Bernard Williams argues that it is unrealistic to hold that there is an exclusive disjunction between moral and prudential motivation. And what about a person, he also asks, who does something in the interests of another and to his own disadvantage because he loves that person, or because he admires him, or respects him, or is a member of his family?[3] None of these reasons has to be either moral or prudential.

Consider Frankena's argument that a conception of morality should enable us to make sense of the question, "Why should I be moral?" It is Prichard's opinion that we shouldn't be able to make sense of the question, that recognizing an action as one's moral duty is just to recognize it as that which one ought to do unqualifiedly and all things considered.[4] There are people who share Prichard's view, but others who do not, who can recognize an action as a moral duty but decide they have reasons not to perform it. These reasons may be based on personal ambition. A student who cheats on a test may admit it to be wrong but feel he cannot afford to be moral given the intense compe-

tition to get into law school. What this suggests is that there is
no common, shared conception of morality to which we may
appeal in trying to decide between a material and a formal
conception.

The issue will remain unresolved as long as we do not ask
which other issues of importance depend on the classification
of an action-guide as a morality. Let us consider the issue of
whether the formal conception is sufficient. Suppose we
eliminate as nonmoral those action-guides that do not require
an agent to consider the interests of others. Why does this matter? For one thing, it reduces the variety of moralities. If we are
interested in deciding whether there is a single true morality,
we need not consider the purely self-regarding action-guide as
a candidate. This move is perfectly legitimate if what we want
to know is whether there is a single true morality among the
ones based on rules requiring the individual to adjust his or her
motivational nature and conduct in consideration of the interests of others. Oppositely, if in asking whether there is a single
true morality we want to know whether there is one action-
guide that is rational for everyone to use, there is good reason
not to arbitrarily exclude a purely egoistic guide from consideration.

Both issues are legitimate and worth addressing, but we
need to decide which we are addressing at a given time. In this
book I shall opt for the material conception. It is worth knowing whether there is one true morality that requires social concern, whether or not there is one action-guide that is rational
for everyone to use. Even if it were rational for some to forgo
acting in the interests of others, the rest of us would want to
know whether there is a single true morality based on rules
requiring social concern.

Now, should we require that a morality be regarded as overriding and supremely authoritative by those who have it? To
do so would be to rule out an issue of importance to many of us
—whether or not an action-guide that requires social concern
should be our supreme guide. Granted that the issue is a non-
issue to those who share Prichard's views, there are enough of
us who think the other way to merit putting the issue on the
table.

Should we add a condition of capacity to be universalized to the material conception? This condition is usually taken to require that a set of rules contain no essential reference to particular agents or patients (those who are acted upon) by way of proper names or definite descriptions. That is, any rule containing such terms must be reformulable in such a way that the terms are replaced by general descriptions. The intuitive rationale is that there must be some general reason why one person should have a duty to act in a certain way while another person does not and a general reason why it is all right to treat one person in a certain way but not all right to treat another person in a different way. The problem with imposing such a condition is that it prevents consideration of some important issues.

Anthropologists and social historians observe that many societies limit the application of prescriptive action-guides that require social concern to members *within* their own societies or to certain classes within their societies. Thus it was permissible to enslave people who fell outside the favored groups but not permissible to do that within the groups. It may be that the discrimination between "in-groups" and "out-groups" is always founded on some sort of error—on mistaken beliefs about the capacities and traits of "inferior" peoples, for instance—but surely that claim cannot be accepted *a priori*. It is at least a possibility that some of the societies in question do not have a condition of capacity to be universalized, that they do not recognize the need to justify the differences in their treatment of people outside the in-group. If we declare that they do not have a morality for that reason, we eliminate a potential kind of diversity in moral beliefs across societies that would be relevant to the issue of absolutism versus relativism. In fact, moralities that can be universalized may be a minority among those action-guides satisfying the material conception. It is possible, furthermore, that the absence of capacity to be universalized is connected with more fundamental features of an action-guide that affect the content of its rules.

Appendix B

Peter Winch's view of magic is similar in some respects to Beattie's but is based on a general theory of rationality and culture. His view is of special interest because it seems to be a rather strong violation of Grandy's principle of humanity. He says that practices such as magic must be viewed in the context of culture and that culture may supply criteria of rationality justifying those practices:

We must, if you like, be open to new possibilities of what could be invoked and accepted under the rubric of 'rationality' — possibilities which are suggested and limited by what we have hitherto so accepted, but not uniquely determined thereby.[1]

Let us consider why Winch believes we do have to do this in the case of the Azande. When he describes the differences between Zande and Western attitudes toward the world, he talks about a difference between conceptions of good and evil, about different ways of making sense of human life. More concretely, he connects our difficulty in understanding Zande rites performed in connection with the growing and harvesting of crops with our inability to think about such matters except in terms of efficiency of production.[2]

   Do the Azande have different criteria of rationality because they do not have as primary goals scientific understanding and efficiency of production? Certainly, we judge the rationality of belief by criteria that have been influenced by science. That is why we (or most of us) dismiss astrology or crystal balls. We want to form beliefs through reliable methods that provide for testing through observation, directly or indirectly. It is plausible enough, therefore, that the Azande do not use some of our criteria for rational belief if Winch is correct in ascribing to them a purpose that conflicts with that of prediction and control. Winch's interpretation, however, makes intelligible the Azande's refusal to reject magic in the face of undermining observational evidence by attributing to them that other purpose. Their refusal is made to appear rational in the widest sense of answering to some purpose. What we have here is not so much a *new* set of criteria for rational belief but a society in which some of our criteria do not have valid application or in which their application is modified in accordance with purposes different from the ones that would motivate their straightforward application.

It is instructive to note that Winch never provides us with *new* criteria for rational belief that are genuine rivals to ours. The Azande do seem to feel the need to make their system of beliefs in magic an internally coherent one. Events that make their rites appear to "work" are taken as confirming instances, and they have a method of explaining away what we would take as disconfirming instances. It is not as if they simply accept such instances as disconfirming and leave it at that. When a Zande consults an oracle and what is foretold does not come about, he may explain that the oracle itself has been influenced by witchcraft or that the question posed was one that could not have been answered by a simple 'yes' or 'no' answer required by the oracle.[3]

As for efficiency of production, it is at best an exaggeration to say that it is rational *per se* to be as concerned with this goal as we have become. There are too many in our own culture who believe that we have gone too far in promoting this goal. Indeed, the anthropologist Robin Horton explains that his decision to live in "still-heavily traditional Africa" lies in the "discovery of things lost at home," including an "intensely poetic quality in everyday life and thought, and a vivid enjoyment of the passing moment" that have been driven out of sophisticated Western life by "the faith in progress."[4] African tribespeople are concerned with producing enough to sustain themselves and their children; they value physical well-being, but surely it is rational to be concerned with the costs of introducing new techniques and modes of organization that promise more of these goods.

The upshot of this discussion of Winch's claims is that fundamental differences in the network of relations among propositional attitudes and the world need not correspond to fundamental differences in criteria of rationality. It seems that we make intelligible the way in which the Azande differ from us by ascribing the basic forms of rationality to them.[5]

Notes

Chapter 1. Introduction to the Strategy of Argument for Moral Relativity and Its Normative Implications

1. Iris Murdoch, *The Sovereignty of the Good* (New York: Schocken Books, 1971), pp. 17-18.

2. 'Absolutist' is sometimes applied to the view that no ineliminable *prima facie* clauses need be present in the statement of moral principles. I do not mean to use the term in this way.

3. John Rawls, "The Independence of Moral Theory," Presidential address to the APA, *Proceedings and Addresses of the APA* 48 (1974-75), p. 7.

Chapter 2. The Importance of Moral Truth

1. Stevenson also gives a "second pattern of analysis" for moral statements, attributing to 'ought' and 'good' a "descriptive meaning," in which properties other than being approved or disapproved by the speaker are attributed to actions, persons, or objects. My criticism of Stevenson, however, is unaffected by this additional analysis. See C. L. Stevenson, *Ethics and Language* (New Haven: Yale University Press, 1944), pp. 20-23, 81-110 for the first pattern; pp. 206-226 for the second pattern.

2. George Pitcher, "On Approval," *Philosophical Review* 67 (1958), pp. 195-211.

3. J. O. Urmson has argued that "This is good" and "I approve of this" cannot be identified, even if the impersonal element in approval is recognized. He points out that one can say "I approve of this, but maybe it is not good." What one would mean is that the reasons one has for approval may be mistaken or outweighed by other considerations. Urmson concludes that "This is good" means "It is correct to approve of this." See his *The Emotive Theory of Ethics* (New York: Oxford University Press, 1968), pp. 58-59.

4. R. M. Hare, *The Language of Morals* (London: Oxford University Press, 1964), pp. 190-191.

5. Hare, *Language of Morals*, pp. 137-197.

6. These analyses are meant to capture the so-called "evaluative meaning" of moral terms. In Hare's view, one has not adequately explained the meaning of 'ought' or 'good' until one has explained how it is used to perform the speech acts they are typically used to perform. His analysis of 'ought' shows how it is used to prescribe an action for a prospective agent. His analysis of 'good' shows how it is used to commend a member of a class.

7. We must distinguish between conclusions that are compatible with Hare's analysis and those conclusions Hare himself has drawn. He does not admit of much significant moral relativity because he believes our choice of 'ought' principles is severely constrained by human nature and the capacity of moral principles to be universalized. If one subscribes to a *moral* principle, one must be ready to apply it to oneself as well as to others, and one must be willing to apply it in all sorts of hypothetical situations in which one finds oneself in the place of others. Until recently, Hare believed that human nature is such that for all but a few "fanatics" there is just a narrow range of principles that would pass this test. See his *Freedom and Reason* (London: Oxford University Press, 1963), p. 192. In "Ethical Theory and Utilitarianism," in *Contemporary British Philosophy*, ed. H. D. Lewis (London: Allen and Unwin, 1976), however, Hare seems to have moved to the position that the fanatic is a defective universalizer.

8. There is, of course, a technical definition of satisfaction that would be out of place here. See Alfred Tarski, "The Concept of Truth in Formalized Languages," in *Logic, Semantics, and Metamathematics* (New York: Oxford University Press, 1956); for a nontechnical introduction, see his "The Semantic Conception of Truth," *Philosophy and Phenomenological Research* 4 (1944), pp. 341-75.

9. Donald Davidson, "Truth and Meaning," in *Philosophical Logic,* ed. J. W. Davis, D. J. Hockney, and W. K. Wilson (Dordrecht: D. Reidel, 1969), p. 6.

10. I take this point from Mark Platts, *Ways of Meaning* (London: Routledge & Kegan Paul, 1979), p. 39.

11. Willard Van Orman Quine, "Two Dogmas of Empiricism," in *From a Logical Point of View,* 2d ed. (New York: Harper, 1961), p. 41.

12. Hilary Putnam gives a plausible explanation of why words such as 'bachelor' give rise to genuinely analytic statements and of why at the same time Quine is right about words such as 'energy'. See "The Analytic and the Synthetic," in *Mind, Language, and Reality,* vol. 2 of two vols. (London: Cambridge University Press, 1975), pp. 52-59.

13. Fred Sommers has pointed out to me that Tarski says nothing about the relation between the truth bearer as a unit and parts of the world. States of affairs are usually connected with statements or propositions in intuitive expressions of the correspondence theory, but Tarski does nothing to elucidate such talk. It is better then, to attribute to him a *realist* theory of truth that constitutes the beginning of a correspondence theory.

Chapter 3. Relativist Analyses of Morality as Social Creation

1. Gilbert Harman, "Moral Relativism Defended," *Philosophical Review* 84 (1975), pp. 3-22; and "Relativistic Ethics: Morality as Politics," *Midwest Studies in Philosophy* 3 (1978), pp. 109-121.

2. Harman defends his explanation of the oddity of the statement by claiming it's not as odd but equally weak to say that what Hitler did was wrong; thus the weakness of the statement that Hitler ought not to have ordered the Holocaust does not fully explain its oddity. But other people do not seem to share Harman's intuition that the second statement is not as odd. He also says that "What Hitler did ought never to have happened" is not as odd but equally weak. But the latter is strong in having practical import for those of us who can do something about the Hitlers before they commit crimes. Keeping the possible point of a statement in mind helps to explain why, as Harman says, it may not be as odd to say Stalin morally ought not to have conducted the purges, on the assumption that Stalin used evil means for good ends. Many of us repeat in much less severe form Stalin's mistake, and we can learn from his.

3. Hector-Neri Castañeda, *The Structure of Morality* (Springfield: Charles C. Thomas, 1974), p. 36.

4. Actually he reverses the variables, but for the sake of uniform notation I shall phrase his analyses to be consistent with the use in this book.

5. Castañeda, *Structure of Morality*, p. 64.

6. The subscript also allows for different kinds of moral 'ought's. See note 5 of chapter four.

7. Castañeda, *Structure of Morality*, pp. 82-96. Castañeda notes that we must be careful in distinguishing what counts as an implied practition and what does not, or we will run into the "Good Samaritan" paradox. He gives the following example of that paradox: suppose that in the B_i of some speaker there is the practition "Smith to pay Jones $500 today;" suppose there is the true proposition that a week from today Smith will murder Jones; these imply the practition "Smith to pay $500 today to the man he will murder a week hence;" and this latter practition seems to imply "Smith to murder Jones." Is the speaker compelled to say that Smith ought to murder Jones? No, says Castañeda, because the conclusion of the chain of inferences is not a practition but a proposition with a truth value. When the act of murdering is mentioned in the practition "Smith to pay $500 today to the man he will murder a week hence," it is considered a "circumstance" and not part of the act that is identified as the object of telling what to do. See *Structure of Morality*, pp. 80-81.

8. Castañeda, *Structure of Morality*, pp. 185-190.

9. Castañeda, *Structure of Morality*, pp. 65-66.

10. Castañeda also labels his theory absolutist, but in a strictly formal sense. There is the common structure that underlies all morality, plus some very general principles that partially characterize the content of the ideal of morality. See *Structure of Morality*, pp. 223-225.

11. I thank Professor Castañeda for clarifying this feature of his position in correspondence with me.

12. Castañeda, *Structure of Morality,* p. 222.

13. Ibid.

14. I should note, however, that Castañeda allows for the possibility of changes in our "moral schemes" that take into account "wider and deeper areas of our personality," changes that result from increase of knowledge. See *Structure of Morality,* p. 220.

15. See Rawls' *A Theory of Justice* (Cambridge: Belknap Press, 1971), pp. 396-97, for his contrast between a "thin" and "thick" theory of the good.

16. Castañeda has replied to me in correspondence that a singular practition is a complex of one or more agents and/or some accusatives and actions. Hence to show how a practition enters into the truth of an "A ought to do X" statement is to show how the agents, accusatives, and the action composing the practition enter into the truth of the statement. I still don't see, however, how this reveals the way in which the *use* of names and descriptions of agents and actions contributes to the truth conditions of "A ought to do X" statements, for the agent and action cannot literally be *parts* of the practition.

17. See Castañeda's "Imperatives, Decisions, and 'Ought's," in *Morality and the Language of Conduct,* ed. Castañeda and George Nakhnikian (Detroit: Wayne State Press, 1963), p. 292.

Chapter 4. The Recommended Relativistic Analysis of Moral "A ought to do X" Statements

1. Roger Wertheimer, *The Significance of Sense* (Ithaca: Cornell University Press, 1972), pp. 92-93.

2. In a book of this scope, I must leave some loose ends. One of them is the problem of specifying identity conditions for possible actions.

3. The feature of relativizing an 'ought' statement to a conditions clause is contained in the following previous analyses: Samuel Wheeler, "The Logical Form of Ethical Language" (Ph.D. dissertation, Princeton University, 1970); Roger Wertheimer, *The Significance of Sense;* Gilbert Harman, "Moral Relativism Defended"; G. H. Von Wright, "A Note on Deontic Logic and Moral Obligation," *Mind* 65 (1956), pp. 507-09; Bas Van Fraasen, "The Logic of Conditional Obligation," *Journal of Philosophy* 30 (1972), pp. 417-438.

4. I am assuming that the set of conditions identified by the clause "under actual conditions C" would be finite, so that this feature of the analysis will dovetail with the possibility of giving a Tarskian truth definition.

5. I should note that Castañeda does not analyze the final 'ought' in the way I do. According to him, "A ought to do X" statements that lack the pushing aspect are distinguished from those that have it by their reference to different sets of practitions and true propositions (see section 3.2). The final 'ought' is an 'ought$_j$' that refers to a set B_j, which contains some practical principles for the resolution of conflicting *prima facie* obligations, while an

'ought$_i$' expressing a *prima facie* obligation may refer to a set B$_i$ that does not contain such practical principles. See Castañeda's *Thinking and Doing* (Dordrecht: D. Reidel, 1976), chapter 7.

6. Castañeda, *Structure of Morality*, p. 17.

7. *A Theory of Justice*, p. 247.

Chapter 5. The Analysis of "A ought to do X" Statements Completed

1. See John Searle, *Speech Acts: An Essay in the Philosophy of Language* (New York: Cambridge University Press, 1969), chapter 7.

2. Saul Kripke, "Naming and Necessity," in *Semantics of Natural Language,* ed. Gilbert Harman and Donald Davidson (Dordrecht: D. Reidel, 1972), p. 302.

3. Hilary Putnam, "The Meaning of 'Meaning' " in *Mind, Language, and Reality*, pp. 227-241; see also Kripke, "Naming and Necessity," pp. 316, 320.

4. Let us be careful in noting what these causal theories are not intended to do for us. They do not tell us what reference *is.* They do not reduce the notion of reference to a relation between speaker and referent that can be described without the use of semantic terms. A dubbing is an act that is giving a name a *reference.* Each speaker in the causal chain, furthermore, resolves to use the name with the same *reference* as the speaker from whom he or she acquired the name. The causal theories simply help us specify reference, not define it. In fact, it may be that we will have to take the notion of reference as a primitive and give up the prospect of carrying out the program of reductive physicalism, if we ever had hopes of doing so. It is important to be clear on the purpose of causal theories because the dubious prospect for reductive physicalism is sometimes taken as a reason for trying to do without a theory of reference in the project of giving truth conditions for a language. Such an argument holds only if we take theories of reference such as Kripke's and Putnam's as attempting to exhaustively analyze the concept of reference in terms of nonlinguistic concepts. Someone who argues for doing without a theory of reference in this way is Donald Davidson. See his "Reality without Reference," in *Reference, Truth and Reality*, ed. Mark Platts (London: Routledge & Kegan Paul, 1980).

5. Evans also believes that members of a linguistic community must *commonly* intend to refer to the object dominantly responsible for their beliefs, for that object to be a true referent of the name. In other words, the object must be a "standard" reference of the name. See "The Causal Theory of Names," in *Naming, Necessity, and Natural Kinds*, ed. Stephen Schwartz (Ithaca: Cornell University Press, 1977), p. 209.

6. James H. Breasted, *The Dawn of Conscience* (New York: Scribner's, 1933), pp. 38-39.

7. See Breasted, *The Dawn of Conscience,* pp. 117-123; also Confucius, *Lun-yü* (Analects) 1:12; and *The Great Learning*, text and chapter 9 of commentary. Translations are given by Wing-tsit Chan, *A Sourcebook in*

Chinese Philosophy (Princeton: Princeton University Press, 1963), pp. 19-20, 91-92.

8. Alasdair MacIntyre, *A Short History of Ethics* (New York: MacMillan, 1973), pp. 5, 8-10, 89-91. His later book, *After Virtue,* expands on this theme. There will be much more discussion of his theory of morality in chapter nine.

9. William Graham Sumner, in *Folkways* (New York: Dover, 1906), claims that this is how all moralities are transmitted. See p. 28.

10. Leonard Trelawny Hobhouse, *Morals in Evolution* (London: Chapman & Hall, 1951), p. 219.

11. *Epistolae* 47.

12. May and Abraham Edel, *Anthropology and Ethics* (Cleveland: Press of Case Western Reserve University, 1968), p. 90.

13. See Saint Augustine, *De imitate Dei* XIX, 15.

14. Edward Westermarck, *The Origin and Development of the Moral Ideas* 2 vols. (London: MacMillan, 1912), vol. 1, p. 695.

15. Eugene D. Genovese, *Roll, Jordan, Roll* (New York: Random House, 1976), pp. 3-7, 75-86, 161-168.

16. It might be held that race-conscious affirmative action programs are counterexamples to my claim that this principle is indubitable, but skin color in itself is not the basis for these programs. It is the fact that people of a certain color have been oppressed in the past or are at the bottom end of gross inequalities.

17. Robert Turnbull, *The Mountain People* (New York: Simon and Schuster, 1972).

Chapter 6. Recommended Relativist Analysis of "X is a good Y" Statements and Consideration of Objections

1. Georg Henrik Von Wright, *The Varieties of Goodness* (New York: Humanities Press, 1963), pp. 1-12.

2. *Morality: An Introduction to Ethics* (New York: Harper, 1972), p. 44.

3. At least it is a realist theory of truth. There may be a question of whether it is a genuine correspondence theory, because Tarski does not explain how a statement that is true under his truth definition really corresponds with any fact or state of affairs in the world. See section 2.4 and note 12 of the second chapter.

4. *Roll, Jordan, Roll,* p. 59; Raimondo Luraghi, *Storia della guerra civile americana* (Turin, 1966), pp. 57, 69.

5. Genovese, *Roll, Jordan, Roll,* p. 41.

6. *Ethics: Inventing Right and Wrong* (New York: Penguin, 1977), pp. 59, 73-76.

7. Mackie, *Ethics,* p. 44.

Chapter 7. Absolutist Analyses of Moral Statements

1. *Reason and Morality* (Chicago: University of Chicago, 1978), p. 66.

2. Gewirth, *Reason and Morality*, p. 81.

3. Thomas Nagel, *The Possibility of Altruism* (Oxford: Clarendon Press, 1970), chapters 9-12.

4. Nagel, *Possibility of Altruism*, chapters 5-8.

5. Besides Gewirth and Nagel, I would place the theories of the following philosophers within the Kantian tradition: Kurt Baier, *The Moral Point of View* (New York: Random House, 1965), and "Moral Reasons and Reasons to be Moral," in *Values and Morals*, ed. Alvin I. Goldman and Jaegwon Kim (Dordrecht: D. Reidel, 1978); Alan Donagan, *The Theory of Morality* (Chicago: University of Chicago Press, 1977); Bernard Gert, *The Moral Rules* (New York: Harper and Row, 1970).

6. *The Theory of Morality*, pp. 232-233.

7. John McDowell, "Virtue and Reason," *Monist* 62 (1979), pp. 331-343.

8. See his "Are Moral Requirements Hypothetical Imperatives?" *Proceedings of the Aristotelian Society* supplementary vol. 41 (1978), pp. 13-29.

9. "Virtue and Reason," p. 346.

10. "Hypothetical Imperatives," p. 20.

11. Foot formerly believed that all virtues had to benefit the possessor. That belief was motivated by her assumption that moral judgments necessarily give reasons for acting to each and every moral agent. She has since dropped the underlying assumption. See "Moral Beliefs," *Proceedings of the Aristotelian Society* 59 (1958-59), pp. 83-104; introduction to *Theories of Ethics*, ed. Philippa Foot (New York: Oxford University Press, 1967), and *Virtues and Vices* (Berkeley, Los Angeles, London: University of California Press, 1978), introduction, pp. xiii-xiv, pp. 1-18.

12. "Morality as a System of Hypothetical Imperatives," *Philosophical Review* 81 (1972), pp. 305-316.

13. "Goodness and Choice," *Proceedings of the Aristotelian Society* supplementary vol. 35 (1961), pp. 50-51; *Virtues and Vices*, p. 137.

14. *Virtues and Vices*, p. 6.

15. G. E. Moore, *Principia Ethica* (London: Cambridge University Press, 1971), pp. 1-36.

16. P. T. Geach, "Good and Evil," *Analysis* 17 (1956), pp. 33-42.

17. *Ethics*, pp. 50-51.

18. See his *Ways of Meaning*, pp. 243-263; and "Moral Reality and the End of Desire," in *Reference, Truth and Reality*, ed. Mark Platts (London: Routledge & Kegan Paul, 1980), pp. 69-82.

19. The motivation for austerity can be stated in another way on the assumption that a coherent sense can be given to the contrast between moral and nonmoral facts: Platts believes in the futility of any attempt to reduce moral claims to nonmoral claims. He uses an analogy to explain his view of the relation between moral and nonmoral facts. Suppose a face can be made out when we look at a certain arrangement of dots on a card. The dot arrangement fixes the face, but we do not see the face by attending to the dots. Similarly, once all nonmoral facts are fixed, so are all the moral facts; but we could know all the nonmoral facts while being in utter ignorance of the moral facts. Platts, however, is not sure that a coherent sense can be

given to the contrast between the moral and nonmoral, so he is content to
state his motivation for austerity in the first way until a coherent sense is
given.

20. Platts, *Ways of Meaning*, p. 263.

21. Platts comes the closest to giving this when he gives the analogy with
the face among the dots, and that analogy is only helpful in illustrating how
attending to the nonmoral facts does not help us perceive the moral ones.

Chapter 8. The Method for Explaining Diversity and Disagreement in Moral
Belief

1. Willard Van Orman Quine, *Word and Object* (Cambridge: MIT Press,
1960), p. 69.

2. Richard Grandy, "Reference, Meaning, and Belief," *Journal of Philosophy* 70 (1973), pp. 441, 443-44.

3. Grandy, p. 443.

4. See *The Golden Bough*, 3d ed., 12 vols. (London: 1936).

5. J. H. M. Beattie, *Other Cultures* (London: 1964). He does not deny
that magic may have the purpose of achieving desired goals, as well as the
symbolic purpose. See his "On Understanding Ritual" in *Rationality*, ed.
Bryan R. Wilson (New York: Harper, 1970).

6. Peter Winch, "Understanding a Primitive Society," in *Rationality*,
p. 100.

7. Winch, pp. 104-105.

8. Richard Solomon, *Mao's Revolution and the Chinese Political Culture*
(Berkeley, Los Angeles, London: University of California Press, 1971), p.
517.

9. Hilary Putnam, *Meaning and the Moral Sciences* (Boston: Routledge &
Kegan Paul, 1978), pp. 62-65; and Alasdair MacIntyre, *After Virtue* (Notre
Dame: University of Notre Dame Press, 1981), pp. 84-97.

10. *After Virtue*, p. 99.

11. David E. Cooper, "Moral Relativism," in *Midwest Studies in Philosophy* 3 (1978), p. 101.

12. Donald Davidson, "Thought and Talk," in *Mind and Language*, ed.
Samuel Guttenplan (London: Oxford University Press, 1975), pp. 20-21.

13. Cooper, p. 104.

Chapter 9. Virtue-Centered and Rights-Centered Moralities

1. *After Virtue*, pp. 146.

2. MacIntyre, *After Virtue*, pp. 160-61.

3. MacIntyre, *After Virtue*, p. 175.

4. MacIntyre, *After Virtue*, p. 178.

5. MacIntyre, *After Virtue*, p. 185.

6. MacIntyre, *After Virtue*, p. 201.

7. MacIntyre, *After Virtue*, p. 211.

8. Richard Wasserstrom has pointed out to me that Americans may not be

able to disclaim responsibility since the law sometimes recognizes receipt of undeserved benefits as a basis for requiring a form of compensation to the victims of injustice.

9. MacIntyre, *After Virtue,* pp. 231-233.

10. MacIntyre, *After Virtue,* p. 245.

11. MacIntyre, *After Virtue,* p. 8.

12. Robert Nozick, *Anarchy, State and Utopia* (New York: Basic Books, 1974), pp. 30-35.

13. MacIntyre, *After Virtue,* p. 208.

14. MacIntyre, *After Virtue,* p. 209.

15. *Two Theories of Morality* (London: Oxford University Press, 1977), pp. 36-38.

16. Book I, chap. 7 (1098a); Book X, chaps. 7 and 8 (1177a-1179a).

17. Book X, chap. 8 (1179a), translation from W. D. Ross, *Ethica Nichomachea* (London: Oxford University Press, 1915).

18. MacIntyre, *After Virtue,* p. 56.

Chapter 10. Moral Relativity Within Virtue-Centered and Rights-Centered Moralities

1. Another disagreement within the rights-centered tradition that reflects indeterminacy and variation in the extension of 'adequate moral system' is the one over abortion, but I shall defer discussion of it until chapter twelve, that concerns the normative implications of moral relativity.

2. *Two Theories of Morality,* p. 42.

3. Kathleen Wilkes, "The Good man and the Good for Man in Aristotle's Ethics," in *Essays on Aristotle's Ethics,* ed. Amélie Oksenberg Rorty (Berkeley, Los Angeles, London: University of California Press, 1980), p. 348.

4. Richard Miller, "Rights and Reality," *Philosophical Review* 90 (1981), pp. 383-407.

5. *A Theory of Justice,* p. 172.

6. *Anarchy, State and Utopia,* pp. 160-164.

7. *Lun-yü:* 1:12, 3:19, 6:25, 8:8. See the translation by Chan in *A Sourcebook in Chinese Philosophy,* pp. 21, 30, 33.

8. *Lun-yü:* 3:12, 5:12, 6:20, 7:20, 7:34, 11:11, 17:19; Chan, pp. 25, 28, 30, 32, 33, 36, 47.

9. For a particularly lucid account of this meaning of rites, see Herbert Fingarette's *The Secular as Sacred* (New York: Harper, 1972).

10. K. J. Dover, *Greek Popular Morality in the Time of Plato and Aristotle* (Berkeley, Los Angeles, London: University of California Press, 1974), p. 117.

11. Dover, *Greek Popular Morality,* p. 125.

12. Wing-tsit Chan, *Sourcebook in Chinese Philosophy,* p. 30; see *Lun-yü:* 4:2, 6:21.

13. Fingarette, *Secular as Sacred,* p. 76.

14. *Meng Tzu Shu* (Book of Mencius): 6A:6; a translation is in Chan, pp. 53-54.

Chapter 11. Comparing the Truth of Virtue-Centered and Rights-Centered Moralities

1. *After Virtue,* p. 115.

2. *Lun-yü:* 8:14; see Chan in *Sourcebook of Chinese Philosophy,* p. 34; see also 14:27-28.

3. *Lun-yü:* 16:1, 14:45; in Chan, pp. 44-45, 43.

4. *Meng Tzu Shu,* 1B:7, 8; Chan, pp. 61-62.

5. *Meng Tzu Shu,* 1B:7; Chan, pp. 61-62.

6. Berlin first calls Locke a "libertarian" but then notes his view that "law ill deserves the name of confinement which hedges us in only from bogs and precipices" and that the end of law is to "preserve and enlarge freedom." See "Two Concepts," pp. 124, 147; John Locke, *Essay Concerning Human Understanding,* Book II, chap. 21, sec. 15; and *Treatise of Government,* sec. 57.

7. The passage Berlin quotes to show that Kant sanctions suppression of lower, empirical selves in favor of true, rational selves is in fact as abstract and as mild as the Locke passage quoted above. See "Two Concepts," p. 148. He does say that Kant's rationalist doctrine led to "an authoritarian state obedient to the directives of an *elite* of Platonic guardians" from steps that "if not logically valid, are historically and psychologically intelligible." See p. 152. But if the steps that led to authoritarianism were *not* logically valid, this causal connection hardly seems to justify placing Kant so clearly in the camp of positive liberty.

8. Berlin, "Two Concepts," no. 1, p. 153.

9. Gerald MacCallum, Jr., "Negative and Positive Freedom," *Philosophical Review* 76 (1967), pp. 312-334.

10. 1278^{a}20.

11. See Y. P. Mei, "Status of the Individual in Social Thought and Practice," in *The Chinese Mind,* ed. Charles Moore (Honolulu: University of Hawaii Press, 1967); and Herbert Fingarette, *The Secular as Sacred,* chapters 1 and 2 for elaboration on this theme.

12. "The Status of the Individual in Chinese Ethics," in *Chinese Mind,* pp. 307-322.

13. Irving Goldman, "The Zuni Indians of New Mexico," in *Cooperation and Competition Among Primitive Peoples,* ed. Margaret Mead (New York: McGraw-Hill, 1937), pp. 313-14.

14. *Anthropology and Ethics,* p. 75.

15. *Anthropology and Ethics,* p. 63.

16. Margaret Mead, "Interpretive Statement," in *Cooperation and Conflict Among Primitive Peoples,* p. 511.

17. Ruth Benedict, *Patterns of Culture* (New York: Penguin, 1934), p. 229.

18. Bernard Mishkin, "The Maori of New Zealand," *Cooperation and Conflict Among Primitive Peoples,* p. 452.

Chapter 12. Tolerance and Nonintervention as Implications of Moral Relativity

1. Geoffrey Harrison, "Relativism and Tolerance," in *Philosophy, Politics and Society,* ed. Peter Laslett and James Fishkin (New Haven: Yale University Press, 1979), pp. 273-290, reprinted from *Ethics* 86 (1976), pp. 122-135.

2. Bernard Williams, *Morality: an Introduction to Ethics* (New York: Harper and Row, 1972), p. 20.

3. Harrison, p. 278.

4. Williams, p. 20.

5. Melville Herskovits, *Cultural Relativism: Perspectives in Cultural Pluralism* (New York: Vintage, 1972), p. 11.

6. Immanuel Kant, *Groundwork of the Metaphysic of Morals,* trans. H. J. Paton (New York: Harper and Row, 1964), p. 97; 2d ed., p. 68; Prussian ed., p. 430.

7. Kant, *Groundwork,* p. 96; 2d ed., p. 66; Prussian ed., p. 429.

8. This answer is suggested by Bruce Aune in *Kant's Theory of Morals* (Princeton: Princeton University Press, 1979), p. 110.

9. As we saw in chapter seven, a contemporary philosopher who also emphasizes the value of noninterference with the ends of others is Alan Gewirth. He defines the generic right to freedom as a right to control whether or not one will participate in "transactions" with agents. One's participation must be subject to one's own unforced consent, given with knowledge of relevant circumstances and in an emotionally calm state of mind. See his *Reason and Morality,* pp. 135-138. One could formulate a relativist argument for tolerance premised on Gewirth's right to freedom, instead of Kant's justification principle. The conclusions will be much the same, although Gewirth's right to freedom has some different implications. The set of actions that a relevantly informed and calm person would consent to is not necessarily the same as the set that the person would accept were he or she relevantly informed and fully rational.

10. The variable schema is borrowed from Harrison, pp. 278-79, so that some of his arguments may be related easily to the ones to be set out here.

11. David Lyons, "Human Rights and the General Welfare," *Philosophy and Public Affairs* 6 (1977), p. 118. Lyons points out that Mill is not like contemporary rule utilitarians in that he applies the general welfare standard to acts as well as rules. See p. 120.

12. See chapter 3 of *On Liberty.*

13. See, for example, Pepita Haezrahi, "The Concept of Man as End-In-Himself," in *Kant: a Collection of Critical Essays,* ed. Robert Paul Wolff (Garden City: Anchor Books, 1967), esp. pp. 312-13.

14. Lawrence Blum, *Friendship, Altruism, and Morality* (London: Routledge & Kegan Paul, 1980), pp. 23-24.

15. Harrison, pp. 280-81.

16. Harrison, p. 281.

17. Harrison, p. 281.

18. Harrison, pp. 281-82.

19. Mary Anne Warren, "On the Moral and Legal Status of Abortion," *Monist* 57 (1973), pp. 43-61; reprinted in *Today's Moral Problems,* 2d ed., ed. Richard Wasserstrom (New York: MacMillan, 1979), pp. 35-51.

20. Michael Tooley, "Abortion and Infanticide," *Philosophy and Public Affairs* 2 (1972), pp. 37-65.

21. L. W. Sumner, *Abortion and Moral Theory* (Princeton: Princeton University Press, 1981), p. 44.

22. See pp. 197-198 in *Abortion and Moral Theory.*

23. Moderates (those who believe that abortions in early pregnancy are permissible while most abortions in late pregnancy are not) also make this argument. See Sumner, *Abortion and Moral Theory,* pp. 59-60, and also Richard Werner, "The Ontological Status of the Unborn," *Social Theory and Practice* 3 (1974), pp. 201-222, reprinted in *Today's Moral Problems,* ed. Wasserstrom, pp. 51-73.

24. See the postscript on infanticide in the Wasserstrom reprint of Warren's article.

25. This point is made by Werner, "On the Ontological Status" in Wasserstrom, p. 62.

26. Philip Devine, *The Ethics of Homicide* (Ithaca: Cornell University Press, 1978), pp. 94-95.

27. Roger Wertheimer makes this point on behalf of the conservative in "Understanding the Abortion Argument," *Philosophy and Public Affairs* 1 (1971), pp. 67-95.

28. Sumner makes this criticism. See *Abortion and Moral Theory,* pp. 102-103.

29. In *Philosophy and Public Affairs* 1 (1971), pp. 47-66.

30. There is another attack on the conservative view that seeks to show that the principle of double effect will justify abortions to protect the mother's health or autonomy and not just to save her life. Since conservatives often use the principle to justify abortions to save the mother's life, this is a serious matter. Conservatives should take the line of reply that is analogous to the one suggested for the Thomson attack: the cost in terms of health, autonomy, and so on, will not balance the fetus' loss of all potential for a rich life. See Sumner, pp. 115-121, for this type of attack.

31. Such is the position of American Citizens Concerned for Life, as reported by the *Boston Globe,* March 12, 1981, p. 20.

32. Roger Wertheimer has argued for a proposal similar to the one made here, in "Understanding the Abortion Argument." He argues that liberals and conservatives are equally justified (his arguments for this are different from mine, however). Then he argues that the state cannot prohibit abortion because it must justify the existence and exercise of its powers through their rational acceptability to its citizens. This proposal is more limited than mine because he holds that:

While any constraint on liberty or any harm to others . . . is *prima facie* objectionable, so that the burden of proof is on its perpetrator, it is not evident that the perpetrator is criticizable when his victims are unsatisfied by an argument they cannot refute. So, for a citizen, but not a state, to act without demonstrable justification is not to act wrongly. (p. 50)

The proposal made in this chapter is based on principles for individual agents, as well as the state, and thus implies that conservatives who promote legal sanctions against abortion are criticizable. Wertheimer has suggested in correspondence with this author that he favors his more limited proposal because of his concern with preserving the rights of freedom of speech and assembly. He believes some distinction must be made between the wrongness of the acts urged in speech and speech itself. It must be granted that it is never wrong to express a view *per se*. It is reasonable, however, to hold that acts of promoting unjustifiable acts by the state can be wrong but at the same time that such acts are not to be prevented (except, perhaps, when the democratic process itself is in "clear and present danger") given the rights of freedom of speech and assembly.

Chapter 13. Moral Relativity and the Problem of Equal Worth

1. Gregory Vlastos, "Justice and Equality," in *Social Justice,* ed. Richard B. Brandt (Englewood Cliffs: Prentice-Hall, 1962), p. 43.

2. Immanuel Kant, *Groundwork of the Metaphysic of Morals,* trans. H. J. Paton, pp. 97-98; 2d ed., pp. 68-69; Prussian ed., pp. 429-30.

3. *A Theory of Justice,* pp. 504-512.

4. Alan Gewirth, *Reason and Morality,* pp. 110-11, 122, 124-25.

5. Joel Feinberg, *Social Philosophy* (Englewood Cliffs: Prentice-Hall, 1973), p. 91.

6. Feinberg, p. 93.

7. Bernard Williams, "The Idea of Equality," in *Philosophy, Politics, and Society,* ed. P. Laslett and W. G. Runciman (New York: Barnes and Noble, 1962), p. 115.

8. Richard Sennett and Jonathan Cobb, *The Hidden Injuries of Class* (New York: Alfred A. Knopf, 1973), pp. 90-104.

9. Sennett and Cobb, p. 104.

10. Sennett and Cobb, pp. 65-66.

11. Sennett and Cobb, pp. 107-118, 131-135.

12. Sennett and Cobb, p. 257.

13. *Chuang Tzu,* chapter 1; I use the translation by Burton Watson, *The Complete Works of Chuang Tzu* (New York: Columbia University Press, 1968), p. 38.

14. *Chuang Tzu,* chapter 9; Watson, p. 110.

15. For an enlightening discussion of the theme of forgetting morality see Antonio S. Cua, "Forgetting Morality: Reflections on a Theme in Chuang

Tzu," *Journal of Chinese Philosophy* 4 (1977), pp. 305-328.

16. Richard Sennett, *The Uses of Disorder* (New York: Vintage, 1970), pp. 141-145.

17. Sennett, *Uses*, p. 161.

18. Harry C. Boyte, "Reagan v. the Neighborhoods," *Social Policy* 4 (1982), pp. 3-8.

19. Robert Paul Wolff, *The Poverty of Liberalism* (New York: Beacon, 1968), pp. 150-160.

20. *Tao Te Ching*, chapter 67; p. 171 in Chan's *A Sourcebook in Chinese Philosophy*.

21. *Tao Te Ching*, chapter 81; pp. 175-76 in Chan.

22. *Tao Te Ching*, chapter 75; p. 174 of Chan.

23. *Tao Te Ching*, chapter 49; p. 163 in Chan.

24. *Tao Te Ching*, chapter 66; p. 171 in Chan.

Appendix A

1. William Frankena, "The Concept of Morality," in *Perspectives on Morality*, ed. K. E. Goodpaster (Notre Dame: University of Notre Dame Press, 1976), p. 125.

2. See *The Structure of a Moral Code* (Cambridge: Harvard University Press, 1957), chapter 5, especially.

3. Bernard Williams, *Morality: An Introduction to Ethics*, p. 76.

4. H. A. Prichard, "Does Moral Philosophy Rest on a Mistake?" *Mind* 21 (1912), pp. 21-37; reprinted in *Readings in Ethical Theory*, ed. Wilfred Sellars and John Hospers, 2d ed. (New York: Appleton-Century Crofts, 1952), pp. 86-96.

Appendix B

1. Peter Winch, "Understanding a Primitive Society," in *Rationality*, ed. Bryan Wilson, p. 100.

2. Winch, p. 106.

3. See E. E. Evans-Pritchard, *Witchcraft, Oracles and Magic Among the Zande* (London: Oxford University Press, 1937), p. 338, 476; also Winch, p. 88.

4. Robin Horton, "African Thought and Western Science," in *Rationality*, p. 170.

5. This position is similar to the one held by Steven Lukes in "Some Problems about Rationality," pp. 207-213, and by Martin Hollis in "The Limits of Irrationality," pp. 214-220, both in *Rationality*.

Bibliography

Aristotle (1915). *Ethica Nichomachea.* Translated by W. D. Ross. London: Oxford University Press.

Aune, Bruce (1979). *Kant's Theory of Morals.* Princeton: Princeton University Press.

Baier, Kurt (1965). *The Moral Point of View.* New York: Random House.

Baier, Kurt (1978). "Moral Reasons and Reasons to be Moral." In *Values and Morals.* Edited by Alvin I. Goldman and Jaegwon Kim. Dordrecht: D. Reidel.

Beattie, J. H. M. (1964). *Other Cultures.* New York: Free Press of Glencoe.

Beattie, J. H. M. (1970). "On Understanding Ritual." In *Rationality.* Edited by Bryan R. Wilson. New York: Harper.

Benedict, Ruth (1934). *Patterns of Culture.* New York: Penguin.

Berlin, Isaiah (1969). "Two Concepts of Liberty." In *Four Essays on Liberty.* London: Oxford University Press.

Blum, Lawrence (1980). *Friendship, Altruism, and Morality.* London: Routledge & Kegan Paul.

Boyte, Harry C. (1982). "Reagan v. the Neighborhoods." *Social Policy* 4: 3-8.

Breasted, James (1933). *The Dawn of Conscience.* New York: Scribner's.

Castañeda, Hector-Neri (1963). "Imperatives, Decisions, and 'Ought's." In *Morality and the Language of Conduct.* Edited by Hector-Neri Castañeda and George Nakhnikian. Detroit: Wayne State Press.

Castañeda, Hector-Neri (1974). *The Structure of Morality.* Springfield: Charles C. Thomas.

Castañeda, Hector-Neri (1975). *Thinking and Doing.* Dordrecht: D. Reidel.

Chuang Tzu (1968). *The Complete Works of Chuang Tzu.* Translated by Burton Watson. New York: Columbia University Press.

Confucius (1963). "Lun-yü (Analects)." Translated by Wing-tsit Chan. In *A Sourcebook in Chinese Philosophy.* Edited by Wing-tsit Chan. Princeton: Princeton University Press.

Cooper, David (1978). "Moral Relativism." *Midwest Studies in Philosophy* 3: 97-108.

237

Cua, Antonio S. (1977). "Forgetting Morality: Reflections on a Theme in Chuang Tzu." *Journal of Chinese Philosophy* 4:305-328.

Davidson, Donald (1969). "Truth and Meaning." In *Philosophical Logic*. Edited by J. W. Davis, D. J. Hockney, and W. K. Wilson. Dordrecht: D. Reidel.

Davidson, Donald (1975). "Thought and Talk." In *Mind and Language*. Edited by Samuel Guttenplan. London: Oxford University Press.

Davidson, Donald (1980). "Reality without Reference." In *Reference, Truth and Reality*. Edited by Mark Platts. London: Routledge & Kegan Paul.

Devine, Philip (1978). *The Ethics of Homicide*. Ithaca: Cornell University Press.

Donagan, Alan (1977). *The Theory of Morality*. Chicago: University of Chicago Press.

Dover, K. J. (1974). *Greek Popular Morality in the Time of Plato and Aristotle*. Berkeley, Los Angeles, London: University of California Press.

Downie, R. S., and Telfer, Elizabeth (1970). *Respect for Persons*. New York: Schocken.

Edel, May and Abraham (1968). *Anthropology and Ethics*. Cleveland: Press of Case Western Reserve University.

Evans-Pritchard, E. E. (1937). *Witchcraft, Oracles and Magic Among the Zande*. London: Oxford University Press.

Evans, Gareth (1977). "The Causal Theory of Names." In *Naming, Necessity, and Natural Kinds*. Edited by Stephen Schwartz. Ithaca: Cornell University Press.

Feinberg, Joel (1973). *Social Philosophy*. Englewood Cliffs: Prentice-Hall.

Fingarette, Herbert (1972). *The Secular as Sacred*. New York: Harper.

Foot, Philippa (1961). "Goodness and Choice." *Proceedings of the Aristotelian Society* 35 (supplementary volume): 45-60.

Foot, Philippa (1967). "Introduction." In *Theories of Ethics*. Edited by Philippa Foot. New York: Oxford University Press.

Foot, Philippa (1972). "Morality as a System of Hypothetical Imperatives." *Philosophical Review* 81: 305-316.

Foot, Philippa (1978). *Virtues and Vices*. Berkeley, Los Angeles, London: University of California Press.

Foot, Philippa (1958-59). "Moral Beliefs." *Proceedings of the Aristotelian Society* 59: 83-104.

Frankena, William (1976). *Perspectives on Morality*. Notre Dame: University of Notre Dame Press.

Frazer, Sir James (1911-1936). *The Golden Bough*. London: MacMillan.

Geach, P. T. (1956). "Good and Evil." *Analysis* 17: 33-42.

Genovese, Eugene (1976). *Roll, Jordan, Roll*. New York: Random House.

Gert, Bernard (1970). *The Moral Rules*. New York: Harper and Row.

Gewirth, Alan (1978). *Reason and Morality*. Chicago: University of Chicago.

Goldman, Irving (1937). "The Zuni Indians of New Mexico." In *Cooperation and Competition Among Primitive Peoples*. Edited by Margaret Mead. New York: McGraw-Hill.

Grandy, Richard (1973). "Reference, Meaning, and Belief." *Journal of Philosophy* 70: 439-452.

Great Learning (1963). Translated by Wing-tsit Chan. In *A Sourcebook in Chinese Philosophy*. Edited by Wing-tsit Chan. Princeton: Princeton University Press.

Haezrahi, Pepita (1967). "The Concept of Man as End-In-Itself." In *Kant: a Collection of Critical Essays*. Edited by Robert Paul Wolff. Garden City: Anchor Books.

Hampshire, Stuart (1977). *Two Theories of Morality*. London: Oxford University Press.

Hare, R. M. (1963). *Freedom and Reason*. London: Oxford University Press.

Hare, R. M. (1964). *The Language of Morals*. London: Oxford University Press.

Hare, R. M. (1976). "Ethical Theory and Utilitarianism." In *Contemporary British Philosophy*. Edited by H. D. Lewis. London: Allen and Unwin.

Harman, Gilbert (1975). "Moral Relativism Defended." *Philosophical Review* 84: 3-22.

Harman, Gilbert (1978). "Relativistic Ethics: Morality as Politics." *Midwest Studies in Philosophy* 3: 109-121.

Harman, Gilbert (1978). "What is Moral Relativism?" In *Values and Morals*. Edited by Alvin I. Goldman and Jaegwon Kim. Dordrecht: D. Reidel.

Harrison, Geoffrey (1976). "Relativism and Tolerance." *Ethics* 86: 122-135.

Herskovits, Melville (1972). *Cultural Relativism: Perspectives in Cultural Pluralism*. New York: Vintage.

Hobhouse, Leonard Trelawny (1951). *Morals in Evolution*. London: Chapman and Hall.

Hsieh Yu-wei (1967). "The Status of the Individual in Chinese Ethics." In *The Chinese Mind*. Edited by Charles Moore. Honolulu: University of Hawaii Press.

Kant, Immanuel (1964). *Groundwork of the Metaphysic of Morals*. Translated by H. J. Paton. New York: Harper and Row.

Kripke, Saul (1972). "Naming and Necessity." In *Semantics of Natural Language*. Edited by Gilbert Harman and Donald Davidson. Dordrecht: D. Reidel.

Ladd, John (1957). *The Structure of a Moral Code*. Cambridge: Harvard University Press.

Lao Tzu (1963). *Tao Te Ching*. Translated by Wing-tsit Chan. In *A Sourcebook in Chinese Philosophy*. Edited by Wing-tsit Chan. Princeton: Princeton University Press.

Lyons, David (1977). "Human Rights and the General Welfare." *Philosophy and Public Affairs* 6: 113-129.

MacCallum, Gerald (1967). "Negative and Positive Freedom." *Philosophical Review* 76: 312-334.

MacIntyre, Alasdair (1973). *A Short History of Ethics*. New York: MacMillan.

MacIntyre, Alasdair (1981). *After Virtue.* Notre Dame: University of Notre Dame Press.

Mackie, J. L. (1977). *Ethics: Inventing Right and Wrong.* Harmondsworth: Penguin.

McDowell, John (1978). "Are Moral Requirements Hypothetical Imperatives?" *Proceedings of the Aristotelian Society* 41 (supplementary volume): 13-29.

McDowell, John (1979). "Virtue and Reason." *Monist* 62: 331-343.

Mead, Margaret (1937). "Interpretive Statement." In *Cooperation and Conflict Among Primitive Peoples.* Edited by Margaret Mead. New York: McGraw-Hill.

Mei, Y. P. (1967). "Status of the Individual in Social Thought and Practice." In *The Chinese Mind.* Edited by Charles Moore. Honolulu: University of Hawaii Press.

Mencius (1963). "Meng Tzu Shu." Translated by Wing-tsit Chan. In *A Sourcebook in Chinese Philosophy.* Edited by Wing-tsit Chan. Princeton: Princeton University Press.

Miller, Richard (1981). "Rights and Reality." *Philosophical Review* 90: 383-407.

Mishkin, Bernard (1937). "The Maori of New Zealand." In *Cooperation and Competition Among Primitive Peoples.* Edited by Margaret Mead. New York: McGraw-Hill.

Moore, G. E. (1971). *Principia Ethica.* London: Cambridge University Press.

Murdoch, Iris (1971). *The Sovereignty of the Good.* New York: Schocken Books.

Nagel, Thomas (1970). *Possibility of Altruism.* Oxford: Clarendon Press.

Nozick, Robert (1974). *Anarchy, State, and Utopia.* New York: Basic Books.

Pitcher, George (1958). "On Approval." *Philosophical Review* 67: 195-211.

Platts, Mark (1979). *Ways of Meaning.* London: Routledge & Kegan Paul.

Prichard, H. A. (1912). "Does Moral Philosophy Rest on a Mistake?" *Mind* 21: 21-37.

Putnam, Hilary (1975). *Mind, Language, and Reality.* London: Cambridge University Press.

Putnam, Hilary (1978). *Meaning and the Moral Sciences.* Boston: Routledge & Kegan Paul.

Quine, Willard Van Orman (1960). *Word and Object.* Cambridge: MIT Press.

Quine, Willard Van Orman (1961). "Two Dogmas of Empiricism." In *From a Logical Point of View.* New York: Harper.

Rawls, John (1971). *A Theory of Justice.* Cambridge: Belknap Press.

Rawls, John (1974-1975). "Presidential address to the APA." *Proceedings and Addresses of the APA* 48: 5-22.

Searle, John (1969). *Speech Acts: An Essay in the Philosophy of Language.* New York: Cambridge University Press.

Sennett, Richard (1970). *The Uses of Disorder.* New York: Vintage.

Sennett, Richard and Cobb, Jonathan (1973). *The Hidden Injuries of Class.* New York: Alfred A. Knopf.

Solomon, Richard (1971). *Mao's Revolution and the Chinese Political Culture*. Berkeley, Los Angeles, London: University of California Press.

Stevenson, C. L. (1944). *Ethics and Language*. New Haven: Yale University Press.

Sumner, L. W. (1981). *Abortion and Moral Theory*. Princeton: Princeton University Press.

Sumner, William Graham (1906). *Folkways*. New York: Dover.

Tarski, Alfred (1944). "The Semantic Conception of Truth." *Philosophy and Phenomenological Research* 4: 341-375.

Tarski, Alfred (1956). "The Concept of Truth in Formalized Languages." In *Logic, Semantics, and Metamathematics*. New York: Oxford University Press.

Thomson, Judith J. (1971). "A Defense of Abortion." *Philosophy and Public Affairs* 1: 47-66.

Tooley, Michael (1972). "Abortion and Infanticide." *Philosophy and Public Affairs* 2: 37-65.

Turnbull, Robert (1972). *The Mountain People*. New York: Simon and Schuster.

Urmson, J. O. (1968). *The Emotive Theory of Ethics*. New York: Oxford University Press.

Van Fraasen, Bas (1972). "The Logic of Conditional Obligation." *Journal of Philosophy* 30: 414-38.

Vlastos, Gregory (1962). "Justice and Equality." In *Social Justice*. Edited by Richard B. Brandt. Englewood Cliffs: Prentice-Hall.

Von Wright, G. H. (1956). "A Note on Deontic Logic and Moral Obligation." *Mind* 65: 507-9.

Von Wright, G. H. (1972). *The Varieties of Goodness*. New York: Humanities Press.

Warren, Mary Anne (1973). "On the Moral and Legal Status of Abortion." *Monist* 57: 43-61.

Warren, Mary Anne (1979). "On the Moral and Legal Status of Abortion, Postscript on Infanticide." In *Today's Moral Problems*. 2d ed. Edited by Richard Wasserstrom. New York: MacMillan.

Werner, Richard (1974). "The Ontological Status of the Unborn." *Social Theory and Practice* 3: 201-222.

Wertheimer, Roger (1971). "Understanding the Abortion Argument." *Philosophy and Public Affairs* 1: 67-95.

Wertheimer, Roger (1972). *The Significance of Sense*. Ithaca: Cornell University Press.

Westermarck, Edward (1912). *The Origin and Development of the Moral Ideas*. London: MacMillan.

Wheeler, Samuel (1970). "The Logical Form of Ethical Language." Ph.D. Dissertation. Princeton University.

Wilkes, Kathleen (1980). "The Good Man and the Good for Man in Aristotle's Ethics." In *Essays on Aristotle's Ethics*. Edited by Amélie Oksenberg Rorty. Berkeley, Los Angeles, London: University of California Press.

Williams, Bernard (1962). "The Idea of Equality." In *Philosophy, Politics, and Society.* Edited by Peter Laslett and W. G. Runciman. New York: Barnes and Noble.

Williams, Bernard (1972). *Morality: An Introduction to Ethics.* New York: Harper.

Williams, Bernard (1974-5). "The Truth in Relativism." *Proceedings of the Aristotelian Society* 75: 215-228.

Winch, Peter (1970). "Understanding a Primitive Society." In *Rationality.* Edited by Bryan R. Wilson. New York: Harper.

Wolff, Robert Paul (1968). *The Poverty of Liberalism.* New York: Beacon.

Index